Words and Phrases Legally Defined

Words and Phrases Legally Defined

SUPPLEMENT 2020

David Hay MA, LLM
of the Inner Temple, Barrister

LexisNexis® UK & Worldwide

United Kingdom   RELX (UK) Limited trading as LexisNexis®,
                        1-3 Strand, London WC2N 5JR and 9-10 St Andrew
                        Square, Edinburgh EH2 2AF
LNUK Global PartnersLexisNexis® encompasses authoritative legal
                        publishing brands dating back to the 19th century
                        including: Butterworths® in the United Kingdom,
                        Canada and the Asia-Pacific region; Les Editions du
                        Juris Classeur in France; and Matthew Bender®
                        worldwide. Details of LexisNexis® locations
                        worldwide can be found at www.lexisnexis.com

© RELX (UK) Limited 2020

Published by LexisNexis

A CIP Catalogue record for this book is available from the British Library.

ISBN for this volume: 9781474314497

Printed in Great Britain by Hobbs the Printers Ltd, Totton, Hampshire

Visit LexisNexis at http://www.lexisnexis.co.uk

Preface

This supplement contains a further selection of definitions from case law and statute.

The law as indicated is that existing at 20 August 2020.

This is the second Supplement to the Fifth Edition to be published. Editorial notes have been revised, particularly reference to Halsbury's Laws of England where volumes have been reissued, or issued for the Fifth Edition.

The style follows that used in the main volumes, which should be consulted first. Notes of statutory repeals or amendments and any other editorial comments are shown in square brackets.

LexisNexis

September 2020

A

ABATEMENT

Of legacy

[For 103 Halsbury's Laws of England (5th Edn) (2010) para 1086 see now 103 Halsbury's Laws of England (5th Edn) (2016) para 1087.]

ABODE

See PLACE OF ABODE

ABEYANCE

Of peerage

[For 79 Halsbury's Laws of England (5th Edn) (2014) para 832 see now 79 Halsbury's Laws of England (5th Edn) (2020) para 830.]

ACCEPTANCE

Of offer

[For 22 Halsbury's Laws of England (5th Edn) (2012) para 251 see now 22 Halsbury's Laws of England (5th Edn) (2019) para 51.]

ACCIDENT

In insurance policy

[For 60 Halsbury's Laws of England (5th Edn) (2011) para 545 see now 60 Halsbury's Laws of England (5th Edn) (2018) para 522.]

ACCORD AND SATISFACTION

[For 22 Halsbury's Laws of England (5th Edn) (2012) para 605 see now 22 Halsbury's Laws of England (5th Edn) (2019) para 396.]

ACT OF GOD

[For 22 Halsbury's Laws of England (5th Edn) (2012) para 478 see now 22 Halsbury's Laws of England (5th Edn) (2019) para 269.]

ADEMPTION

[For 60 Halsbury's Laws of England (5th Edn) (2011) para 455 see now 60 Halsbury's Laws of England (5th Edn) (2018) para 433.]

[For 102 Halsbury's Laws of England (5th Edn) (2010) para 155 see now 102 Halsbury's Laws of England (5th Edn) (2016) para 155.]

ADOPT

[Insolvency Act 1986, Sch B1 para 99(5).] '[70] I should first deal with a preliminary argument that para 99(5) is simply inapplicable in the current situation. Ms Toube QC indicated that some commentators in the market apparently take the view that since Lord Browne-Wilkinson had identified that correction of the mischief in *Nicoll v Cutts* [[1985] BCLC 322, CA] was the reason for the introduction of the forerunner to para 99(5) in the 1986 Act, and since the only identified mischief in *Nicoll v Cutts* was that employees might render services in the insolvency without payment, para 99(5) should be read as having no application whatever unless employees actually rendered services to the company in administration. Hence, so the argument goes, a contract which provides for an employee to be furloughed could never be adopted by administrators under para 99(5).

'[71] I reject that argument. It is certainly true that the mischief in *Nicoll v Cutts* involved an employee not being paid for services that they had rendered in an insolvency. But if Parliament had wanted to limit super-priority for wages and salary to cases where services are actually rendered to a company in administration, it could have said so simply and directly.

Instead it chose to deploy the concept of adoption of the contract of employment itself, and to persist with that concept when making subsequent amendments to the Insolvency Act (first by the Insolvency Act 1994 and secondly by the Enterprise Act 2002 when introducing Sch B1), long after any difficulties with that concept had become apparent.

'[72] Moreover, even in normal circumstances not involving COVID-19 or furlough, there are situations in which an administrator might, without committing any breach or repudiation of an employee's contract of employment, not require the employee to work for a period during the administration, but where it would nevertheless be entirely appropriate for the administrator to be required to continue to pay their wages or salary. To give one example, take an employee who has particular skills or know-how regarding the company's business which would, if available to a competitor, devalue the business which the administrator was seeking to sell. Even if there was no new work for the employee to do in the administration until it was known whether the business could be sold, it would be commercially important for the administrator not to terminate the employee's contract. In that way, the employee would continue to be available to the purchaser of the business, the restrictive covenants in his contract would continue in effect, and the maximum post-termination period of restraint would be available for the potential benefit of the purchaser. Given those benefits to the administration, even if, with the permission of the administrator, the employee were not required to attend the premises to work, it would be wrong if they were not entitled to payment of their wages or salary.

'[73] Moreover, although the coronavirus and the concept of furlough were obviously not foreseen by Parliament when it enacted and amended the relevant insolvency legislation, or by the House of Lords when *Paramount [Powdrill v Watson]* was decided, it is very clear from Lord Browne-Wilkinson's speech ([1995] 2 All ER 65 at 76 and 79, [1995] 2 AC 394 at 441–442 and 445) that promotion of the rescue culture is an important consideration when interpreting the Insolvency Act. In the instant case, a conclusion that because furloughed employees could not provide services, their contracts of employment could not be adopted under para 99(5) would have the unwelcome result that the main statutory provision dealing with the issue of employment in administrations

would have no application and would not enable furloughed wages or salary to be paid as the Scheme plainly envisages. That would be entirely contrary to the rescue culture in the current situation in which such an approach may be needed more than ever before.

'[74] I therefore see no reason whatever to strive to reach a conclusion that para 99(5) is wholly inoperable in the current situation. Instead, if it is possible to do so, para 99(5) should be interpreted to permit the Scheme to be given effect, and thus support the rescue culture and the Government's efforts to deal with the economic consequences of the COVID-19 pandemic.' *Re Carluccio's Ltd (in administration)* [2020] EWHC 886 (Ch), [2020] 3 All ER 291 at [70]–[74], per Snowden J

[Insolvency Act 1986, Sch B1 para 99(5).]
'[53] … When Lord Browne-Wilkinson referred [in *Powdrill v Watson ('Paramount')*] at [1995] 2 All ER 65 at 83, [1995] 2 AC 394 at 449 to "some conduct by the administrator or receiver which amounts to an election to treat the continued contract of employment as giving rise" to super-priority, he was not introducing as a relevant factor the intentions of the administrator, even if objectively determined. He did not, as Mr Smith submitted, require the conduct of the administrator to evidence an election by the administrator. It is a question of law: is the conduct of the administrator such that he must be taken to have to accept that the relevant amounts falling due under the employment contract enjoy super-priority? It is a wholly objective question, focussed entirely on the conduct of the administrator. As Lord Browne-Wilkinson repeatedly said, the issue is whether the office-holder has "continued" the employment of the relevant employees. This is the essence of the test propounded by him. If the office-holder has continued their employment, in other words has taken active steps to continue their employment, that necessarily results in super-priority for the relevant liabilities under the contracts of employment. As earlier noted, and by contrast, doing nothing involves no continuation by the administrators of the employment.

'[54] We agree with the way in which Laddie J summarised the effect of *Paramount* on the meaning of adoption in *Re Antal International Ltd (in admin)* [2003] EWHC 1339 (Ch), [2003] 2 BCLC 406, [2003] BPIR 1067 (at [7]):

"What Lord Browne-Wilkinson was pointing out was that it was important to find some conduct on behalf of the administrator or receiver which could be treated as an election or could be regarded as ... him exercising a choice as to whether or not the contracts of employment were to be adopted".

And again at [12] where he said:

"It is necessary to look at the facts and to decide whether there has been some conduct by the administrator or receiver which can legitimately be treated as an election to continue the contract of employment".'

Re Debenhams Retail Ltd (in administration) [2020] EWCA Civ 600, [2020] 3 All ER 319 at [53]–[54], per David Richards LJ

ADULTERY
[For 72 Halsbury's Laws of England (5th Edn) (2015) para 399 see now 72 Halsbury's Laws of England (5th Edn) (2019) para 394.]

ADMINISTRATION
[For 103 Halsbury's Laws of England (5th Edn) (2010) para 607 see now 103 Halsbury's Laws of England (5th Edn) (2016) para 607.]

ADVANCEMENT
[For 98 Halsbury's Laws of England (5th Edn) (2013) para 516 see now 98 Halsbury's Laws of England (5th Edn) (2019) para 489.]

AFTER-CARE SERVICES
[Mental Health Act 1983, s 117.] '[38] As discussed, in interpreting a statutory provision it is not sufficient to consider the ordinary meanings of the words used and how the same words are used elsewhere in the Act: it is necessary to identify the purpose of the provision, read in its context. The clear purpose of s 117 is to arrange for the provision of services to a person who has been, but is not currently being, provided with treatment and care as a hospital patient. That purpose is implicit in the very expression "after-care", which is used not only in the heading but throughout the body of s 117 in the phrase "after-care services". It is further articulated by the definition of "after-care services" in s 117(6). As specified in s 117(6)(b), to consti-

tute after-care services, the services must have the purpose of "reducing the risk of a deterioration of the person's mental condition (and, accordingly, reducing the risk of the person requiring admission to a hospital again for treatment for mental disorder)". That purpose is only capable of being fulfilled if the person concerned is not currently admitted to a hospital at which he or she is receiving treatment for mental disorder.

...

'[42] On the facts of the present case there is neither any need nor any scope for the claimant to be provided with "after-care services". As he remains in the care of the hospital and its staff even when he goes on the bus trips for which he is granted leave of absence, no question or possibility of "after-care" arises. Nor can it possibly be said in these circumstances that any services provided to the claimant during the trips have the purpose of "reducing the risk of the person requiring admission to a hospital again for treatment for mental disorder", as required by s 117(6)(b). This is not and could not be their purpose because the claimant's return to the hospital at the end of each trip is not a risk which it is the aim of the trip to reduce: it is inevitable, being one of the terms on which leave of absence is granted. In any case, the claimant does not require "admission to a hospital again for treatment" at the end of each trip, as I interpret those words, as he has remained admitted to the hospital for treatment throughout the trip. I would accept that the phrase "admission to a hospital" as it is used in s 117(6), like the phrase "leave hospital" in s 117(1), has to be read in light of the purpose of the provision, and is capable of applying to a person living in the community on leave of absence who is then recalled to hospital. But there is no basis in either the language or the purpose of s 117(6)(b) for regarding a person who returns from a trip during which he has never left the custody of hospital staff as requiring re-admission to the hospital for treatment. That is all the more so when, as noted earlier, one of the very purposes of the leaves of absence granted to the claimant in this case, recorded on the forms signed by the responsible clinician, is "treatment". In other words, the trips are part of the treatment which the hospital is providing to the claimant. Accordingly, the services provided to the claimant in taking him on escorted day trips do not and cannot constitute "after-care services" within the meaning of s 117.

...

'[44] The inescapable conclusion is that the claimant does not "cease to be detained" or "leave hospital" within the meaning of s 117(1) when he is escorted on day trips and is therefore not a person to whom s 117 applies. Moreover, even if this were wrong, I think it clear that the services provided during the trips do not constitute "after-care services" within the meaning of s 117(6) because it is not their purpose to reduce the risk of the claimant requiring admission to a hospital again for treatment for mental disorder; they are part of the treatment which he is currently receiving as a hospital patient. The claimant has at all times remained in the hospital's care.' *R (on the application of CXF (by his mother, his litigation friend)) v Central Bedfordshire Council* [2018] EWCA Civ 2852, [2019] 3 All ER 20 at [38], [42], [44], per Leggatt LJ

AGREED

[Limitation Act 1980, s 10(4): contribution under the Civil Liability (Contribution) Act 1978, s 1, in the case of a settlement is treated as accruing on the 'earliest date on which the amount to be paid ... is agreed'.] '[26] ... It is important to approach the section on the basis that ss 10(3) and (4) are, upon their true construction, intended to be mutually exclusive. I agree with Rix LJ that there can only be one trigger date to start time running under s 10; namely either:
26.1 the date of the judgment or award requiring a payment in cases where such issue is the subject of a judicial or arbitral determination; or
26.2 the date of the agreement to make the payment in a case where the issue is compromised.
'[27] Since there can only be one trigger event, it follows that time cannot start to run where the parties reach an unenforceable agreement as to payment. In such a case the litigation or arbitration remains on foot and time will only start to run under s 10(4) from the date of the subsequent formal agreement or, if the matter cannot be agreed, under s 10(3) from the date of the judgment or award.
'[28] In my judgment Mr Walker QC is right therefore to submit that the proper construction of s 10(4) is that time only starts to run from the date of a binding agreement as to the amount of the compensation payment.
...
'[32] [I]t is open to the parties to reach an immediately binding agreement as to the settlement payment, but leave for later agreement details as to payment terms ... or any liability for costs .... In such cases, time will start to run from the date of the agreement as to the amount of the payment. Equally, it is open to the parties to agree that, to use an expression much used in connection with the current Brexit negotiations, nothing is agreed until everything is agreed. If so, time will not start to run until the date of the subsequent binding agreement as to the payment or, should agreement prove impossible, the judgment or award.' *RG Carter Building Ltd v Kier Business Services Ltd (formerly Mouchel Business Services Ltd)* [2018] EWHC 729 (TCC), [2018] 4 All ER 456 at [26]–[29], [32], per Edward Pepperall QC

ALIEN

[For 4 Halsbury's Laws of England (5th Edn) (2011) para 411 see now 4 Halsbury's Laws of England (5th Edn) (2019) para 411.]

Australia [Commonwealth Constitution, s 51(xix).] '[73] The Commonwealth's concern, that to hold that its legislative power does not extend to treating an Aboriginal Australian as an alien is to identify a race-based limitation on power, is overstated. It is not offensive, in the context of contemporary international understanding, to recognise the cultural and spiritual dimensions of the distinctive connection between indigenous peoples and their traditional lands, and in light of that recognition to hold that the exercise of the sovereign power of this nation does not extend to the exclusion of the indigenous inhabitants from the Australian community.
'[74] The conclusion is not to deny that an attribute of every sovereign state is the power to decide whether an alien is admitted to membership of the community and to expel an alien whom it chooses not to suffer to remain. As Gleeson CJ observed in *Re Minister for Immigration and Multicultural Affairs; Ex parte Te* [(2002) 212 CLR 162; 193 ALR 37; [2002] HCA 48], the exercise of the power is vital to the welfare, security and integrity of the nation. The position of Aboriginal Australians, however, is sui generis. Notwithstanding the amplitude of the power conferred by s 51(xix) it does not extend to treating an Aboriginal Australian as an alien because, despite the circumstance of birth in another country, an Aboriginal Australian cannot be said to belong to another place.
...

'[373] Aboriginal Australians have a unique connection to this country; it is not just ancestry or place of birth or even both. It is a connection with the land or waters under Indigenous laws and customs which is recognised under Australian law. The Australian Citizenship Act has not removed or modified that connection. Nor has the Parliament removed or modified that connection by other legislation. Whether the Parliament could remove or modify that connection need not be decided.

'[374] It is a connection to this country that means that Aboriginal Australians are not foreigners within the constitutional concept of alien under s 51(xix). And it is a connection which means that even if an Aboriginal Australian's birth is not registered and as a result no citizenship is recorded, or an Aboriginal Australian is born overseas without obtaining Australian citizenship, they are not susceptible to legislation made pursuant to the aliens power or detention and deportation under such legislation.' *Love v Commonwealth* [2020] HCA 3, (2020) 375 ALR 597 at [73]–[74], per Bell J and at [373]–[374], per Gordon J

ALLUVION

[For 29 Halsbury's Laws of England (5th Edn) (2014) para 177 see now 29 Halsbury's Laws of England (5th Edn) (2019) para 182.]

AMBIGUITY

Latent ambiguity

[For 102 Halsbury's Laws of England (5th Edn) (2010) para 219 see now 102 Halsbury's Laws of England (5th Edn) (2016) para 220.]

Patent ambiguity

[For 102 Halsbury's Laws of England (5th Edn) (2010) para 219 see now 102 Halsbury's Laws of England (5th Edn) (2016) para 220.]

AMOTION

[For 24 Halsbury's Laws of England (5th Edn) (2010) para 364 see now 24 Halsbury's Laws of England (5th Edn) (2019) para 464.]

ANNUITY

[For 58 Halsbury's Laws of England (5th Edn) (2014) paras 549, 557 see now 99 Halsbury's Laws of England (5th Edn) (2018) paras 152, 159–160.]

ANOTHER PARTY

New Zealand [Funding agreement: by cl 3.2.2, where another party agreed to fund the proceedings, Blue Chip was to procure that party to repay the Funding and to pay the Fee.] '[61] Remember, the Liquidators acted as agent of Blue Chip. Any reference in the Agreement to "the company" incurring an obligation of necessity includes a reference to the Liquidators as agent of the company, with the authority under sch 6 of the Companies Act to conduct the business of the company. In that context, we note that:

(a) it is "the company and [explicitly] the Liquidators" who are to give Commercial Factors the first option;

(b) it is the company, and hence implicitly the Liquidators, who agree not to enter a Funding Agreement "with another party" on any less favourable terms without first reoffering the funding opportunity to Commercial Factors; and

(c) it is the company, and hence implicitly the Liquidators, who contract to procure the funder to pay "before the proceedings are filed or any funding for the proceedings is made available to the company or the liquidators".

'[62] In our view, therefore, when cl 3.2 refers to "another party" it is referring to a party other than the company or the Liquidators. We place particular reliance on the opening words of cl 3.2 in reaching that conclusion. That is, it is the Liquidators who will endeavour to obtain funding for proceedings and it is the Liquidators who, under s 301 of the Companies Act, actually take the proceedings. It would, in those circumstances, be unusual to regard the Liquidators as "another party" for the purposes of cl 3.2.2.' *Commercial Factors Ltd v Meltzer* [2018] NZCA 505, [2019] 2 NZLR 484 at [61]–[62], per Clifford J

ANY

Any appropriate relief

[Cross-Border Insolvency Regulations 2006, SI 2006/1030, Sch 1, art 21.] '[1] This appeal raises important questions about the proper scope of the powers conferred on the English court by the Cross-Border Insolvency Regulations 2006, SI 2006/1030, (the "CBIR") to order a stay of proceedings in this jurisdiction in support of a foreign insolvency proceeding.

...

'[84] It is clear, to my mind, that the present case does not involve an issue of jurisdiction in the former, or what one might call the "strict", sense. The application was made by a foreign representative of a foreign proceeding, duly recognised as such in this jurisdiction under the CBIR. Furthermore, the foreign proceeding was still in progress both when the application was made and when it was determined by the High Court. As Mr Bayfield made clear, the application is made under art 21(1)(a) and (b), which expressly empower the court, "where it is necessary to protect ... the interests of the creditors", to "grant any appropriate relief" at the request of the foreign representative, including a stay of the commencement or continuation of individual actions or proceedings concerning the debtor's assets, rights, obligations or liabilities, or a stay of execution against the debtor's assets to the extent that there has not already been an automatic stay under art 20(1)(a) and (b). As a matter of jurisdiction in the strict sense, the application seems to me to fall squarely within the clear wording of art 21. In particular, I would reject a submission made by Mr Moss that the only purpose of art 21(1)(a) and (b) is to enable the court, upon reorganisation of a foreign *non-main* proceeding, to grant equivalent relief to that automatically conferred by the corresponding paragraphs of art 20(1) in the case of a foreign *main* proceeding. That is no doubt an important function of art 21(1)(a) and (b), but I can see no warrant in the wide language of the paragraphs for confining their scope so narrowly.' *Re OJSC International Bank of Azerbaijan; Bakhshiyeva v Sberbank of Russia* [2018] EWCA Civ 2802, [2019] 2 All ER 713 at [1], [84], per Henderson LJ

Any person

New Zealand [Oranga Tamariki Act 1989, s 15.] '[57] Section 15 of OTA (as it was prior to 1 July 2019 amendments) provided:

> Any person who believes that any child or young person has been, or is likely to be, harmed (whether physically, emotionally, or sexually), ill-treated, abused, neglected, or deprived may report the matter to the chief executive or a constable.

'[58] Presuming (for present purposes) that "any person" includes a person employed by MSD [Ministry of Social Development] or MoE [Ministry of Education], s 15 imposes no duty to report. Rather, as this Court noted in *R v Strawbridge* [[2003] 1 NZLR 683, CA], it confers a "right" to report where the requisite belief is genuine. Meanwhile, as noted by the appellant, s 16 protects the reporter from civil, criminal or disciplinary proceedings, in relation to the disclosure.

...

'[61] The s 19 process is more formal and supervision of it is closer and more prescriptive. We accept that this section is designed for use by state agencies. The procedural requirements in subs (1A) reflect this. But ss 15 and 19 should not be mutually exclusive. A key purpose of the Act is to protect tamariki from harm. The Act's multiple reporting pathways should be construed liberally so as to be consistent with that purpose. There is no reason to read s 15 as if employees of MSD or MoE do not fit the description "any person". On the contrary, this is good reason to construe the phrase as applying to such employees if that would better provide for the safety of tamariki. We think it would. We conclude therefore that both ss 15 and 19 may be used by MSD and MoE employees to report to OT or the police any concerns they may have for the safety of tamariki.' *Attorney-General v J* [2019] NZCA 499, [2020] 2 NZLR 176 at [57]–[58], [61], per Williams J

APPARENT

[For 102 Halsbury's Laws of England (5th Edn) (2010) para 82 see now 102 Halsbury's Laws of England (5th Edn) (2016) para 82.]

ARMS

Court of Chivalry

[For 79 Halsbury's Laws of England (5th Edn) (2014) paras 884, 878–882 see now 79 Halsbury's Laws of England (5th Edn) (2020) paras 880, 874–878.]

ARREST

[For 84 Halsbury's Laws of England (5th Edn) (2013) para 485 see now 84 Halsbury's Laws of England (5th Edn) (2019) para 450.]

ARRESTS, RESTRAINTS AND DETAINMENTS

[For 60 Halsbury's Laws of England (5th Edn) (2011) para 330 see now 60 Halsbury's Laws of England (5th Edn) (2018) para 309.]

ARTICLES

[For 91 Halsbury's Laws of England (5th Edn) (2013) para 529 see now 91 Halsbury's Laws of England (5th Edn) (2019) para 429.]

AS A RESULT OF

Australia '[9] Whether a benefit can be said to be obtained "as a result of" knowing participation in a breach of fiduciary duty by another contrary to the principles of equity is a question of causation or contribution that depends on "a precise examination of the particular facts" of the case, rather than upon attempts to refine the expression "as a result of" as if that phrase has some determinate operation of its own that may be discerned and applied independently of the equitable principle of which it is part. The equitable disgorgement principle with which we are concerned is a "prophylactic rather than a restitutionary principle". It is sufficient to show that the profit would not have been made but for dishonest wrongdoing. Further, whatever may be the position for wrongdoing that is not marked by dishonesty, a defendant cannot avoid liability to disgorge profits dishonestly made by showing that those profits might have been made honestly. ...' *Ancient Order of Foresters in Victoria Friendly Society Ltd v Lifeplan Australia Friendly Society Ltd* [2018] HCA 43, (2018) 360 ALR 1 at [9], per Kiefel CJ, Keane and Edelman JJ

AS OF RIGHT

[For 32 Halsbury's Laws of England (5th Edn) (2012) para 23 see now 32 Halsbury's Laws of England (5th Edn) (2019) para 23.]

ASCERTAIN

[For 91 Halsbury's Laws of England (5th Edn) (2013) para 303 see now 91 Halsbury's Laws of England (5th Edn) (2019) para 304.]

ASSET

Canada '1 At issue in this appeal is whether the interest that the appellant, SA, has in a trust that was set up for her care and maintenance should be treated as an "asset", which would negatively affect her eligibility to participate in a rental subsidy program offered by her landlord, the respondent, Metro Vancouver Housing Corporation ("MVHC").

'**40** The next issue that must be addressed is the meaning of the word "assets" as it is used in the Assistance Application, which is the source of SA's obligation to supply MVHC with information supporting the valuation of her assets if she wishes to be considered for rental assistance. To be clear, the issue in this appeal is not the meaning of the word "assets" *in the abstract*, but rather how that word should be understood in the specific context of MVHC's Rental Assistance Program. In this respect, I agree with the Court of Appeal that the Chambers Judge erred in analyzing this issue at least in part through the lens of the Tenancy Agreement: "[t]he critical document to determine whether to grant rental assistance is the Assistance Application" (para 52).

...

'**46** If the definition in [the Asset Ceiling] policy does not apply, what should the word "assets" be understood to mean? The words in the Assistance Application must be given their ordinary and grammatical meaning in light of the specific context in which they were used (*Sattva* [*Sattva Capital Corp v Creston Moly Corp* 2014 SCC 53, [2014] 2 SCR. 633], at paras 47–48; *Ledcor Construction Ltd v Northbridge Indemnity Insurance Co* 2016 SCC 37, [2016] 2 SCR 23, at para 27). With this in mind, I would observe that the word "asset" is ordinarily used to denote valuable property that a person can use to discharge debts and other liabilities. One of the definitions of the word "asset" in the Oxford English Dictionary (online) is "an item of value owned; spec. an item on a balance sheet representing the value of a resource, right, item of property, etc., placed under an appropriate heading. Frequently coupled with *liability*". Similarly, Merriam-Webster (online) defines the plural word "assets" as "the entire property of a person, association, corporation, or estate applicable or subject to the payment of debts" and the singular word "asset" as "an item of value owned". The Chambers Judge referred to a similar definition from *Black's Law Dictionary* (6th ed 1990), at p 117 (Chambers Judge's Reasons, at para 50):

> Property of all kinds, real and personal, tangible and intangible, including inter alia, for certain purposes, patents and causes of action which belong to any person including a corporation and the estate of a decedent. The entire property of a person, association, corporation, or estate that is applicable or subject to the payment of his or her or its debts.
>
> ...
>
> '**56** A careful reading of documents relevant to the resolution of this appeal leads me to conclude that the word "assets", as it is used in the Assistance Application, is not broad enough to encompass SA's interest in the Trust. Given that the discretion over distributions lies exclusively in the Trustees' hands, SA's interest in the trust property is in the nature of a mere hope of receiving some or all of that property in the future. Unless and until the Trustees actually decide to make distributions in SA's favour, that interest is not in practice something on which she can rely to pay the rent (or to offset other debts and liabilities).' *SA v Metro Vancouver Housing Corp* [2019] SCJ No 4, [2019] 1 SCR 99 at paras 1, 40, 46, 56, per Côté J

ASSIGNMENT

[For 22 Halsbury's Laws of England (5th Edn) (2012) para 333 see now 22 Halsbury's Laws of England (5th Edn) (2019) para 135.]

AT AND FROM

[For 60 Halsbury's Laws of England (5th Edn) (2011) para 249 see now 60 Halsbury's Laws of England (5th Edn) (2018) para 228.]

AT WORK

'**100** ... An employee is "at work", for the purposes of both the Management Regulations [Management of Health and Safety at Work Regulations 1999, SI 1999/3242] and the PPE Regulations [Personal Protective Equipment at Work Regulations 1992, SI 1992/2966], throughout the time when she is in the course of her employment: section 52(1)(b) of the [Health and Safety at Work etc Act 1974]. The point is illustrated by the facts of *Robb v Salamis (M & I) Ltd* [2007] ICR 175. Miss Kennedy in particular, as a home carer, was "at work" when she was travelling between the home of one client and that of another in order to provide them with care. Indeed, travelling from one client's home to another's was an integral part of her work. The meaning of the words "while at work" in regulation 4(1) of the PPE Regulations (and of the equivalent words, "whilst they are at work", in regulation 3(1) of the Management Regulations) is plain. They mean that the employee must be exposed to the risk during the time when she is at work, that is to say, during the time when she is in the course of her employment. They refer to the time when she is exposed to the risk, not to the cause of the risk.' *Kennedy v Cordia (Services) LLP* [2016] UKSC 6, [2016] ICR 325 at para 100, per Lord Reed and Lord Hodge JJSC

ATTAINDER

[For 24 Halsbury's Laws of England (5th Edn) (2012) para 643 see now 24A Halsbury's Laws of England (5th Edn) (2019) para 43.]

ATTEST

[For 102 Halsbury's Laws of England (5th Edn) (2010) para 70 et seq see now 102 Halsbury's Laws of England (5th Edn) (2016) para 70 et seq.]

ATTORNEY

[For 65 Halsbury's Laws of England (5th Edn) (2015) para 435 see now 22 Halsbury's Laws of England (5th Edn) (2020) para 397.]

AUCTION

[For 4 Halsbury's Laws of England (5th Edn) (2011) para 1 see now 4 Halsbury's Laws of England (5th Edn) (2020) para 1.]

AUCTIONEER

[For 4 Halsbury's Laws of England (5th Edn) (2011) para 2 see now 4 Halsbury's Laws of England (5th Edn) (2020) para 1.]

AVERAGE

[For 7 Halsbury's Laws of England (5th Edn) (2011) paras 606–608 see now 7 Halsbury's Laws of England (5th Edn) (2020) paras 553–555.]

General average

[For 60 Halsbury's Laws of England (5th Edn) (2011) para 386 see now 60 Halsbury's Laws of England (5th Edn) (2018) para 364.]

Particular average

[For 60 Halsbury's Laws of England (5th Edn) (2011) para 399 see now 60 Halsbury's Laws of England (5th Edn) (2018) para 377.]

AWARE OF

[Taxes Management Act 1970, s 29(5): 'discovery assessment' allowed where officer could not have been reasonably expected, on the basis of the information made available to him before a specified time, to be 'aware of' the situation mentioned in s 29(1).] '[27] In *Revenue and Customs Comrs v Lansdowne Partners Ltd Partnership* [[2011] EWCA Civ 1578, [2012] STC 544, 81 TC 318], when considering the meaning of "be aware of" for the purposes of s 29(5), it was said that "awareness" was a matter of perception not conclusion and that it was possible to say that an officer was "aware of" something even when he could not at that stage resolve points of law and even though he was not then aware of all of the facts which might turn out to be relevant. Although the word "discover" and the phrase "be aware of" cannot be treated as synonyms, we consider that if it is possible to be aware of something when one does not know all of the relevant facts and one cannot foretell how relevant points of law will be resolved, it cannot be said to be premature for an officer to "discover" that same something even when he knows he is not in possession of all of the relevant facts and does not know how relevant points of law will be resolved.' *Anderson v Revenue and Customs Commissioners* [2018] UKUT 159 (TCC), [2018] 4 All ER 338 at [27], per Morgan J and Judge Berner

B

BAILMENT

[For 4 Halsbury's Laws of England (5th Edn) (2011) paras 101, 106 see now 4 Halsbury's Laws of England (5th Edn) (2020) paras 101, 106.]

BAIRD PRINCIPLE

'[8] But a series of 19th century cases beginning with *Coverdale v Charlton* (1878) 4 QBD 104 and culminating in the decision of the House of Lords in *Mayor of Tunbridge Wells v Baird* [1896] AC 434, [1895–9] All ER Rep Ext 2006, established that the successive statutory provisions for the automatic vesting of proprietary interests in highways in the bodies responsible for their maintenance and repair operated in a much more limited way than would a simple conveyance or transfer of the freehold. First, it was a determinable, rather than absolute, fee simple, which would end automatically if the body responsible for its repair ceased to be so responsible (eg if the road ceased to be a public highway): see *Rolls v Vestry of St George the Martyr, Southwark* (1880) 14 Ch D 785. Secondly it was inalienable, for so long as that responsibility lasted. Thirdly, and most importantly for present purposes, statutory vesting conferred ownership only of that slice of the land over which the highway ran, viewed in the vertical plane, as was necessary for its ordinary use, including its repair and maintenance. Following the example of counsel, I shall call this "the Baird principle".

'[9] That slice of the vertical plane included, of course, the surface of the road over which the public had highway rights, the subsoil immediately beneath it, to a depth sufficient to provide for its support and drainage, and a modest slice of the airspace above it sufficient to enable the public to use and enjoy it, and the responsible authority to maintain and repair it, and to supervise its safe operation. That lower slice was famously labelled 'the top two spits' in *Tithe Redemption Commission v Runcorn Urban DC* [1954] 1 All ER 653 at 661, [1954] Ch 383 at 407. A spit is a spade's depth. Although colourful, that phrase says nothing about the necessary airspace above the surface. Again following counsel's example, I prefer the phrase "zone of ordinary use".

'[10] It is common ground that the zone of ordinary use is a flexible concept, the application of which may lead to different depths of subsoil and heights of airspace being vested in a highway authority, both as between different highways and even, over time, as affects a particular highway, according to differences or changes in the nature and intensity of its public use. A simple footpath or bridleway might only require shallow foundations, and airspace of up to about ten feet, to accommodate someone riding a horse. By contrast a busy London street might require deep foundations to support intensive use, and airspace sufficient to accommodate double-decker buses, and even the overhead electric power cables needed, in the past, by trolley buses and, now, by urban trams.

'[11] The Baird principle was developed so as to limit, in the vertical plane, the defeasible freehold interest automatically vested in the body responsible for the repair of a highway. This was because, in a series of leading judgments, the court regarded this statutory vesting as a form of expropriation of private property rights without compensation, and was therefore concerned to limit its effect strictly to that which was necessary to achieve the Parliamentary objective, that is conferring upon highway authorities sufficient property to enable them to perform their statutory duties of the repair, maintenance and operation of highways. ...' *Southwark London Borough Council v Transport for London* [2018] UKSC 63, [2019] 2 All ER 271 at [8]–[11], per Lord Briggs

BARONET

[For 79 Halsbury's Laws of England (5th Edn) (2014) para 861 see now 79 Halsbury's Laws of England (5th Edn) (2020) para 857.]

BARRATRY

[For 60 Halsbury's Laws of England (5th Edn) (2011) para 333 see now 60 Halsbury's Laws of England (5th Edn) (2018) para 312.]

BED

Of minerals

[For 76 Halsbury's Laws of England (5th Edn) (2013) para 14 see now 76 Halsbury's Laws of England (5th Edn) (2019) para 14.]

Of river

New Zealand [Resource Management Act 1991, s 2.] '[2] This appeal is primarily concerned with the proper interpretation of "bed", as it relates to a river, under s 2 of the RMA. Relevantly, "bed" is defined as "the space of land which the waters of the river cover at its fullest flow without overtopping its banks". The Council contends that the High Court's interpretation (given on appeal from the District Court) was incorrect.

...

'[10] The second judgment was appealed to the High Court where Gendall J considered that Judge Hassan applied the wrong legal test to determining the bed of a river for the purposes of the RMA. The correct legal test was regarded as the "bank to bank" test outlined in *Kingdon v Hutt River Board* (1905) 25 NZLR 145, SC, which stands for the proposition that the bed of a river extends only from bank to bank, and more specifically, is the area within the banks covered by water during the rainy season.

'[11] The High Court held that the words "usual or non-flood" should be implied and read into the RMA definition of "bed" before the words "fullest flow". "Fullest flow" for the purpose of the definition was therefore to be regarded as:

... the river's fullest usual flow over a reasonable period of years of river activity cycles, and not including flood waters that would flow onto the margins and flood plain adjacent to the river.

...

'[36] Of relevance is the fact that the terms "fullest flow" and "banks", used in the definition of "bed" in s 2(1), are not defined in the RMA.

...

'[38] In the present context, the terms "bed" and "river" are used in connection with statutory restrictions on the uses of beds of rivers. ...

...

'[51] To assist the analysis in this case, the following principles emerge from the above common law authorities:

(a) The description of a river or watercourse includes as essential features the channel (or bed) and its banks.

(b) The bed comprises the space between the banks occupied by the river at its fullest flow.

(c) Ascertaining the bed in a given case will require consideration of all relevant geographical, meteorological and hydrological features such as banks, channels, shores, seasonal flows, as well as unseasonable wet weather events which produce a flood where the water overflows the banks and spreads into the surrounding areas.

(d) The bed of a river is not limited to the portion between the banks through which the water flows only in dry weather. Equally, though a river or watercourse is dry for part (even the greater part) of the year, it is nonetheless a river or watercourse.

(e) The bank of a river is the outermost part of the bed and comprises an acclivity or elevation of land above the level of the adjacent land or water, which creates a boundary sufficient to prevent the water from flowing into the neighbouring land.

(f) The banks of some rivers may often be indistinct or indefinite and liable to constant changes, as are the waters or currents in their beds.

(g) All the water contained in the riverbed, between the two banks, or their high-water line on the shore, is river.

(h) Ascertaining the dividing line between the banks and the bed cannot be determined by reference only to the ordinary high water mark or the ordinary low water mark. The task requires examining the banks and the bed and finding where the presence and action of the water are common or usual as apply in ordinary years. Also relevant are the nature of the soils of the bed and the banks and the surrounding vegetation.

(i) The bed of a river is a natural object to be determined not by abstract rules, but by the distinctive appearances they present, particularly in respect of the banks and their soils and vegetation.

...

'[77] It follows that we also agree with the view of Gendall J that a river's "fullest flow" for the purposes of the definition of "bed" must be something less than the point where it floods.

'[78] It was at this point of his analysis that Gendall J invoked the principle (correctly in our view) that the bed of a river comprises those lands covered by water during the ordinary rainy season, but contained within the banks of the river and extending from bank to bank. Such an approach is entirely consistent with the common law and the principles set out in the treatises discussed above.

'[79] Accordingly, we consider that the determination of the "bed" of a river, as defined in s 2(a)(ii), will depend not only on the position of the banks of the river, but also on the water coverage measure as determined by the river's fullest flow which occurs within those banks. This latter criterion is qualified by the words "without overtopping its banks". This qualifying term serves to exclude flows or inundations arising from major storms where the water extends temporarily beyond the banks.

'[80] We would not exclude from consideration in particular cases those features identified in principles (c), (d) and (h) in [51] above. These factors are all endorsed by the common law cases and we see no basis for excluding them in the wording of the s 2 definition of "bed".

...

'[99] For all the above reasons we uphold the interpretation of Gendall J in the High Court as to the meaning of "bed" in relation to a river in s 2(a)(ii) of the RMA definition of "bed".'
Canterbury Regional Council v Dewhirst Land Co Ltd [2019] NZCA 486, [2020] 2 NZLR 10 at [2], [10]–[11], [36], [38], [51], [77]–[80], [99], per Stevens J

BEDROOM

[Housing Benefit Regulations 2006, SI 2006/213, reg B13(5).] '[2] The issue for consideration in this appeal is: what is a "bedroom" for the purpose of reg B13(5)? The size criteria pursuant to B13(5) entitle an HB claimant to

"one bedroom for each of the following categories of person" in occupation of the property. The categories are listed (a) to (e) as at the relevant time of the first respondent's determination.

...

'[37] The methodology of the regulations is that the bedroom is used as a proxy for need. The size criteria/bedroom criteria are a means of quantifying cash entitlement. A "bedroom" does not represent a precise proxy. The Secretary of State accepts that it is an imprecise means of measuring need but it serves the purpose because all persons in housing need a bedroom and thus it is useful. It is also accepted that mismatches can arise but can be met, for example, by DHPs.

'[38] "Bedroom" is an ordinary word which is neither defined nor qualified in the regulations. The word has to be construed and applied in its context having regard to the underlying purposes of the legislation. The underlying purpose of the regulations is to limit HB entitlement to those occupying social housing. The language of the regulations demonstrates that the criteria identified as limiting such benefit is the entitlement of a tenant to a bedroom for persons listed in sub-paras (5) and (6). The assessment is to be carried out by the relevant authority in respect of a notionally vacant house. A point accepted by the first respondent. It is also accepted by the first respondent that B13(5) depersonalises the assessment to be performed such that the characteristics of the particular individuals are irrelevant. It follows that such an assessment is an objective one.

'[39] There is nothing in the regulations to indicate that any such assessment is required to take account of how a property and, in particular, the bedrooms in the property would be used by a particular family unit. Were that to be so, the purpose underlying the legislation would be frustrated as a tenant could, by use of the property, change the objective classification so as to reduce the relevant number of bedrooms. This further demonstrates the objective nature of the assessment and, with it, the interpretation of "bedroom" within B13(5).

...

'[41] For the reasons given I find that pursuant to the size criteria (reg B13(5) of the Housing Benefit Regulations 2006, which entitles the housing benefit claimant to "one bedroom for each of the following categories of person" in occupation of the property) the word "bedroom" should be interpreted as meaning a room capable of being used as a "bedroom" by any of the listed categories and not a room capable of being used as a "bedroom" by the particular claimant. In holding that the correct interpretation was a room capable of being used as a "bedroom" by the particular claimant, the UT erred in law and its decision was wrong.' *Hockley v Secretary of State for Work and Pensions* [2019] EWCA Civ 1080, [2020] 2 All ER 20 at [2], [37]–[39], [41], per Nicola Davies LJ

BENEVOLENT
[For 8 Halsbury's Laws of England (5th Edn) (2015) para 93 see now 8 Halsbury's Laws of England (5th Edn) (2019) para 93.]

BEQUEST
[For 102 Halsbury's Laws of England (5th Edn) (2010) para 286 see now 102 Halsbury's Laws of England (5th Edn) (2016) para 284.]

BETH DIN

Australia '[1] On 14 December 2017, the primary judge, Sackar J, found the appellants guilty of two charges of criminal contempt on the basis that they had threatened the second respondent, Mr Reuven Barukh, with religious sanctions if he did not submit to the jurisdiction of the Sydney Beth Din, a religious court that administers Halacha, or Jewish law: *Live Group Pty Ltd v Ulman* [2017] NSWSC 1759.
...
'[6] According to the appellants, the Beth Din has authority to determine civil disputes between observant Jews, its jurisdiction deriving from the interpretation of Jewish law by the Rabbis who constitute themselves as a Beth Din. In other words, *"their ultimate authority comes from themselves in the sense that as a community of Dayan ... they interpret as best they can ... the Halachic law"*. *Ulman v Live Group Pty Ltd* [2018] NSWCA 338, (2018) 367 ALR 95 at [1], [6], per Bathurst CJ and Beazley P

BILL
[For 96 Halsbury's Laws of England (5th Edn) (2012) para 767 see now 96 Halsbury's Laws of England (5th Edn) (2018) para 376.]

Hybrid bill
[For 96 Halsbury's Laws of England (5th Edn) (2012) para 625 see now 96 Halsbury's Laws of England (5th Edn) (2018) para 225.]

BILL OF LADING
[Delete the entry referenced to 91 Halsbury's Laws of England (5th Edn) (2012) para 377; and for 7 Halsbury's Laws of England (5th Edn) (2015) paras 314, 324 see now 7 Halsbury's Laws of England (5th Edn) (2020) paras 428, 440.]

BLASPHEMY
[Delete the entry referenced to 11(1) Halsbury's Laws of England (4th Edn 2006 Reissue) para 826.]

BLOCKADE
[For 85 Halsbury's Laws of England (5th Edn) (2012) para 614 see now 85 Halsbury's Laws of England (5th Edn) (2020) para 714.]

BODY

Corpse
[For 24 Halsbury's Laws of England (5th Edn) (2010) para 83 see now 24 Halsbury's Laws of England (5th Edn) (2019) para 272.]

BONA VACANTIA
[For 29 Halsbury's Laws of England (5th Edn) (2014) para 149 see now 29 Halsbury's Laws of England (5th Edn) (2019) para 154.]
[For 102 Halsbury's Laws of England (5th Edn) (2010) para 513 see now 102 Halsbury's Laws of England (5th Edn) (2016) para 512.]

BOOTY
[For 85 Halsbury's Laws of England (5th Edn) (2012) para 605 see now 85 Halsbury's Laws of England (5th Edn) (2020) para 705.]

BOUNDARY

[For 4 Halsbury's Laws of England (5th Edn) (2011) para 301 see now 4 Halsbury's Laws of England (5th Edn) (2020) para 301.]

BROKER

[For 91 Halsbury's Laws of England (5th Edn) (2012) para 43 see now 91 Halsbury's Laws of England (5th Edn) (2019) para 42.]

BY REASON OF

New Zealand [Securities Act 1978, s 56(1).] '[129]   If investors establish that they have invested on the faith of the prospectus, it will still be necessary for them to establish that they have sustained loss by reason of the untrue statement. We turn to that aspect of s 56(1) now.

'[130]   The words "loss or damage [investors] may have sustained by reason of such untrue statement" indicate that there must be a nexus between the untrue statement and the loss sustained by the investor. The issue is what type of nexus is required. We consider that the words must be interpreted consistently with the meaning given to the concept of "untrue statement" in terms of s 55(a) (in particular the fact that it refers to an untrue statement, not a materially untrue statement) and the words "on the faith of [the] prospectus" in s 56(1) (particularly that those words do not require proof of actually having read and relied on the untrue statement and, indeed, do not require that an investor has read the prospectus).

'[131]   Given our conclusion that s 55(a) deals with untrue statements, not just materially untrue statements, we see the "by reason of" requirement in s 56 as a mechanism for control-ling the imposition of liability under s 56 (which is consistent with the courts' approach to "legal" causation in other areas).

...

'[134]   We consider that the issue is rather whether loss or damage was sustained "by reason of" an untrue statement in a prospectus. This means that a court must determine whether the effect of the untrue statement was such that the market value of the securities for which the investor subscribed would have been lower than the price paid if the misleading statement had not been made or, put another way, if the prospectus had complied in all respects with the Securities Act and the Securities Regulations. If the price paid by the investor was greater than the price that would have been payable if adequate disclosure had been made in the prospectus, the investor will have suffered loss "by reason of" the untrue statement, assuming the investor has proved he or she invested on the faith of the prospectus in the sense described above.

'[135]   In some cases, the untruth will be egregious and its impact obvious. In that type of case, subscribers may be able to obtain compensation equalling the full amount of their investment under s 56. Their argument would be that revelation of the truth would have revealed that the securities were, in truth, valueless or of such little value that investors would not have invested had the true position been known. In less serious cases, the inquiry will be on whether the revelation of the true position in the prospectus would have indicated the securities had a lower value than the offer price.' *Houghton v Saunders* [2018] NZSC 74, [2019] 1 NZLR 1 at [129]–[131], [134]–[135], per Elias CJ, Glazebrook, O'Regan, Arnold and Kós JJ

C

C.I.F.

[For 91 Halsbury's Laws of England (5th Edn) (2012) para 14 see now 91 Halsbury's Laws of England (5th Edn) (2019) para 15; and for 91 Halsbury's Laws of England (5th Edn) (2012) para 335 see now 7 Halsbury's Laws of England (5th Edn) (2020) para 387.]

CAPTURE

[For 60 Halsbury's Laws of England (5th Edn) (2011) paras 328, 330 see now 60 Halsbury's Laws of England (5th Edn) (2018) paras 307, 309.]

CARGO

Deck cargo

[For 7 Halsbury's Laws of England (5th Edn) (2015) para 456 see now 7 Halsbury's Laws of England (5th Edn) (2020) para 253.]

CARRIAGE OF GOODS

[For 7 Halsbury's Laws of England (5th Edn) (2015) paras 7–27 see now 7 Halsbury's Laws of England (5th Edn) (2020) para 7.]

CARRIER

Private carrier

[For 7 Halsbury's Laws of England (5th Edn) (2015) paras 56–70 see now 7 Halsbury's Laws of England (5th Edn) (2020) paras 10–24.]

CASUAL PROFIT

[For 58 Halsbury's Laws of England (5th Edn) (2014) para 653 see now 99 Halsbury's Laws of England (5th Edn) (2019) para 233.]

CHALLENGE

[For 61 Halsbury's Laws of England (5th Edn) (2010) para 825 see now 61A Halsbury's Laws of England (5th Edn) (2018) para 225.]

CHARGE (NOUN)

[Equality Act 2010, s 165: taxi driver's duty 'not to make any additional charge' for carrying disabled person in wheelchair.] '[17] It is not in dispute between the parties that demanding payment from a wheelchair user for the time it takes to board the taxi would amount to the making of an additional charge for the purposes of s 165(4)(b) and s 165(7) of the EA 2010. …

…

'[19] The main issue on this appeal is whether a "charge" was made by the Appellant by the act of him switching on his taximeter before Ms Vogelman and Ms Creek had boarded, even though Ms Vogelman never entered his taxi, no money was demanded (either expressly or by implication) and they ended up travelling in a different taxi.

…

'[29] The starting point is to note the precise language used in s 165(4)(b). The driver's duty is not "to make any additional charge" as a result of being hired by or on behalf of a disabled person. In this phrase the word "charge" is being used as a noun and not a verb. The online Oxford English Dictionary definitions of "charge" when used as a noun include "a price asked for goods or services" and also "a financial liability or commitment" (see https://en.oxforddictionaries.com/definition/charge).

'[30] The first of these meanings supports, to an extent, Mr Taylor's submission that the point in time when a driver makes an additional charge can only be at the end of the journey because it is then and only then that the precise fare can be ascertained, in other words, only is the price asked. On the other hand, the second definition supports Mr Patience's submission that in a taxi fitted with a taximeter the passenger's obligation is to pay whatever the meter shows at the end of journey, and so the moment the meter is switched on the passenger becomes financially liable for the fare, and it is thus at that point that the driver makes the charge.

'[31] In my judgment it is the second meaning which is to be ascribed to the word "charge" as used in s 165(4)(b), and a taxi driver makes a charge when he switches his taximeter on, and if he does this for a disabled passenger before the passenger and her wheelchair have been loaded into the taxi, there will be an additional charge and thus an offence under s 165(7) even if, for whatever reason, the driver never actually demands the fare.

...

'[35] In my judgment there can be no doubt that no later than the time a taximeter is switched on at the point of hire, an actual financial liability or commitment is imposed on the passenger to pay the amount shown on the meter when the hiring is terminated, and it is therefore at that point that the charge is made for the purposes of s 165(4)(b). ...

...

'[42] For these reasons, in my judgment the words "make an additional charge" in s 165(4)(b) mean to impose an additional financial liability or commitment on a disabled wheelchair user as compared with an able bodied passenger, and such a liability or commitment is imposed no later than the point when a London taxi driver switches on his meter before such a person and their wheelchair have boarded the taxi.' *McNutt v Transport for London* [2019] EWHC 365 (Admin), [2020] 1 All ER 84 at [17], [19], [29]–[31], [35], [42], per Julian Knowles J

CHARITY—CHARITABLE PURPOSES

General meaning [For 8 Halsbury's Laws of England (5th Edn) (2015) para 2 see now 8 Halsbury's Laws of England (5th Edn) (2019) para 2.]

CHARTER VALUES

Canada '61. As this Court explained in *Bell ExpressVu Limited Partnership v Rex*, 2002 SCC 42, [2002] 2 SCR 559, the "Charter values" interpretive principle serves a narrow purpose: when faced with two interpretations—one compliant with the Canadian Charter of Rights and Freedoms ("Canadian Charter"), the other infringing it—courts can apply the presumption of compliance with the Canadian Charter to read the statute in a manner respectful of the Charter value in question. This allows the statute to remain in force—untouched—and interpreted such that it complies with the Canadian Charter. This principle, however, does not allow the courts to generate in the name of Charter values an interpretation unsupported by the text of the statute (*Bell ExpressVu*, at para 62; *R v Clarke* 2014 SCC 28, [2014] 1 SCR 612, at para 12).' *Quebec (Commission des normes, de l'équité, de la santé et de la sécurité du travail) v Caron* [2018] SCJ No 3, [2018] 1 SCR 35 at para 61, per Rowe J

CHARTERPARTY

[For 7 Halsbury's Laws of England (5th Edn) (2015) paras 208, 211 see now 7 Halsbury's Laws of England (5th Edn) (2020) paras 162, 166.]

CHILDREN'S HOME

'[21] A "children's home" is defined in s 1(2) of the Care Standards Act 2000 as "An establishment [which] provides care and accommodation wholly or mainly for children" but this is subject to various qualifications in the Act and regulations which exclude certain types of accommodation from being classified as a "children's home". Thus, for example, s 1(3) provides that "an establishment is not a children's home merely because a child is cared for and accommodated there by a parent or relative of his or by a foster parent", s 1(4A) and (5) exclude hospitals and schools from the definition of a "children's home". Part II of the Care Standards Act makes provision for the registration and regulation of children's homes in England. The Children's Homes (England) Regulations 2015, SI 2015/541, in addition to excluding other types of accommodation from being classified as a "children's home", prescribe a range of quality standards for children's homes and make further wide-ranging provisions designed to ensure the safety and welfare of children in such establishments. ...' *Re B (a child) (Association of Lawyers for Children intervening)* [2019] EWCA Civ 2025, [2020] 3 All ER 375 at [21], per Baker LJ

CHURCHWAY

[For 55 Halsbury's Laws of England (5th Edn) (2012) para 6 see now 55 Halsbury's Laws of England (5th Edn) (2019) para 8; and for 32 Halsbury's Laws of England (5th Edn) (2012) para 37 see now 32 Halsbury's Laws of England (5th Edn) (2019) para 37.]

CIVIL COMMOTION

[For 60 Halsbury's Laws of England (5th Edn) (2011) para 571 see now 60 Halsbury's Laws of England (5th Edn) (2018) para 548.]

CIVIL LIST

[For 29 Halsbury's Laws of England (5th Edn) (2014) para 120 see now 29 Halsbury's Laws of England (5th Edn) (2019) para 125.]

CIVIL PARTNERSHIP

[For 72 Halsbury's Laws of England (5th Edn) (2015) para 3 see now 72 Halsbury's Laws of England (5th Edn) (2019) para 4.]

CLASS

Gift to

[For 102 Halsbury's Laws of England (5th Edn) (2010) para 175 see now 102 Halsbury's Laws of England (5th Edn) (2016) para 175.]

CLASS CLOSURE ORDER

Australia [Civil Procedure Act 2005 (NSW), s 183.] '[33] The principal issue on the appeal was whether order 16 in the present case was within the power granted by s 183 of the Civil Procedure Act. So-called "class closure orders" have been endorsed by the Full Court of the Federal Court as being empowered by s 33ZF of the Federal Court Act, which is equivalent to s 183 of the Civil Procedure Act. The appellants submitted that ss 183 and 33ZF did not support an interpretation empowering the making of order 16 for the purpose of encouraging or facilitating a settlement. Further, it was submitted that even if there was power to make such an order, the discretion to make order 16 here miscarried.

...

'[62] Jargon abounds in cases arising under Pt 10 of the Civil Procedure Act. Order 16 describes itself as a "class closure order". "Class closure" is not a statutory term. Part 10 authorises a wide range of representative proceedings which may, but need not, concern an "open class". That is to say, Part 10 permits representative proceedings to be brought on behalf of Group Members who may (but need not necessarily) be identifiable on a list.

'[63] As it happens, practical considerations often result in representative proceedings being commenced on behalf of an open class, although that need not be so. Insofar as it was repeatedly submitted that "closure", whether at all or particularly before any settlement, was necessary, that is not so as a matter of demonstrable historical fact.

'[64] Critically, one of the few mandatory requirements in Pt 10 is for all Group Members to be given the right to "opt out" prior to the commencement of the initial hearing: s 162. That right is supported by requirements of notice: s 175(1)(a). But there is no requirement to "close" an open class before any hearing, including the hearing of common questions, even if that hearing about common questions also includes the hearing of claims for actual loss by the representative applicant and individual Group Members.

'[65] Part 10 deals expressly with the possibility of settlement but only by imposing an additional requirement of court approval: s 173(1). Part 10 says nothing about an obligation to "close" a class before a settlement is achieved or before mediation occurs.

'[66] That legislative framework tends strongly against an implication that there must be power to make an order extinguishing the rights of an unregistered Group Member in advance of any settlement being achieved (or even attempted) in order to facilitate settlement of the claims of Group Members who choose to register their claims.

'[67] Practical considerations may in many cases make it desirable to convert an "open" class to a "closed" or fully identified class of Group Members. This may occur in a number of ways. For very many years this occurred by courts permitting an amendment to the originating process so as to narrow the group definition so that it applied only to persons who in addition to having a claim against the defendant had also registered themselves or had retained the same firm of solicitors or agreed to a funding agreement with an external funder.

...

'[78] Of course, neither "class closure" nor "closed class" is a statutory term. Both terms describe the effect of amendments to originating process and pleadings or the operation of court orders upon the legal rights of Group Members in representative proceedings.

...

'[114] Nevertheless, order 16 in the present case is beyond the power conferred by s 183. This is not because settlement of proceedings is not a desirable aim. Plainly it is. I do not, however, accept as the respondents submitted that the "supplementary" power in s 183 was intended to provide a power of contingently extinguishing Group Members' claims so that "realistic settlement discussions may take place" by "seeking to crystallise the outer sum being claimed".

...

'[119] There are two significant matters to consider. The first is that the scheme of Part 10 is inconsistent with an interpretation of s 183 as empowering the Court to make orders for pre-settlement class closure. ...' *Haselhurst v Toyota Motor Corp Australia Ltd (t/a Toyota Australia)* [2020] NSWCA 66, (2020) 379 ALR 556 at [33], [62]–[67], [78], [114], [119], per Payne JA

CLEARLY ABUSIVE

New Zealand [Immigration Act 2009, s 140(3): A refugee and protection officer may refuse to consider a subsequent claim for recognition as a refugee or a protected person if the officer is satisfied that the claim: (a) is manifestly unfounded or clearly abusive; or (b) repeats any claim previously made (including a subsequent claim).] '[58] Woodhouse J considered it preferable in approaching the issue of whether WK's fourth claim was "clearly abusive" to take "[a]ll relevant factors" into account, rather than to define that term by reference "to a set of circumstances" or "synonyms". The Judge accepted that a "clearly abusive" claim could include one that is lodged to prolong the appeal or deportation process, but that the circumstances in which a clearly abusive claim may arise were not exhaustive.

...

'[60] The RPO [Refugee and Protection Officer] concluded that WK's fourth claim was "clearly abusive". That finding rested on the history of WK's claims and the timing of his fourth claim. ...

'[61] We consider that such a conclusion would not have been available to the RPO unless, as Woodhouse J observed, "[a]ll relevant factors" had been taken into account. In the circumstances of the present case, the relevant factors would necessarily include the particulars of the subsequent claim. The effect of the RPO's assessment was that WK's fourth claim based on his social media activities did not give rise to any essentially different risk of refoulement. It follows in those circumstances that, even on the test contended for by Mr Pidgeon, the RPO was permitted to draw an adverse inference from the timing of WK's fourth claim to conclude it was clearly abusive. This is particularly so when set against the history of his previous claims and the unmeritorious nature of WK's subsequent claim. In the circumstances, we, like Woodhouse J, consider that the RPO's finding was reasonably available to him.' *WK v Refugee and Protection Officer* [2018] NZCA 258, [2019] 2 NZLR 223 at [58], [60]–[61], per Mander J

CODICIL

[For 102 Halsbury's Laws of England (5th Edn) (2010) para 1 see now 102 Halsbury's Laws of England (5th Edn) (2016) para 1.]

COLLIERY

[For 76 Halsbury's Laws of England (5th Edn) (2013) para 15 see now 76 Halsbury's Laws of England (5th Edn) (2019) para 15.]

COLLISION

Collision clause in marine policy

[For 60 Halsbury's Laws of England (5th Edn) (2011) para 336 see now 60 Halsbury's Laws of England (5th Edn) (2018) para 315.]

COMMERCIAL PRACTICE

[Consumer Protection from Unfair Trading Regulations 2008, SI 2008/1277, reg 2(1); European Parliament and Council Directive 2005/29/EC (Unfair Practices Directive), art 2.] '[41] [I]n my judgment, a commercial practice for the purposes of art 2(d) of the Directive (and thus reg 2(1) of the 2008 Regulations) may be constituted by or derived from a test purchase made of a product (including a service) that is generally promoted to and intended for purchase by consumers, even where the purchaser may not himself be a consumer. Specifically, the giving to the test purchaser of an invoice or other document incorporating false information as to a main characteristic of the product (including the execution of a service) that would mislead the average consumer into paying for services that he has not received (which he would not otherwise have done) is a commercial practice which is a misleading action for the purposes of regs 5 and 9 of the 2008 Regulations, being "directly connected with the promotion, sale or supply of a product to ... consumers".' *Warwickshire County Council v Halfords Autocentres Ltd (Competition and Markets Authority intervening)* [2018] EWHC 3007 (Admin), [2019] 2 All ER 69 at [41], per Hickinbottom LJ

COMMODITY EXCHANGE

[Commercial Agents (Council Directive) Regulations 1993, SI 1993/3053, reg 2(2)(b): Regulations not to apply tp commercial agents when they operate on commodity exchanges or in the commodity market.] '[76]   Taking first the concept of a "commodity exchange", I am unable to agree with the judge that an exchange in its historical and commercial sense is simply a place for sales to take place. No one, for example, would reasonably describe a supermarket as an exchange. Nor are the facts that the class of persons able to buy is restricted and the process of selling regulated sufficient to make a place where sales take place an exchange. An auction house, for example, where only people who satisfy specified criteria are permitted to bid and where sales are conducted in accordance with the auctioneer's rules would not be regarded in the commercial world as an exchange. The nature of an "exchange", as I believe the term would generally be understood, is a place where trading takes place among members of the exchange and subject to its rules. The corresponding phrases in the French and German text ("les bourses du commerce" and "Handelsbörsen") have a similar connotation. Thus, well known examples of commodity exchanges in the UK are the London Commodity Exchange, which in 1996 merged to become part of the London International Financial Fu-

tures Exchange ("LIFFE"), and the London Metal Exchange. Trading on such exchanges was traditionally conducted by open outcry, but now generally takes place electronically. Most of the trading on modern commodity exchanges is in futures and options but, like the judge, I see no reason to regard the availability of trading in such contracts as an essential characteristic. What would in my view be regarded as an essential feature of a commodity exchange is that the commodities (or rights to buy and sell commodities) which are traded on the exchange can be freely bought and sold among the participants.
...
'[85]   I would accordingly hold that, in acting as a commercial agent for Pluczenik in negotiating purchases of rough diamonds from De Beers, Nagel was not operating on a commodity exchange or in the commodity market and that its activities were therefore within the scope of the Directive and the Regulations. It follows that on the termination of the agency contract Nagel was entitled to compensation from Pluczenik under reg 17." *W Nagel (a firm) v Pluczenik Diamond Co NV* [2018] EWCA Civ 2640, [2019] 2 All ER 194 at [76], [85], per Leggatt LJ

COMMODITY MARKET

[Commercial Agents (Council Directive) Regulations 1993, SI 1993/3053, reg 2(2)(b): Regulations not to apply tp commercial agents when they operate on commodity exchanges or in the commodity market.] '[77]   I agree with the judge that the fact that the Directive [Council Directive 86/653/EEC on the co-ordination of the laws of member States relating to self-employed commercial agents] uses two different expressions ("commodity exchanges" and "the commodity market" in the English version) indicates that the two expressions must be intended to have different, even if overlapping, meanings. Thus, the phrase "the commodity market" must be wider than simply connoting the sum of all commodity exchanges; otherwise its inclusion would be superfluous. But equally, the phrase "the commodity market" must be given a meaning which does not make the inclusion of the reference to "commodity exchanges" superfluous. That is achieved, as it seems to me, by interpreting "commodity exchanges" as typical or paradigmatic instances of "the commodity market". Thus, transactions negotiated or concluded in the commodity mar-

ket are transactions of a similar kind as those which are negotiated or concluded on a commodity exchange. So understood, the commodity market encompasses any general trading in commodities that takes place in the open market.
...

'[85] I would accordingly hold that, in acting as a commercial agent for Pluczenik in negotiating purchases of rough diamonds from De Beers, Nagel was not operating on a commodity exchange or in the commodity market and that its activities were therefore within the scope of the Directive and the Regulations. It follows that on the termination of the agency contract Nagel was entitled to compensation from Pluczenik under reg 17.' *W Nagel (a firm) v Pluczenik Diamond Co NV* [2018] EWCA Civ 2640, [2019] 2 All ER 194 at [77], [85], per Leggatt LJ

COMMON CARRIER

[For 7 Halsbury's Laws of England (5th Edn) (2015) para 3 see now 7 Halsbury's Laws of England (5th Edn) (2020) para 3.]

COMPOSITION

[For 5 Halsbury's Laws of England (5th Edn) (2013) para 856 see now 5 Halsbury's Laws of England (5th Edn) (2020) para 40, n 2.]

CONDITION

Conditions precedent and subsequent

[For 102 Halsbury's Laws of England (5th Edn) (2010) para 129 see now 102 Halsbury's Laws of England (5th Edn) (2016) para 129.]

CONDITIONAL DISCHARGE

[Mental Health Act 1983, s 73(2): tribunal must in specified circumstances direct conditional discharge of a patient who is subject to a restriction order.] '[28] The MHA is silent: it says nothing about the type or content of the conditions which may be imposed by the Secretary of State or the FtT [First-tier Tribunal]. In this respect it has remained unchanged since the 1959 Act. There are several possibilities: (1) that the FtT cannot impose a condition of detention in a hospital but the Secretary of State

may do so; (2) that neither may do so; (3) that both may impose a condition of detention in a place which is not a hospital within the meaning of the MHA whether or not the patient consents; (4) that both may do so but only if the patient consents; and (5) that neither may do so.

'[29] There is of course the argument that a condition which amounts to a detention or deprivation of liberty could nonetheless serve the rehabilitative purpose of the power of conditional discharge. Just as there is nothing in the MHA which permits it, there is nothing in the MHA which prohibits it. The thinking of the experienced Upper Tribunal in *RB* [*Secretary of State for Justice v RB* [2010] UKUT 454 (AAC)] (para [21] above) is worthy of respect. The main textual argument in favour of a power to impose such a condition is that a conditionally discharged patient remains "liable to be detained" within the meaning of the MHA (see para [18] above). As such, he is more akin to a hospital patient who has been given leave of absence than to a patient who is subject to a community treatment order. "Discharge" therefore cannot mean "discharge from compulsion". Although it must mean "discharge from the hospital where he is currently detained", it need not mean any more than that, and so could encompass a range of possible arrangements. Furthermore, although it is clear that the FtT cannot impose a condition of detention in a hospital for treatment, because by definition the FtT is not satisfied that the grounds for such detention exist (para [10] above), the same is not true of the Secretary of State. He has power to discharge the patient conditionally irrespective of whether the grounds for detention in hospital still exist.' *Secretary of State for Justice v MM* [2018] UKSC 60, [2019] 2 All ER 749 at [28]–[29], per Lady Hale P

CONSIDERATION

[Value Added Tax: whether overpayments in respect of parking at 'pay and display' car parks, where a customer who did not have correct change paid more than the stipulated amount, were consideration.] '[6] Article 1(2) of Council Directive 2006/112/EC on the common system of value added tax ("the Principal VAT Directive") explains that the principle of the common system of VAT "entails the application to goods and services of a general tax on consumption exactly proportional to the price of the goods and services". Amongst the transactions subject to VAT are "the supply of services for consideration within the territory of a Member State by a taxable person acting as such" (art 2(1)(c)). By art 73, in respect of a supply of goods or services:

"the taxable amount shall include everything which constitutes consideration obtained or to be obtained by the supplier, in return for the supply, from the customer or a third party ..."

'[7] Provisions to similar effect are to be found in the Value Added Tax Act 1994. Under s 4(1), VAT is to be charged on "any supply of goods or services made in the United Kingdom, where it is a taxable supply made by a taxable person in the course or furtherance of any business carried on by him". "Supply" includes "all forms of supply, but not anything done otherwise than for a consideration" (s 5(2)(a)).

'[8] The word "consideration", which features in both arts 2(1)(c) and 73 of the Principal VAT Directive and s 5(2)(a) of the 1994 Act, does not in the VAT context refer to what might be deemed "consideration" for the purposes of domestic contract law but has an autonomous EU-wide meaning (see eg *Staatssecretaris van Financiën v Coöperative Aardappelenbewaarplaats* (Case 154/80) EU:C:1981:38, [1981] ECR 445, [1981] 3 CMLR 337 ("the *Dutch potato* case"), at para 9 of the judgment of the Court of Justice. "[T]he concept of the supply of services effected for consideration within the meaning of art 2(1) of the Sixth Directive [ie the predecessor of the Principal VAT Directive] presupposes the existence of a direct link between the service provided and the consideration received" (*Apple and Pear Development Council v Customs and Excise Comrs* (Case 102/86) EU:C:1988:120, [1988] 2 All ER 922, [1988] ECR 1443, at para 12 of the Court of Justice's judgment; see also eg *Commission of the European Communities v Finland* (Case C-246/08) EU:C:2009:671, [2009] ECR I-10605, at para 45 of the Court of Justice's judgment). A supply of services is effected "for consideration", and hence is taxable, "only if there is a legal relationship between the provider of the service and the recipient pursuant to which there is reciprocal performance, the remuneration received by the provider of the service constituting the value actually given in return for the service supplied to the recipient" (*Tolsma v Inspecteur der Omzetbelasting Leeuwarden* (Case C-16/93) EU:C:1994:80, [1994] STC 509, [1994] ECR I-743, at para 14 of the Court of Justice's judgment; see also eg

Geemente Borsele v Staatssecretaris van Financiën, Staatssecretaris van Financiën v Geemente Borsele (Case C-520/14) EU:C:2016:334, [2016] STC 1570, at para 24 of the Court of Justice's judgment).

'[9] The authorities also show that "consideration" is a "subjective value" in the sense that "the basis of assessment for the provision of services is the consideration actually received and not a value assessed according to objective criteria" (the *Dutch potato* case, at para 13 of the judgment). In *Campsa Estaciones de Servicio SA v Administración del Estado* (Case C-285/10) EU:C:2011:381, [2011] STC 1603, the Court of Justice explained in para 28 of its judgment:

"According to settled case law ..., the taxable amount for the supply of goods or services for consideration is the consideration actually received for them by the taxable person. That consideration is thus the subjective value, that is to say, the value actually received, and not a value estimated according to objective criteria."

...

'[11] In the present case, the UT [Upper Tribunal], upholding the FTT's [First-tier Tribunal's] decision, considered that in the hypothetical example set out in para [3] above the taxable amount and consideration for VAT purposes was the full £1.50 actually paid rather than the £1.40 tariff for up to an hour's parking. ...

...

'[18] English law, of course, generally adopts an objective approach when deciding what has been agreed in a contractual context. Here, it seems to me that, taken together, the tariff board and the statement that "overpayments" were accepted and no change given indicated, looking at matters objectively, that NCP was willing to grant an hour's parking in exchange for coins worth at least £1.40. In the hypothetical example, the precise figure was settled when the customer inserted her pound coin and 50p piece into the machine and then elected to press the green button rather than cancelling the transaction. The best analysis would seem to be that the contract was brought into being when the green button was pressed. On that basis, the pressing of the green button would represent acceptance by the customer of an offer by NCP to provide an hour's parking in return for the coins that the customer had by then paid into the machine. At all events, there is no question of the customer having any right to repayment of 10p. The contract price was £1.50.

'[19] This is the contractual analysis in the hypothetical example where the customer has only a pound coin and a 50p piece, and therefore has no alternative but to pay £1.50 if she wishes to park in the car park. However, the analysis is the same even if it is possible for the customer to obtain the right coins, for example by obtaining change from another user of the car park. If the customer nevertheless chooses to insert £1.50 and presses the green button, it remains the case that she has accepted the offer to provide an hour's parking at that price.
...

'[22] In the circumstances, I agree with the UT and FTT that, in the hypothetical example, the consideration and taxable amount was £1.50. Like the UT, I consider that, "[i]f a customer pays £1.50, that amount is the value given by the customer and received by the supplier in return for the right to park for up to an hour". That means that NCP's present appeal should be dismissed.' *National Car Parks Ltd v Revenue and Customs Commissioners* [2019] EWCA Civ 854, [2019] 3 All ER 590 at [6]–[9], [11], [18]–[19], [22], per Newey LJ

CONTEMPT OF COURT
[For 22 Halsbury's Laws of England (5th Edn) (2012) para 2 see now 24 Halsbury's Laws of England (5th Edn) (2019) para 2.]

CONTRACT
[For 22 Halsbury's Laws of England (5th Edn) (2012) para 201 see now 22 Halsbury's Laws of England (5th Edn) (2019) para 1.]

Contract of record
[For 22 Halsbury's Laws of England (5th Edn) (2012) para 215 see now 22 Halsbury's Laws of England (5th Edn) (2019) para 11.]

Contract made by deed
[For 22 Halsbury's Laws of England (5th Edn) (2012) para 216 see now 22 Halsbury's Laws of England (5th Edn) (2019) para 12.]

Executed contract
[For 22 Halsbury's Laws of England (5th Edn) (2012) para 205 see now 22 Halsbury's Laws of England (5th Edn) (2019) para 6.]

Executory contract
[For 22 Halsbury's Laws of England (5th Edn) (2012) para 205 see now 22 Halsbury's Laws of England (5th Edn) (2019) para 6.]

Illegal contract
[For 22 Halsbury's Laws of England (5th Edn) (2012) para 452 see now 22 Halsbury's Laws of England (5th Edn) (2019) para 243.]

Simple contract
[For 22 Halsbury's Laws of England (5th Edn) (2012) para 218 see now 22 Halsbury's Laws of England (5th Edn) (2019) para 14.]

Void contract
[For 22 Halsbury's Laws of England (5th Edn) (2012) para 207 see now 22 Halsbury's Laws of England (5th Edn) (2019) para 4.]

Voidable contract
[For 22 Halsbury's Laws of England (5th Edn) (2012) para 207 see now 22 Halsbury's Laws of England (5th Edn) (2019) para 4.]

CONTRIBUTION

Insurance
[For 60 Halsbury's Laws of England (5th Edn) (2011) paras 233–234 see now 60 Halsbury's Laws of England (5th Edn) (2018) paras 212–213.]

CONTRIBUTORY
[For 17 Halsbury's Laws of England (5th Edn) (2011) para 661 et seq see now 17 Halsbury's Laws of England (5th Edn) (2017) para 599 et seq.]

CORPORATION

Corporation aggregate
[For 24 Halsbury's Laws of England (5th Edn) (2010) para 312 see now 24 Halsbury's Laws of England (5th Edn) (2019) para 412.]

Corporation sole

[For 24 Halsbury's Laws of England (5th Edn) (2010) para 314 see now 24 Halsbury's Laws of England (5th Edn) (2019) para 414.]

COSTS

[For 29 Halsbury's Laws of England (5th Edn) (2014) para 310 see now 29 Halsbury's Laws of England (5th Edn) (2019) para 310.]

Of appeal

[For 12 Halsbury's Laws of England (5th Edn) (2015) para 1737 et seq see now 12A Halsbury's Laws of England (5th Edn) (2015) para 1680 et seq.]

COURT

[For 24 Halsbury's Laws of England (5th Edn) (2010) para 606 see now 24A Halsbury's Laws of England (5th Edn) (2019) para 6.]

Court of a State

Australia [Commonwealth Constitution, Ch III; Judiciary Act 1903 (Cth), s 39.] '[172] As was apparent from the summary of the submissions which I have set out above, each of the parties approached the question of whether the Tribunal [New South Wales Civil and Administrative Tribunal] was a "court of a State" for the purpose of Ch III of the Constitution in a somewhat different fashion. The applicant and the Commonwealth approached it as a matter of construing the legislation which established the body, while the contradictors suggested that, if all the indispensable features of a "court" were present, then it was a "court of a State" for the purpose of Ch III of the Constitution irrespective of whether the State legislature intended to create it as such.

'[173] In the present case, I do not think that the different approaches yield different results. It will be unusual to find that the legislature created a body with all the essential characteristics of a "court" for the purpose of Ch III of the Constitution while not intending it to be a "court" in some other sense.

'[174] In *Pompano* [*Assistant Commissioner Condon v Pompano Pty Ltd* (2013) 252 CLR 38; 295 ALR 638; [2013] HCA 7] at [125], the majority stated that "independence and impartiality are defining characteristics of all of the courts of the Australian judicial system". Similarly, Gageler J emphasised at [182]–[183]

that, for a court to be able to act judicially, it "must have institutional integrity: it must 'be and appear to be an independent and impartial tribunal'", citing *Forge* [*Forge v Australian Securities and Investments Commission* (2006) 228 CLR 45; 229 ALR 223; 59 ACSR 1; [2006] HCA 44] at [78]; *Bradley* [*North Australian Aboriginal Legal Aid Service Inc v Bradley* (2004) 218 CLR 146; 206 ALR 315; [2004] HCA 31] at [29].

'[175] However, there are three things to be noted in this context. The first is that, as was pointed out in *Bradley* at [30], "no exhaustive statement of what constitutes [the minimum standard] in all cases is possible". The second is that it is clear that a "court of a State" does not have to be solely constituted by judges with the same terms of appointment as s 72 of the Constitution provides for judges of federal courts: see *Commonwealth v Hospital Contribution Fund of Australia* (1982) 150 CLR 49 at 61; 40 ALR 673 at 682 (*Hospital Contribution Fund*); *Forge* at [40]–[41].

'[176] The third matter is this. The fact that the Tribunal has some of the "trappings" or features of a court does not necessarily mean it is a "court of a State" for the purpose of Ch III of the Constitution. ...

...

'[184] Applying these principles to the present case, I am of the view that, although the Tribunal has many of the features of a "court" and can, in a number of areas, exercise State judicial power, it is not a "court of a State" for the purpose of Ch III of the Constitution. My reasons are set out below. While none of these may be decisive individually, in combination, they lead to the clear conclusion that the Tribunal is not a "court of a State".

...

'[190] The combination of these factors means that, in my view, the State legislature did not intend the Tribunal to be a "court of a State" for the purpose of Ch III of the Constitution and that the Tribunal did not have the necessary degree of independence and impartiality to constitute such a court. Thus, irrespective of the approach adopted, the same conclusion is reached.

...

'[192] In these circumstances, I am of the opinion that the Tribunal was not a "court of a State" for the purpose of Ch III of the Constitution or s 39 of the Judiciary Act 1903 (Cth).' *Attorney-General (NSW) v Gatsby (2018 of 66655)* [2018] NSWCA 254, (2018) 361 ALR 570 at [172]–[176], [184], [190], [192], per Bathurst CJ

CORONAVIRUS
In this Act: 'coronavirus' means severe acute respiratory syndrome coronavirus 2 (SARS-CoV-2); 'coronavirus disease' means COVID-19 (the official designation of the disease which can be caused by coronavirus)' (Coronavirus Act 2020, s 1(1))

COURT MARTIAL
[For 3 Halsbury's Laws of England (5th Edn) (2011) paras 633, 638 see now 3 Halsbury's Laws of England (5th Edn) (2019) paras 534, n 1, 534, 538.]

COVENANT
[For 32 Halsbury's Laws of England (5th Edn) (2012) para 448 see now 32 Halsbury's Laws of England (5th Edn) (2019) para 448.]

CRIMINAL CAUSE OR MATTER
[Senior Courts Act 1981, s 18(1)(a): no appeal to Court of Appeal from any judgment of the High Court in any 'criminal cause or matter'; appeal against refusal of judicial review of decision to discontinue prosecutions.] '[22] In my opinion, it is wholly plain that the judgment below was in a "criminal cause or matter". That being so, by reason of the provisions of s 18(1) of the 1981 Act no appeal lies to this court.

'[23] It does no harm first to view the matter without reference to authority. In the present case, there had been ongoing criminal proceedings in the Crown Court. The decision of the CPS was to discontinue those criminal proceedings. How, it may be asked, can a judgment upholding such a decision be anything other than in a criminal matter? Mr Schama could give no sensible answer.
...

'[25] At all events, what cannot here validly be maintained is that there is no criminal cause or matter involved simply and solely because the decision under challenge is a decision of the executive sought to be challenged on public law grounds in judicial review proceedings. Such an approach most emphatically is not the law.' *R (on the application of Thakrar) v Crown Prosecution Service* [2019] EWCA Civ 874, [2020] 1 All ER 704 at [22]–[23], [25], per Davis LJ

CROWN EMPLOYMENT
[Employment Rights Act 1996, s 191.] '[23] Section 191(3) provides that "In this Act 'Crown employment' means employment under or for the purposes of a government department or any officer or body exercising on behalf of the Crown functions conferred by a statutory provision". Clearly, "employment" in this section cannot mean "employment under a contract" because it would then add nothing to the definition in s 230(3). The predecessor to s 191 was inserted into the Industrial Relations Act 1971 because historically Crown servants had not been seen to be employed under contracts of service and had not been able to complain of wrongful dismissal. The object was to enable them to complain of unfair dismissal and enjoy the other employment rights listed in s 191(2). Thus, argues the appellant, s 191 is apt to give her the protection of Pt IVA even if she is not employed under a contract.

'[24] The definition in s 191(3) has two limbs: employment under or for the purposes of a government department; and employment under or for the purposes of an officer or body exercising on behalf of the Crown functions conferred by a statutory provision. For the reasons given earlier, it is impossible to regard the judiciary as employed under or for the purposes of the Ministry of Justice. They are not civil servants or the equivalent of civil servants. They do not work for the ministry. It is slightly more plausible to regard them as working under or for the purposes of the Lord Chief Justice, who since the 2005 Act [Constitutional Reform Act 2005], has had statutory responsibilities in relation to the judiciary: under s 7 of that Act, he is responsible for the maintenance of appropriate arrangements for the welfare, training and guidance of the judiciary of England and Wales (within the resources provided by the Lord Chancellor) and for their deployment and the allocation of work within the courts. As already noted, he also shares some responsibility for appointments, discipline and removal with the Lord Chancellor. But it is difficult to think that, by conferring these functions upon the Lord Chief Justice, the 2005 Act brought about such a fundamental change in the application of s 191. Judges do not work "under and for the purposes of' those functions of the Lord Chief Justice but for the administration of justice in the courts of England and Wales in accordance with their oaths of office. Mutatis mutandis, the same reasoning would apply to the identical definition of crown employment in art 236(3) of the Employment Rights (Northern Ireland) Order 1996, SI 1996/1919.

'[25] It is perhaps worth noting that s 83(2) and (9) of the Equality Act 2010, passed since the 2005 Act, defines "employment" as covering "Crown employment" as defined in s 191 of the 1996 Act. But it also makes express provision, in ss 50 and 51, prohibiting discrimination in relation to, among other things, appointment to public offices. These are defined to include officers appointed by or on the recommendation of a member of the executive (such as the Lord Chancellor) or by the Lord Chief Justice or Senior President of Tribunals. Thus judicial office-holders are clearly protected by these provisions, which would have been quite unnecessary had they already been protected as persons in Crown employment. Sections 50 and 51 do not apply in Northern Ireland, but this does not affect the force of this point.' *Gilham v Ministry of Justice* [2019] UKSC 44, [2020] 1 All ER 1 at [23]–[25], per Lady Hale P

CUSTOM

[For 32 Halsbury's Laws of England (5th Edn) (2012) paras 1, 6 see now 32 Halsbury's Laws of England (5th Edn) (2019) paras 1, 6.]

CY-PRÈS

Application to charity

[For 8 Halsbury's Laws of England (5th Edn) (2015) para 209 see now 8 Halsbury's Laws of England (5th Edn) (2019) para 207.]

D

DAMAGE

Pecuniary damage

[For 29 Halsbury's Laws of England (5th Edn) (2014) para 312 see now 29 Halsbury's Laws of England (5th Edn) (2019) para 312.]

DAMAGES

[For 29 Halsbury's Laws of England (5th Edn) (2014) para 304 see now 29 Halsbury's Laws of England (5th Edn) (2019) para 304.]

Aggravated damages

[For 29 Halsbury's Laws of England (5th Edn) (2014) para 322 see now 29 Halsbury's Laws of England (5th Edn) (2019) para 322.]

Liquidated damages

[For 29 Halsbury's Laws of England (5th Edn) (2014) para 311 see now 29 Halsbury's Laws of England (5th Edn) (2019) para 311.]

Liquidated damages and penalty distinguished

[For 29 Halsbury's Laws of England (5th Edn) (2014) para 551 see now 29 Halsbury's Laws of England (5th Edn) (2019) paras 550–551.]

Nominal damages

[For 29 Halsbury's Laws of England (5th Edn) (2014) paras 319–320 see now 29 Halsbury's Laws of England (5th Edn) (2019) paras 319–320.]

Prospective damages

[For 29 Halsbury's Laws of England (5th Edn) (2014) para 314 see now 29 Halsbury's Laws of England (5th Edn) (2019) para 314.]

Special damages

[For 29 Halsbury's Laws of England (5th Edn) (2014) para 317 see now 29 Halsbury's Laws of England (5th Edn) (2019) para 317.]

Statutory damages

[For 29 Halsbury's Laws of England (5th Edn) (2014) para 302 see now 29 Halsbury's Laws of England (5th Edn) (2019) para 302.]

DE BONIS NON

[For 103 Halsbury's Laws of England (5th Edn) (2010) para 793 see now 103 Halsbury's Laws of England (5th Edn) (2016) para 793.]

DEDICATION

[For 55 Halsbury's Laws of England (5th Edn) (2012) para 111 see now 55 Halsbury's Laws of England (5th Edn) (2019) para 142.]

DEED

[For 32 Halsbury's Laws of England (5th Edn) (2012) paras 201, 208 see now 32 Halsbury's Laws of England (5th Edn) (2019) paras 201, 208.]

DEED POLL

[For 32 Halsbury's Laws of England (5th Edn) (2012) para 203 see now 32 Halsbury's Laws of England (5th Edn) (2019) para 203.]

DEFAMATION

[For 32 Halsbury's Laws of England (5th Edn) (2012) paras 510, 543 see now 32 Halsbury's Laws of England (5th Edn) (2019) paras 509, 543.]

DELIVERY

Of goods

[For 91 Halsbury's Laws of England (5th Edn) (2012) para 161 see now 91 Halsbury's Laws of

England (5th Edn) (2019) para 164; and for 91 Halsbury's Laws of England (5th Edn) (2012) paras 161–193 see now 91 Halsbury's Laws of England (5th Edn) (2019) paras 164–196.]

DEMISE

Of monarch

[For 29 Halsbury's Laws of England (5th Edn) (2014) para 11 see now 29 Halsbury's Laws of England (5th Edn) (2019) para 11.]

DEMURRAGE

[For 7 Halsbury's Laws of England (5th Edn) (2015) para 288 see now 7 Halsbury's Laws of England (5th Edn) (2020) para 332.]

DEPENDENT RELATIVE REVOCATION

[For 102 Halsbury's Laws of England (5th Edn) (2010) para 108 see now 102 Halsbury's Laws of England (5th Edn) (2016) para 108.]

DEPOSIT

Of chattel

[For 4 Halsbury's Laws of England (5th Edn) (2011) para 111 see now 4 Halsbury's Laws of England (5th Edn) (2020) para 111.]

DEPRIVATION OF LIBERTY

[Mental Health Act 1983, s 17A: detained patient may in specified circumstances be discharged from hospital under a community treatment order ('CTO'); Human Rights Act 1998, Sch 1, Pt I, art 5 (right to liberty).] '[18] The Welsh Ministers are entirely correct in what they say about the legal effect of a CTO. But it does not follow that the patient has not in fact been deprived of his liberty as a result of the conditions to which he is subject. The European Court of Human Rights has said time and time again that the protection of the rights contained in the European Convention must be practical and effective. When it comes to deprivation of liberty, they and we must look at the concrete situation of the person concerned: has he in fact been deprived of his liberty? Otherwise, all kinds of unlawful detention might go unremedied, on the basis that there was no

power to do it. That is the antithesis of what the protection of personal liberty by the ancient writ of habeas corpus, and now also by art 5 of the Convention, is all about.

'[19] Since the judgment in the Upper Tribunal, this case has proceeded on the basis that the factual circumstances in which PJ found himself under the CTO conditions did amount to a deprivation of liberty. Charles J found that the MHRT had applied the wrong test, but neither made the determination for himself nor sent the case back for the MHRT to do so. But it is enough for our purposes to proceed on the basis that there was a deprivation of liberty on the ground. The question is whether the RC has power, under the MHA, to impose conditions which have that effect.' *Welsh Ministers v PJ* [2018] UKSC 66, [2019] 2 All ER 766 at [18]–[19], per Lady Hale P

'[28] For what it is worth, in the case of *Secretary of State for the Home Dept v JJ* [2007] UKHL 45, [2008] 1 All ER 613, [2008] 1 AC 385, it was taken for granted that a curfew enforced by electronic tagging, clocking in and clocking out, and arrest or imprisonment for breach was a "classic detention or confinement" (para [59]). The only question was whether it was also a deprivation of liberty within the meaning of art 5 of the ECHR [European Convention on Human Rights], which leads on to the second issue.

'[29] Mr Tam makes an alternative argument in this Court which was not open to him in the courts below. This is that the concept of imprisonment for the purpose of the tort of false imprisonment should now be aligned with the concept of deprivation of liberty within the meaning of art 5 of the ECHR. The classic definition of this concept is taken from *Guzzardi v Italy* (App no 7367/76) (1980) 3 EHRR 333, [1980] ECHR 7367/76, at para 92:

> "In order to determine whether someone has been 'deprived of his liberty' within the meaning of article 5, the starting point must be his concrete situation and account must be taken of a whole range of criteria such as the type, duration, effects and manner of implementation of the measure in question."

'The ECHR distinguishes between the deprivation and restriction of liberty and the court emphasised that this was a matter of degree rather than nature or substance (para 93). This multi-factorial approach is very different from the approach of the common law to imprisonment.

'[30] In *Austin v Metropolitan Police Comr* [2007] EWCA Civ 989, [2008] 1 All ER 564, [2008] QB 660, the Court of Appeal held that "kettling" the claimants for several hours at Oxford Circus was indeed imprisonment at common law, but that it was justified by the common law principle of necessity; however, it was not a deprivation of liberty within the meaning of art 5, a conclusion with which both the House of Lords and the European Court of Human Rights agreed: [2009] UKHL 5, [2009] 3 All ER 455, [2009] AC 564, and *Austin v UK* (App no 39692/09) (2012) 32 BHRC 618, (2012) 55 EHRR 14. The trial judge's observation that there could be imprisonment at common law without there being a deprivation of liberty under art 5 and vice versa was cited by the Court of Appeal with apparent approval (para [87]). That observation was repeated by the Court of Appeal in *Walker v Comr of the Police of the Metropolis* [2014] EWCA Civ 897, [2015] 1 WLR 312, [2015] 1 Cr App Rep 283, where it was held to be false imprisonment for a police officer to stand in the front doorway of a house so as to prevent the claimant from leaving, even for a very short time, but it was not a deprivation of liberty within the meaning of art 5.

'[31] By contrast, when the *Bournewood* case [*R v Bournewood Community and Mental Health NHS Trust, ex p L* [1998] 3 All ER 289, [1999] AC 458, HL) reached the European Court of Human Rights, that court held that the patient had been deprived of his liberty within the meaning of art 5: *HL v UK* [(2004) 81 BMLR 131, (2004) 40 EHRR 761, ECtHR]. This is thought to be the only case going the other way. Imprisonment for the purpose of the tort of false imprisonment can take place for a very short period of time, whereas a number of factors are relevant to whether there has been a deprivation of liberty. On the other hand, imprisonment may be justified at common law in circumstances which are not covered by the list of possibly permissible deprivations of liberty in art 5(1) of the ECHR.

'[32] Mr Tam argues that the time has now come to align the two concepts: specifically to align the concept of imprisonment with the concept of deprivation of liberty. He says this because, in *Secretary of State for the Home Dept v JJ* [2007] UKHL 45, [2008] 1 All ER 613, [2008] 1 AC 385, while the House of Lords held, by a majority, that a 16-hour curfew was a deprivation of liberty, Lord Brown of Eaton-under-Heywood expressed the view that an eight-hour curfew, such as this, would not be such a deprivation.

'[33] It is, of course, the case that the common law is capable of being developed to meet the changing needs of society. In Lord Toulson's famous words in *Kennedy v Charity Commission* [2014] UKSC 20, [2014] 2 All ER 847, [2015] AC 455 (at [133]), "it was not the purpose of the [Human Rights Act 1998] that the common law should become an ossuary". Sometimes those developments will bring it closer to the ECHR and sometimes they will not. But what Mr Tam is asking this Court to do is not to develop the law but to make it take a retrograde step: to restrict the classic understanding of imprisonment at common law to the very different and much more nuanced concept of deprivation of liberty under the ECHR. The Strasbourg court has adopted this approach because of the need to draw a distinction between the deprivation and the restriction of physical liberty. There is no need for the common law to draw such a distinction and every reason for the common law to continue to protect those whom it has protected for centuries against unlawful imprisonment, whether by the State or private persons.

'[34] The Court of Appeal in Austin and in Walker were right to say that there could be imprisonment at common law without there being a deprivation of liberty under art 5. Whether they were also right to add 'and vice versa' may be open to doubt in the light of the *Bournewood* saga, but it is not necessary for us to express an opinion on the matter.' *R (on the application of Jalloh (formerly Jollah)) v Secretary of State for the Home Department* [2020] UKSC 4, [2020] 3 All ER 449 at [28]–[34], per Lady Hale

DEROGATION FROM GRANT

[For 32 Halsbury's Laws of England (5th Edn) (2012) para 258 see now 32 Halsbury's Laws of England (5th Edn) (2019) para 258.]

DESCENDANT

[For 102 Halsbury's Laws of England (5th Edn) (2010) para 339 see now 102 Halsbury's Laws of England (5th Edn) (2016) para 338.]

DESERTION

Matrimonial causes

[For 72 Halsbury's Laws of England (5th Edn) (2015) para 397 see now 72 Halsbury's Laws of England (5th Edn) (2019) para 392; and for 72 Halsbury's Laws of England (5th Edn) (2015) para 411 see now 72 Halsbury's Laws of England (5th Edn) (2019) para 406.]

DESIGN

[For 79 Halsbury's Laws of England (5th Edn) (2014) paras 711–712 see now 79 Halsbury's Laws of England (5th Edn) (2020) paras 648, 684.]

DESTRUCTION

Of will

[For 102 Halsbury's Laws of England (5th Edn) (2010) para 94 see now 102 Halsbury's Laws of England (5th Edn) (2016) para 94.]

DETAINED

[Mental Health Act 1983, s 117: duty to provide after-care services to a patient who has ceased to be detained under s 3.] '[5] By s 117(1):

"This section applies to persons who are detained under section 3 above … and then cease to be detained and (whether or not immediately after so ceasing) leave hospital."

It is the meaning of the final words of this provision which is at the centre of this dispute.
…
'[15] The first issue raised by the claim, and the main issue raised on this appeal, is whether, when he goes on an escorted day trip for which he is granted leave of absence under s 17, the claimant is a person to whom s 117 of the Act applies. This depends on whether, when he goes on such trips, the claimant "ceases to be detained and … leaves hospital" within the meaning of s 117(1).
…
'[32] I accept the starting point of the claimant's argument that the term "detained" as it is generally used in the Act refers to detention in a hospital. This is confirmed by the recent decision of the Supreme Court in *Secretary of State for Justice v MM* [2018] UKSC 60,

[2019] 2 All ER 749, [2018] 3 WLR 1784, which held that there is no power under the Act to impose a condition of detention in a place which is not a hospital (save for the emergency powers under ss 135 and 136 to detain a person at a place of safety). But I do not accept that, as a matter of language, it is inappropriate to describe a patient who is permitted to leave the hospital premises to go on a short escorted trip and then return as a person who is still "detained" in the hospital. That description may reasonably be used to refer to the person's general situation, even if the person is not confined within the hospital premises at all times.
'[33] That the term "detained" not only can be but is actually used in the Act in this more general sense is confirmed by the decision of the Court of Appeal in *B v Barking, Havering and Brentwood Community Healthcare NHS Trust* [1999] 1 FLR 106, (1999) 47 BMLR 112.
…

'[35] I am not suggesting that the decision in the *B v Barking* case determines what is meant by the phrase "cease to be detained" in s 117(1) of the Act. But it does show that the term "detained" is capable of being used, and is used in at least one place in the Act, to encompass a person who is on leave of absence under s 17 from the hospital in which he or she is detained.
…
'[38] As discussed, in interpreting a statutory provision it is not sufficient to consider the ordinary meanings of the words used and how the same words are used elsewhere in the Act: it is necessary to identify the purpose of the provision, read in its context. The clear purpose of s 117 is to arrange for the provision of services to a person who has been, but is not currently being, provided with treatment and care as a hospital patient. That purpose is implicit in the very expression "after-care", which is used not only in the heading but throughout the body of s 117 in the phrase "after-care services". It is further articulated by the definition of "after-care services" in s 117(6). …
'[39] Interpreting s 117(1) in the light of this purpose, I readily accept that there will be cases in which a patient granted leave of absence from hospital under s 17 does "cease to be detained" and "leave hospital" within the meaning of s 117(1) so as to become eligible to receive after-care services during the period of their absence. I would also accept the submission

made by Mr Wise QC that it is not necessary in order to trigger s 117 that the person concerned should have been "discharged" from hospital in either of the two senses, discussed in the *MM* case at paras [19]–[20], in which that term is used in the Act. I see no reason why s 117 should not apply to a person who is living in the community on leave of absence–either full-time or for part of the week like the claimant in the *Barking* case–without having been conditionally discharged from hospital under s 42(2) or 73(2) of the Act, let alone "absolutely" discharged from the liability to be detained.

...

'[44] The inescapable conclusion is that the claimant does not "cease to be detained" or "leave hospital" within the meaning of s 117(1) when he is escorted on day trips and is therefore not a person to whom s 117 applies. ...' *R (on the application of CXF (by his mother, his litigation friend)) v Central Bedfordshire Council* [2018] EWCA Civ 2852, [2019] 3 All ER 20 at [5], [15], [32]–[33], [35], [38]–[39], [44], per Leggatt LJ

DEVASTAVIT

[For 103 Halsbury's Laws of England (5th Edn) (2010) para 1246 see now 103 Halsbury's Laws of England (5th Edn) (2016) para 1244.]

DEVIATION

Of ship

[For 60 Halsbury's Laws of England (5th Edn) (2011) para 313 see now 60 Halsbury's Laws of England (5th Edn) (2018) para 292.]
[For 7 Halsbury's Laws of England (5th Edn) (2015) para 249 see now 7 Halsbury's Laws of England (5th Edn) (2020) para 280.]

DEVOLVE—DEVOLUTION

[For 103 Halsbury's Laws of England (5th Edn) (2010) para 916 see now 103 Halsbury's Laws of England (5th Edn) (2016) para 916; and for 103 Halsbury's Laws of England (5th Edn) (2010) paras 916–954 see now 103 Halsbury's Laws of England (5th Edn) (2016) paras 916–955.]

DISCLAIMER

By trustee in bankruptcy

[For 5 Halsbury's Laws of England (5th Edn) (2013) paras 490–506 see now 5 Halsbury's Laws of England (5th Edn) (2020) paras 473–488.]

DISCOVER

[For 59 Halsbury's Laws of England (5th Edn) (2014) para 2219 see now 99 Halsbury's Laws of England (5th Edn) (2018) para 672.]
[Taxes Management Act 1970, s 29 ('discovery assessment'): power to make an assessment if an inspector 'discovers' that tax which ought to have been assessed has not been assessed or an assessment to tax is insufficient or relief is excessive.] '[11] ... In the present appeal, it is not in dispute that the concept of a "discovery" by an officer involves the application of a subjective test, as to the officer's state of mind, and an objective test as to whether it is open to an officer to have that state of mind.

...

'[28] ... Having reviewed the authorities, we consider that it is helpful to elaborate the test as to the required subjective element for a discovery assessment as follows:

"The officer must believe that the information available to him points in the direction of there being an insufficiency of tax."

That formulation, in our judgment, acknowledges both that the discovery must be something more than suspicion of an insufficiency of tax and that it need not go so far as a conclusion that an insufficiency of tax is more probable than not.

...

'[30] The officer's decision to make a discovery assessment is an administrative decision. We consider that the objective controls on the decision making of the officer should be expressed by reference to public law concepts. Accordingly, as regards the requirement for the action to be "reasonable", this should be expressed as a requirement that the officer's belief is one which a reasonable officer could form. It is not for a tribunal hearing an appeal in relation to a discovery assessment to form its own belief on the information available to the officer and then to conclude, if it forms a different belief, that the officer's belief was not reasonable.' *Anderson v Revenue and Customs Commission-*

ers [2018] UKUT 159 (TCC), [2018] 4 All ER 338 at [11], [28], [30], per Morgan J and Judge Berner

DISFRANCHISEMENT

[For 24 Halsbury's Laws of England (5th Edn) (2010) para 351 see now 7 Halsbury's Laws of England (5th Edn) (2019) para 451.]

DISPROPORTIONATELY SEVERE

See also CRUEL AND UNUSUAL PUNISH-MENT; INHUMAN OR DEGRADING PUN-ISHMENT

New Zealand New Zealand Bill of Rights Act 1990, s 9: right not to be subjected to cruel, degrading, or disproportionately severe treatment or punishment.] '[170] As in the ICCPR [International Covenant on Civil and Political Rights], there are degrees of reprehensibility evident in ss 9 and 23(5). Section 9 is concerned with conduct on the part of the state and its officials which is to be utterly condemned as outrageous and unacceptable in any circumstances. Section 23(5), which is confined in application to persons deprived of their liberty, proscribes conduct which is unacceptable in our society but of a lesser order, not rising to a level deserving to be called outrageous.

'[171] All forms of conduct proscribed by s 9 are of great seriousness. Without attempting exhaustive definitions, they can be understood in the New Zealand context in the following way. The worst is torture, which involves the deliberate infliction of severe physical or mental suffering for a particular purpose, such as obtaining information. Treatment or punishment that lacks such an ulterior purpose can be characterised as cruel if the suffering that results is severe or is deliberately inflicted. In the s 9 context, treatment or punishment is degrading if it gravely humiliates and debases the person subjected to it, whether or not that is its purpose.

'[172] The last of the matters listed in s 9 is treatment or punishment that is "disproportionately severe". This expression has no counterpart in the overseas instruments discussed above, but must take its colour from the rest of s 9 and therefore from the jurisprudence under those overseas instruments. I have concluded that the words "disproportionately severe" must have been included to fulfil much the same role as "inhuman" treatment or punishment plays in

art 7 of the ICCPR, and to perform the same function as the gloss of "gross disproportionality" does for s 12 of the Canadian Charter. There might not otherwise be a classification in s 9 to catch behaviour which does not inflict suffering in a manner or degree which could be described as cruel, and cannot be said to be degrading in its effect, but which New Zealanders would nevertheless regard as so out of proportion to the particular circumstances as to cause shock and revulsion.

...

'[176] It is therefore apparent that "disproportionately severe", appearing in s 9 alongside torture, cruelty and conduct with degrading effect, is intended to capture treatment or punishment which is grossly disproportionate to the circumstances. Conduct so characterised can, in my view, when it occurs in New Zealand, be fairly called "inhuman" in the sense given to that term in the jurisprudence under art 7 of the ICCPR.' *Taunoa v Attorney-General* [2007] NZSC 70, [2008] 1 NZLR 429 at [170]–[172], [176], per Blanchard J

DISQUALIFIED

[For 89 Halsbury's Laws of England (5th Edn) (2011) paras 281–284 see now 89 Halsbury's Laws of England (5th Edn) (2018) paras 289–292.]

DISTRESS

[For 32 Halsbury's Laws of England (5th Edn) (2012) para 901 see now 62 Halsbury's Laws of England (5th Edn) (2016) para 282n.]

DISTURB

New Zealand [Wildlife Act 1953, s 2: hunting or killing in relation to any wildlife includes pursuing, disturbing, or molesting.] '[69] In common usage, it is possible to disturb something without intending to do so. We agree with the Court of Appeal that, as with the word killing, disturbing is a word that prohibits a result and not an action. It follows that an intention to disturb need not be proved. While this imposes strict liability for a disturbance, we have already noted the imposition of strict liability is consistent with the overall statutory scheme, which clearly contemplates liability under s 63A for accidental acts.

'[70] Beyond that however, settling on a meaning for this word becomes more difficult. The *Oxford English Dictionary* lists among possible meanings:

(a) "To agitate and destroy (quiet, peace, rest); to break up the quiet, tranquillity, or rest of (a person, a country, etc); to stir up, trouble, disquiet."

(b) "To throw into a state of physical agitation, commotion, or disorder; to agitate."

(c) "To agitate mentally, discompose the peace of mind or calmness of (any one); to trouble, perplex."

(d) "To interfere with the settled course or operation of; to put out of its course; to interrupt, derange, hinder, frustrate."

(e) "To move anything from its settled condition or position; to unsettle."

...

'[72] We start from the premise that, as appears from the dictionary definition, the word "disturb" can carry many different meanings. We accept Shark Experience's argument that a definition of "disturb" which captures acts breaking up the peace or tranquillity of protected wildlife would cast too broad a net. It would result in criminalising actions such as walking through the bush, or swimming in the sea, since each of those will often result in startling wildlife, and some of that wildlife may be protected. Such conduct would be criminalised even though it carried with it no real risk of harm to the wildlife. We are confident it was not Parliament's intention to expose people to the risk of criminal liability in such circumstances.

'[73] That favours a narrower construction, as does the statutory context. The statutory purpose suggests a meaning for the word "disturbing" which prohibits conduct carrying a real risk of significant harm. If "disturbing" is construed to have a meaning closer to harm in this way, it fits both with the dictionary definition of disturbing and the purpose of the Act.

'[74] Construing the word in its statutory context and, in particular, placing it within the context of the list of the other prohibited actions, leads us to conclude that what is intended to be prohibited is action which physically or mentally agitates the protected wildlife to a level creating a real risk of significant harm. Such an interpretation is consistent with the meaning of the verb "disturb" in its common usage sense. It imbues the conduct thereby

prohibited with a character in keeping with the other prohibited acts: conduct which carries a real risk of significantly harming a protected animal.

...

'[93] ... In the s 2(1) definition of "hunt or kill": "disturbing" means an action which physically or mentally agitates the protected animal to a level creating a real risk of significant harm.' *Shark Experience Ltd v PauaMAC5 Inc* [2019] NZSC 111, [2019] 1 NZLR 791 at [69]–[70], [72]–[74], [93], per Winkelmann CJ

DIVERT

[For 55 Halsbury's Laws of England (5th Edn) (2012) paras 811–813 see now 55 Halsbury's Laws of England (5th Edn) (2019) paras 831–833.]

DIVORCE

[For 72 Halsbury's Laws of England (5th Edn) (2015) para 396 et seq see now 72 Halsbury's Laws of England (5th Edn) (2019) para 391 et seq.]

DONATIO MORTIS CAUSA

[For 103 Halsbury's Laws of England (5th Edn) (2010) para 921 see now 103 Halsbury's Laws of England (5th Edn) (2016) para 921.]

DURATION OF WORKING TIME

[Agency Workers Regulations 2010, SI 2010/93, regs 5, 6.] '[28] Mr Glyn's core submission, pleaded as ground (1) of the Grounds of Appeal and amplified by certain particular points pleaded as ground (2), was that the ET [Employment Tribunal] and the EAT [Employment Appeal Tribunal] had erred in law by failing to give reg 6(1)(b) what he said was its literal, natural and correct meaning. He contended that the phrase in reg 6(1) "terms and conditions relating to ... duration of working time" naturally refers to any term dealing with the amount of time that a worker works and accordingly naturally covers the term in a contract that specifies the amount of work that the worker is both entitled and required to work. Accordingly, if the term of a comparator's contract of employment specified a 39-hour week the Claimant's entitlement under reg 5(1) to "the same ... conditions" meant that he was entitled to work that number of hours. He submitted that that construction was consistent with the purpose of the Directive and in particular with the principle of equal treatment stated in art 5.

'[29] I do not accept either that that construction represents the natural meaning of the phrase "duration of working time" in reg 6(1)(b) or that it is consistent with the purpose of the legislation. My reasons are as follows.

'[30] I start with the words themselves. If one writes the definition of "working time" from para (5)(a) into para (1)(b), it reads:

"... the duration of any period during which [the] individual is working, at the disposal of [his or her] employer ... and carrying out [his or her] activity or duties".

There are elements of repetition or overlap in that definition and for present purposes I can shorten it to "the duration of any period during which the individual is working". (It would be possible to add in the other kinds of "working time" specified at para 5(b) and (c), but that would unnecessarily complicate the exercise.)

'[31] Even without any statutory context, I do not think it is natural to describe a term specifying the number of hours in the working week as relating to the "duration" of the "period" during which an individual is working. Mr Glyn referred us to the definition of "duration" in *Black's Law Dictionary* as "the length of time something lasts" or "the length of time; a continuance of time" and offered his own paraphrase "the time during which something continues". We need not be pinned to a specific definition, but I agree that "duration" connotes the length of a period of time. It seems to me to follow in the ordinary case that the period in question should be continuous, and indeed both the *Black*'s definition and Mr Glyn's incorporate that concept. That would mean that in this context the "periods" of time to whose duration reg 6(1)(b) refers are periods during which the worker is working continuously (ignoring rest-breaks), such as the working day or shift. Outside such a period the worker is neither

working nor at the disposal of his or her employer nor carrying out any activity or duties. Regulation 5(1) would accordingly not apply to a term specifying a 39-hour working week, which will necessarily involve several discrete periods of work. Not only is that a correct use of language but it is in accordance with ordinary usage: you would not describe someone working full-time as working for a "period" of (say) 39 hours. At para 14 of his skeleton argument Mr Glyn summarises his position by adopting the shorthand "a quantity of time". But that is not accurate, because it does not incorporate the notion of a continuous period. It allows Mr Glyn to advance the apparently obvious proposition that 39 hours is "a quantity of time": no doubt in one sense it is, but it is not necessarily, and is not in this context, the duration of a period.

'[32] The position becomes clearer still when one takes into account the wider context. I have noted at para [17] above the correlations of heads (b)–(f) in reg 6(1) with the subject-matter, and language, of the WTR [Working Time Regulations 1998, SI 1998/1833]. In the light of that, it seems to me plain (subject to para [34] below) that reg 6(1)(b) is intended to refer to terms which set a maximum length for any such period, as the WTR does. ...

'[33] That is how both the ET and the EAT read it: see para 49 of the ET's Reasons and para 44(a) and (b) of the EAT's judgment. I believe that they were right; and on that basis the Regulations do not entitle agency workers to work the same number of contractual hours as a comparator.' *Kocur v Angard Staffing Solutions Ltd* [2019] EWCA Civ 1185, [2020] 1 All ER 791 at [28]–[33], per Underhill VP

DURESS

[For 22 Halsbury's Laws of England (5th Edn) (2012) para 292 see now 22 Halsbury's Laws of England (5th Edn) (2019) para 92.]

[For 76 Halsbury's Laws of England (5th Edn) (2013) para 837 see now 47 Halsbury's Laws of England (5th Edn) (2014) para 37.]

E

EASEMENT

New Zealand '[56] For an interest in land to be an easement, it must possess the following three characteristics:

(a) There must be a dominant tenement (the land deriving the benefit of the easement) and a servient tenement (the land over which the easement is exercisable). In this case, the dominant tenement is the Boatyard land and the servient tenement is the reserve.

(b) The right must accommodate (that is, confer a benefit on) the dominant tenement as opposed to a personal benefit on the owner of the dominant tenement.

(c) The right claimed must be capable of being the subject matter of the grant of an easement. This incorporates a number of requirements: that the easement be in sufficiently clear terms; that it is not so precarious that it is liable to be taken away by the servient owner; that it is not so extensive or invasive as to oust the servient owner from the enjoyment and control of the servient tenement; and that it does not impose on the servient owner an obligation to spend money or do anything beyond mere passivity.'

[Note: See *Re Ellenborough Park* [1956] Ch 131 at 163, CA (Eng). The additional requirement referred to in that case, that the owners of the dominant and the servient tenements must be different persons, is no longer a requirement in New Zealand: see the Land Transfer Act 2017, s 108(3). It is possible to have an easement in gross in New Zealand (that is, an easement in favour of a specified person, rather than specified land): see the Property Law Act 2007, s 291. Under that Act and the Land Transfer Act 2017, the terminology used in connection with easements is 'burdened land' rather than servient tenement and 'benefited land' rather than dominant tenement.]

Schmuck v Opua Coastal Preservation Inc [2019] NZSC 118, [2019] 1 NZLR 750 at [56], per O'Regan J

EDITION

[For 85 Halsbury's Laws of England (5th Edn) (2012) para 704, notes 2–3 see now 85 Halsbury's Laws of England (5th Edn) (2020) para 804.]

EDITOR

[For 85 Halsbury's Laws of England (5th Edn) (2012) para 732 see now 85 Halsbury's Laws of England (5th Edn) (2020) para 825.]

EFFECTS

In will: generally

[For 102 Halsbury's Laws of England (5th Edn) (2010) para 290 see now 102 Halsbury's Laws of England (5th Edn) (2016) para 288.]

EJUSDEM GENERIS

[For 32 Halsbury's Laws of England (5th Edn) (2012) para 435 see now 32 Halsbury's Laws of England (5th Edn) (2019) para 435.]

ELDEST

[For 102 Halsbury's Laws of England (5th Edn) (2010) para 335 see now 102 Halsbury's Laws of England (5th Edn) (2016) para 333.]

EMPLOYEE

Casual employee

Australia [Fair Work Act 2009 (Cth), ss 86, 95, 106.] '[31] The meaning of casual employee as used in the expression "other than casual employees" in s 86 of the FW Act (dealing with entitlements to annual leave), s 95 of the FW Act (dealing with entitlements to personal/carer's leave) and s 106 of the FW Act (dealing with compassionate leave) was not in contest. It was accepted that in *Skene* [*WorkPac Pty Ltd v Skene* (2018) 264 FCR 536; 362 ALR 311; [2018] FCAFC 131], a Full Court of this Court (Tracey, Bromberg and Rangiah JJ) correctly determined that a casual employee is an employee who has no firm advance commitment from her or his employer to continuing and indefinite work according to an agreed pattern of work ("**firm advance commitment**").' *WorkPac Pty Ltd v Rossato* [2020] FCAFC 84, (2020) 378 ALR 585 at [31], per Bromberg J

EMPLOYMENT
[Double Taxation Relief (Taxes on Income) (South Africa) Order 2002, SI 2002/3138, arts 7, 14. If taxpayer was self-employed, by virtue of art 7, which applied to business profits, he was taxable in South Africa. If not, and the income was employment income, he was taxable in the UK by virtue of art 14. Income Tax (Trading and Other Income) Act 2005, s 15: in the case of a person who performs the duties of employment as a diver or diving supervisor in the UK or Continental Shelf, performance of the duties of employment is treated for income tax purposes as the carrying on of a trade in the United Kingdom.] '[11] So the first question is: what is the meaning of "employment" for the purposes of UK tax law? If UK tax law does not provide a complete answer then the second question is: what does "employment" mean under the general law of the UK?

'[12] For the purposes of UK taxation, s 4 of the Income Tax (Earnings and Pensions) Act 2003 ('the 2003 Act') contains a partial definition of "employment". It provides:

"In the employment income Parts 'employment' includes in particular–
(a) any employment under a contract of service,
(b) any employment under a contract of apprenticeship, and
(c) any employment in the service of the Crown."

'[13] Since this is not an exhaustive definition, but only an inclusive one, I consider that the meaning of the word "employment" has to

be supplemented, where necessary, by the meaning of that word under the general law of England and Wales. This is expressly permitted by art 3(2) of the treaty. Although the partial definition of "employment" in the tax legislation prevails over the meaning of that word under the general law of England and Wales, where the definition is incomplete it is permissible to resort to other laws of the contracting state. For the purposes of the preliminary issue we must, I think, assume that Mr Fowler carried out his diving activities under a contract of service. On that assumption, his activities fell within the express definition of 'employment'.

...
'[35] In the first place, I agree with Lewison LJ (at [30] of his judgment) that the real question is: how far does the deeming provision in s 15(2) of the 2005 Act extend? On any view, the starting point of the analysis must be that, on the assumed facts for the purposes of the preliminary issue, Mr Fowler was in reality an employed person when he performed the relevant seabed diving activities, with the consequence that his earnings from that employment were employment income within the charge to tax under Pt 2 of ITEPA 2003. In other words, Mr Fowler satisfied the conditions which have to be fulfilled if s 15 of the 2005 Act is to apply at all: see sub-s (1). But sub-s (2) then states, and this is of course the crucial deeming provision:

"The performance of the duties of employment is instead treated for income tax purposes as the carrying on of a trade in the United Kingdom."

...
'[39] The unambiguous effect of the deeming in s 15(2) is therefore that the performance by Mr Fowler of the relevant diving activities is treated as the carrying on by him of a trade, giving rise to trading income charged to tax under Pt 2 of the 2005 Act. This treatment entirely displaces the charge to tax on employment income, under Pt 2 of the 2003 Act, which would have applied in the absence of s 15. Furthermore, to the extent that Mr Fowler's activities were comprised in the deemed trade, they could not simultaneously be regarded for any income tax purposes as performance by him of the duties of his actual employment. The charges to tax on employment income and trading income are mutually exclusive.' *Fowler v Revenue and Customs Commissioners* [2018]

EWCA Civ 2544, [2019] 1 All ER 717 at [11]–[13], per Lewison LJ (dissenting) and at [35], [39], per Henderson LJ

ENACTMENT

[For 96 Halsbury's Laws of England (5th Edn) (2012) para 609 see now 96 Halsbury's Laws of England (5th Edn) (2018) para 209.]

ENEMY

[For 3 Halsbury's Laws of England (5th Edn) (2011) para 194 et seq see now 3 Halsbury's Laws of England (5th Edn) (2019) para 462 et seq.]

EQUIVALENT PERIOD OF COMPENSATORY REST

[Working Time Regulations 1998, SI 1998/1833 (WTR), reg 24: if the application of reg 12 (allowing a rest break of an uninterrupted period of not less than 20 minutes) was excluded by reg 21(f) (workers in railway transport), employer must wherever possible allow a worker to take 'an equivalent period of compensatory rest'.] '[42] I begin with the question whether it is necessary as a matter of law for an "equivalent period of compensatory rest" within the meaning of reg 24(a) to consist of an uninterrupted 20 minutes. …

'[43] The starting-point must be that reg 24 is only engaged because the WTR, following the Directive [Directive 2003/88/EC], provides that in the case of the kinds of work identified in reg 21 an employer is not required to afford workers rest breaks satisfying the requirements of reg 12. That being so, the description of the compensatory rest required under reg 24(a) as "equivalent" cannot be intended to import the identical obligation that would have applied under reg 12. Rather, the intention must be that the rest afforded to the worker should have the same value in terms of contributing to his or her well-being. That is what Lady Smith says at para [13] of her judgment in *Hughes* [*Hughes v Corps of Commissionaires Management Ltd (No 2)* [2011] EWCA Civ 1061, [2011] IRLR 915, [2012] 1 CMLR 649] (see para [36] above), with which I agree (subject to one immaterial caveat): it should be noted that she was sitting with (highly-experienced) lay members, and the views of the EAT on matters of this

kind should be respected wherever possible. Although on the appeal only one aspect of the EAT's reasoning was formally in issue this Court certainly endorsed its view that the requirements of reg 12 and reg 24 cannot be identical. Indeed at para [23], albeit in a part of the judgment dealing with a different issue, Elias LJ said in terms:

"… the concept of an equivalent period of compensatory rest under reg 24(a) cannot be a period identical to a reg 12 break. It is something given in place of that break."

'[44] Whether the rest afforded in any given case is "equivalent", in the sense explained by Lady Smith, must be a matter for the informed judgment of the (specialist) employment tribunal. There is no basis in principle for the proposition that only an uninterrupted break of 20 minutes can afford an equivalent benefit in that sense; and the provision for a collective or workforce agreement to make some different arrangement would be meaningless if that were so. I can see no reason why a single uninterrupted break of 20 minutes will always be better than, say, two uninterrupted breaks of 15 minutes one-third and two-thirds through the shift. The evidence referred to at para [28] above provides other illustrations of how different kinds of rest may be thought appropriate in particular cases.' *Crawford v Network Rail Infrastructure Ltd* [2019] EWCA Civ 269, [2019] 2 All ER 1095 at [42]–[44], per Underhill VP

ESCROW

[For 32 Halsbury's Laws of England (5th Edn) (2012) para 237 see now 32 Halsbury's Laws of England (5th Edn) (2019) para 237.]

ESPIONAGE

Australia '[109] The primary judge held that the applicant had used the word "espionage" in his imputation 5(a) in its ordinary and natural meaning, namely the practice of spying, or of employing spies, citing the *Oxford English Dictionary Online* and the *Macquarie Dictionary*. His Honour stated that—

[A] spy is someone who spies upon, or watches, someone secretly or who is employed by a government to obtain information or intelligence relating to the military or naval or governmental affairs of one or more other countries, or to collect intelligence of any other kind.

'[110] His Honour held at [85]–[87] that paragraph 14(a) of the respondents' particulars might have been unobjectionable were it not accompanied by the alternative in (b), which is not a natural or ordinary meaning of "espionage". His Honour held that paragraph 14 was embarrassing because it sought to expand espionage to encompass vague and imprecise concepts which were not within the natural and ordinary meaning of the word "espionage". His Honour further observed that the activities alleged in paragraphs 15 to 17 of the particulars, such as the making of donations, offers, provision of trips, or access to persons of influence in China, were not within the ordinary meaning of the word "espionage" either. His Honour stated that he did not consider that the respondents could justify an imputation of "espionage" by redefining that word in their particulars and then using that bespoke sense to justify the imputation as redefined. However, his Honour stated that it was not necessary to decide the question, because his Honour considered that the particulars had more fundamental flaws.
...
'[172] Before the primary judge, the applicant submitted that "espionage" meant "spying". The primary judge accepted that submission, holding that "spying" was the natural and ordinary meaning of "espionage". His Honour did not say anything to suggest that there was any relevant ambiguity in the applicant's imputation 5(a) and its employment of the term "espionage". If his Honour had thought there was ambiguity, then he could have required the applicant to amend further the statement of claim to make the meaning of espionage explicit in the pleading. Before this Court, senior counsel for the applicant continued to submit that "espionage" in the applicant's imputation (a) meant "spying", and accepted that in confining the imputation to espionage in this way, the applicant had made a forensic choice.
'[173] The amendments made to the Criminal Code (Cth) by the National Security Legislation Amendment (Espionage and Foreign Interference) Act 2018 (Cth), to which the parties referred in argument, draw a distinction between espionage (Division 91), and foreign interference (Division 92). For the purposes of the Criminal Code, the content of both concepts is found in the statute, and they are different. In this case, we are not concerned with a statutory

concept of "espionage", but with the content of the imputation alleged by the applicant. Whatever possible views there might be of the meaning of the word "espionage" generally, or in particular contexts, it is tolerably clear that for the purposes of the applicant's imputation (a), the applicant's case is that "espionage" has a meaning akin to "spying", and does not extend to the broader concepts such as those that were alleged by the respondents in their bespoke definition of "espionage" in paragraph 14(b) of their particulars which extend to influence, and attempted influence. We agree with the primary judge's opinion that the concepts into which the respondents sought to extend the meaning of espionage were vague and imprecise. In accordance with the relevant principles in *Sutherland v Stopes* [[1925] AC 47, HL], *Chakravarti [Chakravarti v Advertiser Newspapers Ltd* (1998) 193 CLR 519; 154 ALR 294; [1998] HCA 37], and *Hore-Lacy [Hore-Lacy v Cleary* (2007) 18 VR 562; [2007] VSCA 314], the respondents' defence of justification should be directed to the substance or sting of the applicant's meaning, or a permissible variant of it. We consider that there is a substantial difference between "espionage" as it is employed in the applicant's imputation 5(a), and the breadth of the respondents' case, with the consequence that the respondents' case relating to "espionage" is not responsive. The breadth of the respondents' case is manifested in paragraph 59(g) of their particulars which we set out at [111] above, which contains the only direct allegation of espionage by the applicant. That allegation is descriptive of political influence, and is far removed from the sense in which the applicant's imputation 5(a) is to be understood.' *Australian Broadcasting Corp v Chau Chak Wing* [2019] FCAFC 125, (2019) 371 ALR 545 at [109]–[110], [172]–[173], per Besanko, Bromwich and Wheelahan JJ

ESTRAYS

[For 29 Halsbury's Laws of England (5th Edn) (2014) para 286 see now 29 Halsbury's Laws of England (5th Edn) (2019) para 291.]

EXCEEDED

[Abortion Act 1967, s 1(1)(a): legal termination of pregnancy by a registered medical practitioner.] '[1] The issue in this case is the correct interpretation of the words, 'the pregnancy has not exceeded its twenty-fourth week' in s 1(1)(a) of the Abortion Act 1967 ('the 1967 Act').

...

'[57] In my judgment the correct construction of the words "the pregnancy has not exceeded its twenty-fourth week" in s 1(1)(a) of the 1967 Act is that a woman will have exceeded her 24th week of pregnancy once she is 24 weeks + 0 days pregnant, or in other words, from midnight on the expiration of her 24th week of pregnancy, as stated in the Decision Letter [letter clarifying the Department of Health and Social Care's interpretation of the legal time limit].' *R (on the application of British Pregnancy Advisory Service) v Secretary of State for Health and Social Care* [2019] EWHC 1397 (Admin), [2019] 4 All ER 661 at [1], [57], per Supperstone J

EXECUTOR

[For 103 Halsbury's Laws of England (5th Edn) (2010) para 606 see now 103 Halsbury's Laws of England (5th Edn) (2016) para 606.]

EXIT DAY

'Exit day' means 31 January 2020 at 11 pm. ... In this Act references to before, after or on exit day, or to beginning with exit day, are to be read as references to before, after or at 11 pm on 31 January 2020 or (as the case may be) to beginning with 11 pm on that day. (European Union (Withdrawal) Act 2018, s 20(1), (2) (amended by SI 2019/859 and SI 2019/1423)

EXONERATION

[For 5 Halsbury's Laws of England (5th Edn) (2013) para 674 see now 5 Halsbury's Laws of England (5th Edn) (2020) para 657.]

EXPENSES

Expenses incurred

[Political Parties, Elections and Referendums Act 2000, s 111(2): referendum expenses.] '[36] We turn to the question of what is meant by "expenses incurred" in the definition of "referendum expenses" in s 111(2) of PPERA quoted at para [26] above. The claimant's case is that in the definition the term "expense"

means no more than an outflow of economic benefit and that to "incur" an expense simply means to bring upon oneself an expense or render oneself liable to an expense. Thus, "expenses" may be "incurred" by voluntarily making a payment which diminishes a person's assets as well as by assuming an obligation or liability to make such a payment. Counsel for the claimant submitted that this interpretation is consistent both with the ordinary dictionary meanings of the words and with the purpose of the legislation.

...

'[41] As a matter of ordinary English usage, the phrase "expenses incurred" is, we apprehend, most naturally understood in the broad sense contended for by the claimant. It is natural to describe a person as having incurred an expense whenever he or she has spent money or incurred a liability which in either case reduces his or her financial resources. This is also the sense in which accountants typically use the term – albeit with greater precision than in ordinary usage. For example, FRS 102, the Financial Reporting Standard applicable in the UK, defines "expenses" as "decreases in economic benefits during the reporting period in the form of outflows or depletions of assets or incurrences of liabilities that result in decreases in equity, other than those relating to distributions to equity investors". The concept is similarly defined in the Conceptual Framework for Financial Reporting issued by the International Accounting Standards Board. Under s 121 of PPERA, a permitted participant who incurs referendum expenses exceeding £250,000 during any referendum period is required to appoint an auditor to prepare a report on its return to the Electoral Commission. It would be reasonable to expect an auditor appointed for this purpose, unless otherwise instructed, to apply standard accounting concepts in verifying that the return gives a true and fair view of the expenses incurred by the permitted participant during the referendum period.

'[42] We do not accept that as a matter of ordinary language incurring an expense means the same as incurring a liability, as was argued on behalf of Vote Leave. An "expense" and a "liability" are different concepts. Certainly, someone who, for example, purchases goods under a contract and thereby incurs a liability to pay for them would naturally be said to have incurred an expense. But so too would someone who makes a donation to a charity. In the ordinary meaning of the words an expense can just as well be incurred by making a payment voluntarily without any obligation to do so as by undertaking an obligation to make a payment: the value of the person's assets is equally diminished in each case. It is also to be expected that, if the intention were to restrict the meaning of "referendum expenses" to expenses which there is a liability to pay, the legislation would say so expressly and that the word "liable" or "liability" would appear in the definition.' *R (on the application of the Good Law Project) v Electoral Commission (Vote Leave Ltd and another, interested parties)* [2018] EWHC 2414 (Admin), [2019] 1 All ER 365 at [36], [41]–[42], per Leggatt LJ

EXTRAORDINARY TRAFFIC

[In the final paragraph, for the words 'in the High Court or (where not exceeding £500) in the county court' substitute 'in the County Court'. For 55 Halsbury's Laws of England (5th Edn) (2012) paras 316–318 see now 55 Halsbury's Laws of England (5th Edn) (2019) paras 341, 345–347.]

F

FACILITIES FOR ... RECREATION

[Ministry of Housing and Local Government Provisional Order Confirmation (Greater London Parks and Open Spaces) Act 1967, Sch 1, art 7(1)(a)(v): power for local authority in any open space to provide and maintain 'indoor facilities for any form of recreation whatsoever'; whether this included a day nursery for pre-school children.] '[21] Ms Wakefield supported the judge's interpretation of "recreation". She accepted that the children at the proposed nursery would engage in play and therefore in recreation, but the purposes of the interested party's facility were not so limited. At least for the purposes of sub-para (v) it was necessary to ask whether the purpose was wholly or mainly recreation. If one asked that question, the answer was that the interested party's nursery was obviously not within sub-para (v).

'[22] I agree with Ms Wakefield that, to come within sub-para (v), the facilities must be wholly or mainly for recreation. I would accept that a facility which is wholly or mainly for recreation is not disqualified because some necessary ancillary activity will also be carried on there. Thus an indoor recreational facility for children does not become disqualified under sub-para (v) because it is pointed out that children learn through play, and that the children are thereby being provided with a form of education. The purpose of the facility remains wholly or mainly recreational. It is not enough, however, that recreation occurs or may occur within the facility. So to construe art 7(1) would give the local authority free rein to provide any service to the public by means of an indoor facility in an open space provided they included a play area within the facility. Sub-paragraph (v) does not permit additional or different facilities which do not meet the description "recreation".

...

'[24] To my mind, therefore, the proposed facilities do not fall within sub-para (v) for essentially two reasons. Firstly, the proposed facility is more in the nature of a school than a recreational facility. ... Secondly, the proposed facility will offer services which are not a necessary or inherent part of recreation and which go far beyond it, by providing all-day child care for pre-school children while their parents are at work or engaged elsewhere. ...

...

'[26] ... . It is possible that there may be a penumbra around the terms "facilities for ... recreation" in sub-para (v), but the meaning of the term itself is a question of law which the court can and must decide. Given the conclusion I have reached, the question of whether the proposed nursery school is wholly or mainly for recreation is, in my judgment, only capable of being answered in the negative.' *R (on the application of Muir) v Wandsworth Borough Council (Smart Pre-Schools Ltd, interested party)* [2018] EWCA Civ 1035, [2018] 4 All ER 422 at [21]–[22]. [24], [26], per Floyd LJ

FAIR (NOUN)

[For 71 Halsbury's Laws of England (5th Edn) (2013) paras 802–803 see now 71 Halsbury's Laws of England (5th Edn) (2020) paras 702–703.]

FAIR COMMENT

See now HONEST OPINION

[For 32 Halsbury's Laws of England (5th Edn) (2012) paras 637–638 see now 32 Halsbury's Laws of England (5th Edn) (2019) paras 637–638.]

FAMILY ARRANGEMENT

[For 91 Halsbury's Laws of England (5th Edn) (2012) paras 903, 906 see now 91 Halsbury's Laws of England (5th Edn) (2019) paras 789, 792.]

FEDERAL BOARD, COMMISSION OR OTHER TRIBUNAL

Canada [*Federal Courts Act*, RSC 1985, c F-7, s 2.] '18. The *Federal Courts Act* does not allow for judicial review of parliamentary activities. Indeed, ss 18 and 18.1 only grant the Federal Court jurisdiction to judicially review action taken by "any federal board, commission or other tribunal". A "federal board, commission or other tribunal" is defined in the Act, subject to certain exceptions, as a body exercising statutory powers or powers under an order made pursuant to a prerogative of the Crown (s 2; see also *Strickland v Canada (Attorney General)* 2015 SCC 37, [2015] 2 SCR 713, at para 64). Section 2(2) specifies that "federal board, commission or other tribunal" does not include "the Senate, the House of Commons, any committee or member of either House". Thus, I agree that s 2(2) is designed "to preclude judicial review of the legislative process at large" (CA reasons, at para 32). As I will explain further below, Cabinet and ministers do not act pursuant to statutory powers when developing legislation; rather, they act pursuant to powers under Part IV of the *Constitution Act, 1867*. As such, when developing legislation, they do not act as a "federal board, commission or other tribunal" within the meaning of s 2 (see *Shade v Canada (Attorney General)* 2003 FCT 327, 230 FTR.53, at para 34).' *Mikisew Cree First Nation v Canada (Governor General in Council)* [2018] SCJ No 40, [2018] 2 SCR 765 at para 18, per Karakatsanis J

FENCE

[For 4 Halsbury's Laws of England (5th Edn) (2011) para 350 see now 4 Halsbury's Laws of England (5th Edn) (2019) para 349.]

FINANCIALLY INDEPENDENT

[Nationality, Immigration and Asylum Act 2002, s 117B(3).] '[51] Section 117B(3) of the 2002 Act ... provides that it is in the public interest, and in particular in the interests of the economic well-being of the UK, that persons who remain here are "financially independent". Then the subsection proceeds to give two reasons why their financial independence is in the public interest.
...

'[55] The parties are correct to join in submitting to this court that financial independence in s 117B(3) means an absence of financial dependence upon the state. Why would it be "in the public interest" that they should not be financially dependent on other persons? Why would it in particular be "in the interests of the economic well-being of the United Kingdom" that they should not be dependent on them? Sales LJ suggested, at para [64], that the financial support provided to Ms Rhuppiah by her father and Ms Charles might cease, whereupon the obligation to maintain her would probably fall upon the state; but a cessation of a person's employment would probably have the same result. Indeed the present case is a good example of the sometimes flimsy distinction between employment and third party support. Anyone other than Ms Rhuppiah who provided extensive caring services to Ms Charles would need to be paid; and it is but an incident of their close friendship and of Ms Rhuppiah's legal inability to have taken employment prior to 9 February 2018 that instead the provision to her has taken the form of largely free board and lodging.

'[56] Regard must moreover be had to the first of the two reasons given in s 117B(3) for its statement as to where the public interest lay: "because such persons ... are not a burden on taxpayers". It was the view of Sales LJ at para [65] that, if the phrase "financially independent" referred to independence of the state, the quoted words were close to tautological. Had those words been part of the statement as to where the public interest lay, one might more readily have agreed with his view. But they are not part of the statement. They are part of the explanation for it and in my view they unequivocally support the construction of s 117B(3) now agreed between the parties.' *Rhuppiah v Secretary of State for the Home Department* [2018] UKSC 58, [2019] 1 All ER 1007 at [51], [55]–[56], per Lord Wilson JSC

FINISHED OR MANUFACTURED INDIGENOUS TIMBER PRODUCT

New Zealand [Forests Act 1949, ss 2(1), 67C: swamp kauri may be exported if it constitutes any finished or manufactured indigenous timber product, regardless of the source of the timber used in the product.] '[52] Under para (a) of the definition of finished or manufactured indigenous timber product, whether a product is in its final form and ready for use or installation is judged by considering the product itself. Logs will almost always require modification before being ready for use or installation. Merely labelling a log a totem or temple pole does not change this. The definition must also be interpreted in light of its purpose. Two main (related) purposes of the introduction of Part 3A were to curtail the export of indigenous logs and woodchips and to ensure that value was added in New Zealand. Also relevant is the scheme of the Act which suggests that something more should be done after milling for a product to be exported under s 67C(1)(b).

'[53] Against that background a log cannot be a finished or manufactured indigenous timber product unless the work on it is so extensive that it has lost its identity as a log. Surface carving or decoration, however elaborate, is unlikely to cause such a loss of identity. In most cases, any value added in New Zealand by surface carving or decoration is likely to be minimal.

'[54] A slab of swamp kauri labelled a table top would not fit within para (a) of the definition. The use as a table could not be discerned from the product itself. Further, a table top is not a product in its own right and thus is not ready to be installed in a larger structure.

'[55] For similar reasons, we also accept NEPS' submission that a table top, exported as a timber slab without routing, legs, or fixings, does not fall within para (b). Further, an unfinished "table top", in the form of a rough sawn or dressed timber slab or similar, would in any event be excluded from the definition of finished or manufactured indigenous timber product by para (c). Paragraph (c) operates to limit the export of items that, whatever the label attached to them, are in reality unfinished timber and have not had the level of domestically added value that was the purpose of the export restrictions.

'[56] We do not, however, accept NEPS' submission that a complete table will be excluded by para (c) in all cases where the table top could be classified as dressed or rough sawn timber. Whether a complete (or kitset) table comes within the exclusion in paragraph (c) will depend on whether the table in question has a high degree of similarity to dressed or rough sawn timber or building materials in general.

'[57] This will be a factual question assessed by considering the product itself at the time of export. We do note that, where the adding of legs or other mountings can be seen as a device to avoid the exclusion clause, then it would be excluded by para (c) and may well not even come within para (a). At the other end of the scale, a crafted rustic bespoke table would clearly come within para (a) (or (b) if in kitset form) and would not come within the exclusion in para (c), even if the table had a table top that, considered alone, could be classified as rough sawn timber.' *Northland Environmental Protection Society Inc v Chief Executive of the Ministry for Primary Industries* [2018] NZSC 105, [2019] 1 NZLR 257 at [52]–[57], per Glazebrook J

FIRE

[For 60 Halsbury's Laws of England (5th Edn) (2011) para 566 see now 60 Halsbury's Laws of England (5th Edn) (2018) para 543.]

Loss by fire: marine insurance

[For 60 Halsbury's Laws of England (5th Edn) (2011) para 325 see now 60 Halsbury's Laws of England (5th Edn) (2018) para 304.]

FLOTSAM

[For 29 Halsbury's Laws of England (5th Edn) (2014) para 185n see now 29 Halsbury's Laws of England (5th Edn) (2019) para 190 n 3.]

FOOT OR END

[For 102 Halsbury's Laws of England (5th Edn) (2010) paras 65–66 see now 102 Halsbury's Laws of England (5th Edn) (2016) paras 65–66.]

FOR ANY OTHER PURPOSE CONNECTED WITH ANY SUCH LAND

New Zealand [Reserves Act 1977, s 48(1)(f): administering body of the reserve, with the consent of the Minister of Conservation or their delegate, may grant rights of way and other easements over the reserve 'for any other purpose connected with' land not forming part of the reserve.] '[113] We conclude that the Court of Appeal was correct that there is no justification to read down the meaning of the phrase "for any other purpose connected with any such land" in s 48(1)(f) to exclude easements for commercial activities.' *Schmuck   v*

Opua Coastal Preservation Inc [2019] NZSC 118, [2019] 1 NZLR 750 at [113], per O'Regan J

FOR OR IN CONNECTION WITH THE PROVISION OF A DWELLING

[Defective Premises Act 1972, s 1: duty owed by a person taking on work 'for or in connection with the provision of a dwelling'.] '[38] In the present case the context includes the whole of s 1(1), not just the words: "A person taking on work for or in connection with the provision of a dwelling". This includes that the duty relates to how "the work which he takes on is done" and that it is done "with proper materials". The focus is therefore very much on the doing of work.

'[39] That work also has to relate to the "provision of a dwelling". This suggests the bringing of that dwelling into physical existence or its creation. This is consistent with how these words have been interpreted in other cases. For example, *Jacobs v Morton & Partners (a firm)* (1994) 43 ConLR 124 at 135, (1994) 72 BLR 92 at 105: "In my judgment, this phrase connotes the creation of a new dwelling" per Mr Recorder Jackson QC; *Saigol v Cranley Mansions Ltd* (6 July 1995) [1995] Lexis Citation 1860: "Mr Ticciati was in my view correct in submitting the 'provision' was a word which prima facie involved the creation of something new" per Hutchison LJ.

'[40] The emphasis is therefore on those who do work which positively contributes to the creation of the dwelling. That may include architects and engineers who prescribe how the dwelling is to be created, not just those who physically create it. It does not, however, include those whose role is the essentially negative one of seeing that no work is done which contravenes building regulations. Building control ensures that the dwelling is legal and properly certified, but it does not positively contribute to the provision or creation of that dwelling.

...

'[42] That an AI's [approved inspector's] function is far removed from the work of the provision or creation of the dwelling is borne out by the fact that an AI has no statutory power to order changes to be made to plans for works, or to building work which is ongoing or completed. The powers of the AI are confined to refusing to issue a plans certificate or final certificate in the face of non-compliant work.

Moreover, unlike the local authority, the AI has no power to impose conditions or prescribe modifications to the works and the relevant enforcement powers are left entirely with the local authority.

'[43] An AI therefore has no statutory power to influence the design or construction of a building in any way, save to stipulate that it must comply with the law. In certifying, or refusing to certify, plans and works, the AI is not engaged in the positive role of the provision or creation of the relevant building, but performs the essentially negative regulatory role of checking for compliance against prescribed criteria.

'[44] For all these reasons, and those given by Mr Townend and the judge, I consider that the judge was correct to conclude that an AI performing statutory functions does not fall within s 1(1) DPA 1972 on its natural and ordinary meaning.' *Lessees and Management Company of Herons Court v Heronslea Ltd* [2019] EWCA Civ 1423, [2020] 2 All ER 145 at [38]–[40], [42]–[44], per Hamblen LJ

FREE ON BOARD

[For 91 Halsbury's Laws of England (5th Edn) (2012) para 14 see now 91 Halsbury's Laws of England (5th Edn) (2019) para 15.]

FLOTSAM

[For 29 Halsbury's Laws of England (5th Edn) (2014) para 185n see now 29 Halsbury's Laws of England (5th Edn) (2019) para 190 n 3.]

FREIGHT

[For 7 Halsbury's Laws of England (5th Edn) (2015) para 568 et seq see now 7 Halsbury's Laws of England (5th Edn) (2020) para 352 et seq.]

Dead freight

[For 7 Halsbury's Laws of England (5th Edn) (2015) para 460 see now 7 Halsbury's Laws of England (5th Edn) (2020) para 374.]

FRUSTRATION

[For 22 Halsbury's Laws of England (5th Edn) (2012) para 468 see now 22 Halsbury's Laws of England (5th Edn) (2019) para 259.]

FUNDAMENTAL

New Zealand [Crimes Act 1961, s 385(1)(c): appeal to be allowed if there was a miscarriage of justice.] '[25] Some errors are so serious that they cannot be saved by the proviso; put another way, in such a case the appeal will be allowed even if the appellate court is satisfied of the defendant's guilt. Such errors are characterised as "fundamental" or "radical" or said to go to "the root of the proceedings" or to "undermine the integrity of the trial" so that it has lost the character of a fair trial according to law. ...

'[26] There exists no taxonomy of errors that are classified as fundamental; rather, incurability depends on the appellate court's assessment of the significance of the error in the context of the trial. In *Randall v R* [[2002] UKPC 19, [2002] 1 WLR 2237], Lord Bingham, delivering the judgment of the Privy Council, explained that:

> There will come a point when the departure from good practice is so gross, or so persistent, or so prejudicial, or so irremediable that an appellate court will have no choice but to condemn a trial as unfair and quash a conviction as unsafe, however strong the grounds for believing the defendant to be guilty.

'[27] This Court held in *Matenga* [*R v Matenga* [2009] NZSC 18, [2009] 3 NZLR 145] that the New Zealand Bill of Rights Act 1990 guarantees of a fair trial and an appeal do not require that an appeal should be allowed and a retrial ordered whenever there has been a miscarriage at the first trial. The Court cited *R v Condon* [[2006] NZSC 62, [2007] 1 NZLR 300], in which it adopted the passage just cited from *Randall* when discussing the requirements of a fair trial and held that a "fundamentally flawed" trial is an unfair trial for the purposes of s 25(a) of the Bill of Rights Act.

'[28] The language of fundamental error sets a deliberately high threshold to ensure the proviso can do the work for which it was designed. As this Court recognised in *Matenga*, it is a necessary, and usually sufficient, condition for use of the proviso that the appellate court be satisfied of the defendant's guilt:

> ... the decision to confirm a jury verdict, despite something having gone wrong, depends upon whether the appellate court considers a guilty verdict was inevitable on the basis of the whole of the admissible evidence (including any new evidence).'

Lundy v R [2019] NZSC 152, [2020] 1 NZLR 1 at [25]–[28], per Miller J

G

GALE

[For 76 Halsbury's Laws of England (5th Edn) (2013) para 614 see now 76 Halsbury's Laws of England (5th Edn) (2019) para 610.]

GIFT

Class gift

[For 102 Halsbury's Laws of England (5th Edn) (2010) para 175 see now 102 Halsbury's Laws of England (5th Edn) (2016) para 175.]

GOODS

New Zealand [Biosecurity Act 1993, s 116: power to seize and dispose of unauthorised goods.] '[21] Three key arguments were advanced to say that the trees subject to the notices and directions were not "unauthorised goods", and accordingly that the exercise of powers under s 116 was unlawful …

…

'[52] There is a further significant issue. The vast majority of the trees that are subject to the s 116 notice are now growing in the ground. Some have reached their second or third season. This calls into question whether they can be now subject to the exercise of power under s 116. The unauthorised goods, or goods that have been in contact with other authorised goods, must be "goods" as defined. The definition in s 2 is:

> **goods** means all kinds of moveable personal property.

'[53] As Mr Greig submitted, s 116 should be contrasted with other terminology used in other sections of the Act. For example, the powers of examination in s 121 covers organisms, organic material, as well as other goods or material. The words "organic material" and "organism" are subject to their own clear definitions in s 2. The more restricted use of the concept of "goods" in s 116 is significant. It shows that the text, in light of the scheme and purpose of the Act, is intended to have its limits.

'[54] The distinction between personal property and real property is subject to a rich vein of case law. As a general proposition, trees planted in the ground are not treated as moveable property. On this basis any trees that remained in pots, or in other equivalent containment, would be goods but any such trees that had been planted would not be. There is the further complexity here that some of the trees in the ground are dug up and transported once sold by a nursery.

'[55] I accept the argument of Mr Fong that the meaning to be given to "goods" or "moveable property" will be highly dependent on the context. He challenged the idea that the reach of s 116 could turn on the arbitrary actions of the owner of the tree. But Parliament has provided limits on when property can be traced from unauthorised goods for the purposes of s 116. Here a large number of trees are now planted in the land and producing fruit. In some cases, those trees have been in the environment for years. There may have been other trees in the vicinity of these trees. In most cases the situation here seems to be beyond the outer limits of the reach of s 116. So I do not accept that the point made by the applicants is a technicality. Rather it goes to the heart of the intended reach of s 116. It is the Ministry that is pushing its application beyond its technical limits.' *Waimea Nurseries Ltd v Director-General for Primary Industries* [2018] NZHC 2183, [2019] 2 NZLR 107 at [21], [52]–[55], per Cooke J

In marine insurance policy

[For 60 Halsbury's Laws of England (5th Edn) (2011) para 287 see now 60 Halsbury's Laws of England (5th Edn) (2018) para 266.]

GROUND RENT
[For 27(1) Halsbury's Laws of England (4th ed) para 212 at p 202, ft 1 see now 62 Halsbury's Laws (5th Edn) (2016) para 236, n 1.]

H

HABEAS CORPUS

Ad testificandum or ad respondendum

[For 85 Halsbury's Laws of England (5th Edn) (2012) para 457, n 12 see now 85 Halsbury's Laws of England (5th Edn) (2020) para 455, n 12.]

HABITUAL RESIDENCE

See RESIDE—RESIDENCE

HEIRLOOMS

[For 103 Halsbury's Laws of England (5th Edn) (2010) para 928 see now 103 Halsbury's Laws of England (5th Edn) (2016) para 928.]

HIGHWAY

[For 55 Halsbury's Laws of England (5th Edn) (2012) paras 1–8 see now 55 Halsbury's Laws of England (5th Edn) (2019) paras 1–8.]

'[6]   The word highway has no single meaning in the law but, in non-technical language, it is a way over which the public have rights of passage, whether on foot, on horseback or in (or on) vehicles. At common law, at least prior to 1835, there was, generally speaking, no necessary connection between those responsible for the maintenance and repair of a public highway and those with a proprietary interest in the land over which it ran. Prima facie the inhabitants of the parish through which the highway ran would be responsible for its repair, but they were not a corporate body suitable to hold ownership rights in relation to it: see Sauvain on Highway Law (5th edn, 2013) at para 3–05. As he puts it:

"It was left to statute, therefore, to create an interest in land which was to be held by the body on whom the duty to repair had fallen."

Parliament began this task, in a rudimentary way, in s 41 of the Highways Act 1835, continued it in s 68 of the Public Health Act 1848, s 96 of the Metropolis Management Act 1855 and s 149 of the Public Health Act 1875. They all provided for a form of automatic vesting of a property interest in the land over which the highway ran in favour of the body responsible for its maintenance and repair.

...

'[31]   The Court of Appeal concluded that "highway" as used in art 2 [of the GLA Roads and Side Roads (Transfer of Property etc) Order 2000, SI 2000/1552] and s 265 [of the Highways Act 1980] had a clear common law meaning, limited in the vertical plane to the zone of ordinary use. I respectfully disagree. The word "highway" is not a defined term, either in the 1980 Act, in the Transfer Order or in the GLA Act [Greater London Authority Act 1999]. There is a limited explanation, in s 328 of the 1980 Act that:

"In this Act, except where the context otherwise requires, 'highway' means the whole or a part of a highway other than a ferry or waterway ..."

This is largely circular so far as concerns the core meaning of "highway" and, in any event, subject to context. It does not follow that the interpreter is therefore required to find some uniform meaning of the word "highway" wherever it is used, either in the relevant legislation or, as the Court of Appeal thought, at common law.

'[32] There is in my view no single meaning of highway at common law. The word is sometimes used as a reference to its physical elements. Sometimes it is used as a label for the incorporeal rights of the public in relation to the locus in quo. Sometimes, as here, it is used as the label for a species of real property. When used within a statutory formula, as here, the word necessarily takes its meaning from the context in which it is used.

'[33] In agreement with counsel and with the Court of Appeal, I do consider that the meaning of art 2 is to be found by an examination of the meaning of the almost identically worded s 265. This is not merely because of the linguistic similarity between those two provisions, but because the whole of the structure for the transfer of property and liabilities in the Transfer Order is closely modelled on the pre-existing structure of the provisions in s 265 relating to trunk roads.

'[34] It is tempting but, in my view, wrong to assume that, where ss 263 and 265 both refer to "highway" as a label for real property rights which are to be vested in a highway authority, the word "highway" must therefore have precisely the same meaning in both sections. This is not merely because the word appears as part of two quite differently worded provisions. Rather, it is because, although now lying almost side by side in a consolidating statute, the two sections have completely different ancestry, and serve two very different purposes. As already noted, s 263 takes away from private ownership only those rights in the vertical plane of the highway which are necessary to enable the highway authority to perform its statutory functions of operation, maintenance and repair. By contrast, s 265 merely transfers rights in the vertical plane already owned by one public authority to a successor public authority, so that the successor can stand in the shoes of its predecessor so far as ownership is concerned. ...' *Southwark London Borough Council v Transport for London* [2018] UKSC 63, [2019] 2 All ER 271 at [6], [31]–[34], per Lord Briggs

The highway, in so far as it is vested in the former highway authority

[The GLA Roads and Side Roads (Transfer of Property etc) Order 2000, SI 2000/1552, art 2(1)(a), which had been modelled on the Highways Act 1980, s 265, transferred to TfL 'the highway, in so far as it is vested in the former highway authority'.] '[29] In my judgment art 2(1)(a) transfers to TfL ownership of all that part of the vertical plane relating to a GLA road vested in the relevant council on the operative date, but only to the extent that ownership was then vested in the council in its capacity as former highway authority. That is, in my view, the true meaning of the phrase "the highway, in so far as it is vested in the former highway authority". ...' *Southwark London Borough Council v Transport for London*

[2018] UKSC 63, [2019] 2 All ER 271 at [29], per Lord Briggs

HONEST OPINION

[For 32 Halsbury's Laws of England (5th Edn) (2012) paras 637–638 (on fair comment) see now 32 Halsbury's Laws of England (5th Edn) (2019) para 632.]

HOTCHPOT

[For 91 Halsbury's Laws of England (5th Edn) (2012) para 825 see now 91 Halsbury's Laws of England (5th Edn) (2012) para 718.]

HUNT

New Zealand [Wildlife Act 1953, s 63A: offence to hunt or kill any absolutely or partially protected marine wildlife.] '[62] It is implicit in the prohibited act of "hunting" that the defendant intends to hunt. To hunt something, you must intend to catch or kill it. It is not possible to accidentally or unintentionally hunt an animal.

...

'[93] ... In the s 2(1) definition of "hunt or kill": "hunting" means an intentional act committed if a person is proved to have had an intent to hunt.' *Shark Experience Ltd v Paua-MAC5 Inc* [2019] NZSC 111, [2019] 1 NZLR 791 at [62], [93], per Winkelmann CJ

HUNT OR KILL

New Zealand [Wildlife Act 1953, s 63A: a specific offence to 'hunt or kill' certain marine wildlife (including great white sharks). Whether shark cage diving was hunting or killing.] '[29] As the parties acknowledge, the definition is particularly difficult to construe. Part of that difficulty lies in the use of the words "hunt" and "kill" in accordance with their usual meaning as part of an extended definition of the expression "hunt or kill". Part lies in the fact that the overall statutory scheme has been repeatedly amended over the course of the sixty-plus years since its enactment, causing the Act to lose some coherence.

'[30] Shark Experience maintains that the ordinary and grammatical reading of the s 2 definition is that the words "pursuing, disturbing, or molesting" are connected to, and qualified by, the words "hunt or kill". Ms Grey for Shark Experience argues that it is an available interpretation that all of the relevant actions, "pursuing, disturbing, or molesting", are to be read as connected to the words "to hunt or kill". On this reading, what is prohibited is disturbance of protected wildlife connected to hunting or killing, and pursuing or molesting protected wildlife in the course of hunting or killing.

...

'[33] It is helpful at this point to repeat the definition of "hunt or kill" in s 2:

hunt or kill, in relation to any wildlife, includes the hunting, killing, taking, trapping, or capturing of any wildlife by any means; and also includes pursuing, disturbing, or molesting any wildlife, taking or using a firearm, dog, or like method to hunt or kill wildlife, whether this results in killing or capturing or not; and also includes every attempt to hunt or kill wildlife and every act of assistance of any other person to hunt or kill wildlife

'[34] On our analysis, the definition of "hunt or kill" operates on three levels as follows:

(a) The first level is "includes the hunting, killing, taking, trapping, or capturing of any wildlife by any means;". This describes the non-extended meaning of hunting, killing, trapping or capturing, actions that would be captured in accordance with common usage of these words.

(b) The second level is "and also includes pursuing, disturbing, or molesting any wildlife, taking or using a firearm, dog, or like method to hunt or kill wildlife, whether this results in killing or capturing or not;". We read this as extending the meaning of the expression "hunt or kill" beyond the common usage of those words to include both acts incidental to hunting or killing wildlife ("taking or using a firearm, dog, or like method to hunt or kill wildlife"), and also to other kinds of potentially harmful actions ("pursuing, disturbing, or molesting any wildlife") that are not necessarily connected to hunting or killing in a common usage sense.

(c) The third and final level is "and also includes every attempt to hunt or kill wildlife and every act of assistance of any

other person to hunt or kill wildlife". As is common ground, this deals with attempts or the giving of assistance.

...

'[40] On our approach, the definition of "hunt or kill" can be seen as a list of prohibited actions relating to wildlife. The choice of the phrase "hunt or kill" as the defined term does not have any particular significance in determining the meanings of the items in the list. It might be thought improbable or unlikely that the phrase "hunt or kill" was chosen as a catch-all phrase for a collection of prohibited actions, some unrelated to hunting or killing in their common usage. But in other, later, Acts, the use of this phrase in just that manner is beyond question. ...

...

'[92] To conclude this interpretative analysis, we are satisfied that the definition of "hunt or kill" captures within the s 63A offence conduct which is unconnected to the common usage meaning of hunting and killing, extending to pursuing, molesting and disturbing protected wildlife, whether or not those prohibited acts take place in the course of, or for the purpose of, hunting or killing or otherwise. We are satisfied that the overall statutory scheme supports this interpretation, as does the Act's purpose. This interpretation does not lead to incoherence in the statutory scheme, nor to over or indeterminate criminalisation. The nature of the prohibited acts, together with the availability of the s 68B and common law "no fault" defence, create a coherent framework from which exposure to criminal liability can be sufficiently predicted.

'[93] We summarise the nature of the prohibited acts as follows. In the s 2(1) definition of "hunt or kill":

(a) "hunting" means an intentional act committed if a person is proved to have had an intent to hunt;

(b) "killing" means causing the death of a protected animal. An intention to kill need not be proved;

(c) "pursuing" means to intentionally chase but does not include luring or attracting or merely following the animal at a safe distance;

(d) "disturbing" means an action which physically or mentally agitates the protected animal to a level creating a real risk of significant harm; and

(e) "molesting" means intentionally troubling, distressing or injuring a protected animal.

'[94] There is no requirement to prove an intent to commit the offence in s 63A. Aside from the prohibited act of "hunting", there is also no requirement to prove that any of the prohibited acts listed above are committed in the course of, or for the purpose of, hunting or killing in the ordinary usage sense of those words. Attempting any of the prohibited acts would also constitute an offence under s 63A.
...

'[123] The Court of Appeal's declaration that "Shark cage diving is an offence under s 63A Wildlife Act 1953" is set aside.' *Shark*

Experience Ltd v PauaMAC5 Inc [2019] NZSC 111, [2019] 1 NZLR 791 at [29]–[30], [33]–[34], [40], [92]–[92], [123], per Winkelmann CJ

HYPOTHECATION

[For 7 Halsbury's Laws of England (5th Edn) (2012) para 506 see now 7 Halsbury's Laws of England (5th Edn) (2020) para 539.]

I

IP COMPLETION DAY

'IP completion day' means 31 December 2020 at 11 pm. ... In this Act references to before, after or on IP completion day, or to beginning with IP completion day, are to be read as references to before, after or at 11 pm on 31 December 2020 or (as the case may be) to beginning with 11 pm on that day. (European Union (Withdrawal Agreement) Act 2020, s 39(1), (2))

IMPLIED TERM

[For 22 Halsbury's Laws of England (5th Edn) (2012) paras 364–376 see now 22 Halsbury's Laws of England (5th Edn) (2019) paras 163–175.]

IMPRISONMENT

[Curfew imposed by Home Secretary on foreign national awaiting deportation; whether amounting to imprisonment.] '[1] The right to physical liberty was highly prized and protected by the common law long before the United Kingdom became party to the European Convention on Human Rights ("ECHR"). A person who was unlawfully imprisoned could, and can, secure his release through the writ of habeas corpus. He could, and can, also secure damages for the tort of false imprisonment. This case is about the meaning of imprisonment at common law and whether it should, or should not, now be aligned with the concept of deprivation of liberty in art 5 of the ECHR.
...
'[24] As it is put in *Street on Torts* (15th edn, 2018), by Christian Witting, p 259, "False imprisonment involves an act of the defendant which directly and intentionally (or possibly negligently) causes the confinement of the claimant within an area delimited by the defendant." The essence of imprisonment is being made to stay in a particular place by another

person. The methods which might be used to keep a person there are many and various. They could be physical barriers, such as locks and bars. They could be physical people, such as guards who would physically prevent the person leaving if he tried to do so. They could also be threats, whether of force or of legal process. A good example is *R v Rumble* [2003] EWCA Crim 770, [2003] 1 Cr App Rep (S) 618, 167 JP 205. The defendant in a magistrates' court who had surrendered to his bail was in custody even though there was no dock, no usher, nor security staff and thus nothing to prevent his escaping (as indeed he did). The point is that the person is obliged to stay where he is ordered to stay whether he wants to do so or not.
'[25] In this case there is no doubt that the defendant defined the place where the claimant was to stay between the hours of 11 pm and 7 am. There was no suggestion that he could go somewhere else during those hours without the defendant's permission. ...
'[26] The fact that the claimant did from time to time ignore his curfew for reasons that seemed good to him makes no difference to his situation while he was obeying it. Like the prisoner who goes absent from his open prison, or the tunneller who gets out of the prison camp, he is not imprisoned while he is away. But he is imprisoned while he is where the defendant wants him to be.
'[27] There is, of course, a crucial difference between voluntary compliance with an instruction and enforced compliance with that instruction. The Court of Appeal held that this was a case of enforced not voluntary compliance and I agree. It is not to be compared with those cases in which the claimant went voluntarily with the sheriff's officer. There can be no doubt that the claimant's compliance was enforced. He was wearing an electronic tag which meant that leaving his address would be detected. The monitoring company would then telephone him to find out where he was. He was warned in the clearest possible terms that breaking the curfew could lead to a £5,000 fine or imprisonment for

up to six months or both. He was well aware that it could also lead to his being detained again under the [Immigration Act 1971]. All of this was backed up by the full authority of the State, which was claiming to have the power to do this. The idea that the claimant was a free agent, able to come and go as he pleased, is completely unreal.' *R (on the application of Jalloh (formerly Jollah)) v Secretary of State for the Home Department* [2020] UKSC 4, [2020] 3 All ER 449 at [1], [24]–[27], per Lady Hale

IN THE PRESENCE OF

[For 102 Halsbury's Laws of England (5th Edn) (2010) para 70 see now 102 Halsbury's Laws of England (5th Edn) (2016) para 70.]

INCAPACITATED FOR WORK OUTSIDE THE POLICE FORCE

Australia [Police Regulation (Superannuation) Act 1906 (NSW), s 10(1A)(b)(ii): superannuation amount commensurate with incapacity for work outside the police force.] '[17] As was observed at the outset, s 10(1A)(b)(ii) permits of a constructional choice. On one view of its terms, it provides for an "additional amount" of annual superannuation allowance for a "disabled member of the police force" who is incapacitated for work outside the police force regardless of the cause of the member's incapacity for work outside the police force. The alternative view is that it provides for an "additional amount" of annual superannuation allowance for a "disabled member of the police force" who is incapacitated for work outside the police force only if the incapacity for work outside the police force results from a specified infirmity of body or mind determined, in accordance with s 10B, to have been caused by the member having been hurt on duty when a member of the police force.

'[23] Turning next to s 10(1A)(c), the statutory exclusion of s 10(1A)(b) where s 10(1A)(c) applies, and vice versa, conveys that "incapacitated" in the expression "totally incapacitated for work outside the police force" in s 10(1A)(c) has the same meaning as "incapacity" in the expression "incapacity for work outside the police force" in s 10(1A)(b)(ii).

'[24] Contrary to the respondent's submissions, it is also apparent that "incapacitated for work outside the police force" in s 10(1A)(c) must mean incapacitated for work outside the police force from the specified infirmity of body or mind which rendered the member incapable of exercising the functions of a police officer and which was caused by being hurt on duty. That is implicit in the requirement in s 10(1A)(c)(ii) that the additional amount of between 12.25 and 27.25 per cent of attributed salary payable under s 10(1A)(c)(i) in respect of the disabled member's incapacity for work outside the police force be commensurate with the abnormality of the risks to which the member was exposed. As the chapeau to s 10(1A)(c) makes clear, the risks are those that cause the member to be hurt on duty. The provision thereby draws a clear link between the additional amount payable and the event of the member being hurt on duty.

'[29] Taking those considerations together conveys that the preferable view of s 10(1A)(b)(ii) is that, like s 10(1A)(c), it contemplates only one kind of incapacity for work outside the police force, being incapacity the result of the specified infirmity of body or mind determined to have been caused by the member being hurt on duty when a member of the police force.

'[40] In the result, it should be held that, upon the proper construction of s 10(1A)(b) of the Act, the expression "member's incapacity for work outside the police force" means the member's incapacity from a specified infirmity of body or mind determined pursuant to s 10B or on appeal to have been caused by the member being hurt on duty when he or she was a member of the police force. …' *SAS Trustee Corp v Miles* [2018] HCA 55, (2018) 361 ALR 206 at [17], [23]–[24], [29], [40], per Kiefel CJ, Bell and Nettle JJ

INCHMAREE CLAUSE

[For 60 Halsbury's Laws of England (5th Edn) (2011) para 335 see now 60 Halsbury's Laws of England (5th Edn) (2018) para 314.]

INCIDENTAL DEMAND

Canada [Civil Code of Québec ('CCQ'), art 3139: where a Québec authority has jurisdiction to rule on the principal demand, it also has jurisdiction to rule on an incidental demand or a cross demand.] '155 The Court must nevertheless bear in mind that art 3139 *CCQ* is a jurisdiction-*granting* provision, and that its operation assumes that, absent this provision, the court would not be competent, in the jurisdictional sense, to hear the "incidental demand or ... cross demand": Saumier [Saumier, Geneviève. "The Recognition of Foreign Judgments in Quebec — The Mirror Crack'd?" (2002), 81 *Can Bar Rev* 677], at p 703; *Spar* [*Spar Aerospace Ltd v American Mobile Satellite Corp* 2002 SCC 78, [2002] 4 SCR 205], at para 22 ("[t]hese rules [in Book Ten of the *CCQ*] cover a broad range of interrelated topics, including: the jurisdiction of the court (art 3136, 3139 and 3148 *CCQ*)" (emphasis added)). In my view, the term "incidental demand", as that term appears in art 3139 CCQ, is sufficiently broad to cover voluntary and forced intervention of third persons in the proceeding, including an incidental demand in warranty, and the consolidation of proceedings, whether or not they involve the same parties, and whether or not they arise from the same source or from related sources: see arts 184 to 190 and 210 of the new *Code of Civil Procedure*, CQLR, c C-25.01 ("new *CCP*"); see also Côté J's reasons, at paras 206 and 283 ("there is no doubt that [the precise meaning of 'incidental demand'] must be defined on the basis of Quebec procedural law"). Indeed, this point finds ample support in the Quebec doctrine. ...

...

'157 Further, an "incidental demand" is not limited to a recourse in warranty: see, eg, art 184 para 3 of the new *CCP*. A *plaintiff* thus has the right to force the intervention of a third person in order to fully resolve the dispute: see *Bourdages v Québec (Gouvernement du) (Ministère des Transports)* 2016 QCCS 5066; *Fonds d'assurance responsabilité professionnelle du Barreau du Québec v Gariépy*, 2005 QCCA 60, at para 33. ...' *Barer v Knight Brothers LLC* [2019] SCJ No 13, [2019] 1 SCR 573 at paras 155, 157, per Brown J

INCUMBRANCE

[For 27(1) Halsbury's Laws (4th edn reissue) para 81 see now 62 Halsbury's Laws of England (5th Edn) (2016) para 98.]

INDEMNITY

[For 60 Halsbury's Laws of England (5th Edn) (2011) para 3 see now 60 Halsbury's Laws of England (5th Edn) (2018) para 3.]

INDENTURE

[For 32 Halsbury's Laws of England (5th Edn) (2012) para 203 see now 32 Halsbury's Laws of England (5th Edn) (2019) para 203.]

INELIGIBILITY PERIOD

Australia [Migration Act 1958 (Cth), s 494AA.] '[93] The "ineligibility period" is defined as "the period from the time of the unauthorised entry until the time when the person next ceases to be an unlawful non-citizen". So, like the operation of this term (differently defined) in s 494AB, the starting point for s 494AA, in terms of the time period, is when an individual enters Australia.

'[94] There is no meaning4 attributed by the statute to the term "ineligible". The applicant contends the use of a word such as "ineligible" connotes a temporal restriction. I do not agree. Eligibility, or ineligibility, in many statutory contexts, can fix on a person's characteristics or circumstances, on factual matters external to a person, or on periods of time. I accept it is a somewhat curious word to use as part of a definition in a privative clause, however Parliament has used it and the Court must strive to give it meaning. I consider it is clear enough from the context in which the compound phrase "ineligibility period" is used ("period" signalling a length of time) that, read with the prohibitions in s 494AA(1), the intention is to mark out, by reference to events occurring during a period of time, a category of proceeding that is "ineligible" for the exercise of jurisdiction by any Court except the High Court. As I say, it may not be the heights of drafting elegance, but I consider it is clear this is what is intended.' *DBE17 (by his litigation guardian Arthur) v Commonwealth* [2018] FCA 1307, (2018) 361 ALR 423 at [93]–[94], per Mortimer J

INFECTION

[For 85 Halsbury's Laws of England (5th Edn) (2012) para 625 see now 85 Halsbury's Laws of England (5th Edn) (2020) para 725.]

INHERENT VICE

[For 60 Halsbury's Laws of England (5th Edn) (2011) para 344 see now 60 Halsbury's Laws of England (5th Edn) (2018) para 323.]

INNUENDO

[For 32 Halsbury's Laws of England (5th Edn) (2012) para 547 see now 32 Halsbury's Laws of England (5th Edn) (2019) para 547.]

INSTRUMENT

[For 32 Halsbury's Laws of England (5th Edn) (2012) para 340 see now 32 Halsbury's Laws of England (5th Edn) (2019) para 340.]

Under hand

[For 32 Halsbury's Laws of England (5th Edn) (2012) para 339 see now 32 Halsbury's Laws of England (5th Edn) (2019) para 339.]

INSURABLE INTEREST

[For 60 Halsbury's Laws of England (5th Edn) (2011) para 357 see now 60 Halsbury's Laws of England (5th Edn) (2018) para 336.]

INSURANCE

[For 60 Halsbury's Laws of England (5th Edn) (2011) para 2 see now 60 Halsbury's Laws of England (5th Edn) (2018) para 2.]

Contingency insurance

[For 60 Halsbury's Laws of England (5th Edn) (2011) para 746 see now 60 Halsbury's Laws of England (5th Edn) (2018) para 717.]

Double insurance

[For 60 Halsbury's Laws of England (5th Edn) (2011) para 229 see now 60 Halsbury's Laws of England (5th Edn) (2018) para 208.]

Industrial assurance

[For 60 Halsbury's Laws of England (5th Edn) (2011) para 479 see now 60 Halsbury's Laws of England (5th Edn) (2018) para 457.]

INVESTIGATION

Australia [Australian Crime Commission Act 2002 (Cth), s 7C.] '[96] The word "investiga-tion" must, of course, be construed in the context of the Act read as a whole and in a manner consistent with the statutory purpose: *Project Blue Sky Inc v Australian Broadcasting Authority* (1998) 194 CLR 355; 153 ALR 490. In its ordinary meaning, the word may be understood as referring to an inquisitorial activity and so must have as its subject matter something that is capable of forming the basis of an inquiry. An investigation is something that is capable of generating material to be employed in the fulfilment of its stated purpose. However, in the particular statutory context, and in light of what is said below, the material need not necessarily be in the nature of "evidence" at least if that word is intended to refer to evidentiary material gathered solely to aid in the proof of a criminal charge.

'[97] It must also be accepted that the word "investigation", in context, must refer to an activity that is capable of producing outcomes of a kind that are contemplated by the Act: see s 7A(c) and (d); see also *XXVII* [*XXVII v Commonwealth* (2017) 265 A Crim R 519; [2017] FCA 320] at [119]–[120]. However, the Act does not require that an investigation have a "conclusion" in the sense of a fixed end date or pre-determined terminating event: *XXVII* at [117]–[124]; see also *XXVII* at [42] (Dowsett J), [77]–[89] (Wigney J) and [155] (Bromwich J). Moreover, by s 7C(3) and (4)(c) of the Act, it is apparent that the permissible purpose of an investigation will include the understanding, disrupting or preventing the criminal activity to which the investigation relates. These are words of broad import. There is nothing in the text or context of the provisions to suggest that "understanding, disrupting or preventing" the activity must be achieved by the sole means of gathering evidence for use in the trial of a criminal charge. The amendment to s 7C(3) of the Act (introduced after the High Court delivered judgment in *X7*), makes that clear.

'[98] As to the asserted requirement that an investigation have an organising principle, to my mind that should go without saying. However, to identify that requirement does little to inform the question of how wide or varied the subject matter of a single investigation may permissibly be.

'[99] In my view, the permissible scope of an investigation is not to be found in the meaning of the word "investigation". Rather, the permissible scope of an investigation must be discerned from the whole of the phrase "investigate matters relating to federally relevant criminal activity" as those are the words that the Legislature has used in s 7C(1)(c) to define the limits of the Board's authorisation function. The phrase must, of course, be construed in its statutory context (including in the context of the condition imposed by s 7C(3)). It is a defined phrase embedded with further terms that are themselves expressly and comprehensively defined.

...

'[102] With one qualification, on the proper construction of the Act the Board may authorise an investigation the subject matter of which is described in terms as wide as the language of the statute permits. The qualification is that the subject matter and scope of the investigation must be something in respect of which the mandatory condition in s 7C(3) can be fulfilled in a real and practical sense if the investigation is to be validly determined to be special. In other words, the matters to be investigated cannot be defined in such ephemeral or ill-defined terms that consideration cannot meaningfully be given, and a decision cannot meaningfully be made, as to whether ordinary police methods of investigation into the matters are likely to be effective at understanding, disrupting or preventing the federally relevant criminal activity to which the investigation relates. ...'
CXXXVIII v Commonwealth of Australia [2019] FCAFC 54, (2019) 366 ALR 436 at [96]–[99], [102], per Charlesworth J

J

JETTISON

[For 60 Halsbury's Laws of England (5th Edn) (2011) para 332 see now 60 Halsbury's Laws of England (5th Edn) (2018) para 311.]

JOINTURE

[For 98 Halsbury's Laws of England (5th Edn) (2013) para 502 see now 91 Halsbury's Laws of England (5th Edn) (2019) para 524.]

JUDGMENT

Declaratory

[For 61 Halsbury's Laws of England (5th Edn) (2010) para 690 see now 61A Halsbury's Laws of England (5th Edn) (2018) para 107.]

JURISDICTION

[For 24 Halsbury's Laws of England (5th Edn) (2010) para 623 see now 24A Halsbury's Laws of England (5th Edn) (2019) para 23.]

JURISDICTIONAL FACT

Australia '[188] Judicial review for "jurisdictional fact" has been accompanied by an acute debate as to terminology. One aspect of that debate is whether a "jurisdictional fact" must have an objective existence in fact, as opposed to being a subjective state of mind. This was favoured by (among others) Spigelman CJ in *Timbarra Protection Coalition Inc v Ross Mining NL* (1999) 46 NSWLR 55; 102 LGERA 52; [1999] NSWCA 8 and Professor Aronson (see M Aronson, M Groves and G Weeks, *Judicial Review of Administrative Action and Government Liability* (Lawbook Co 2017), para [4.470]). However, the High Court has deployed the concept more broadly, including

when the availability of a power is dependent upon a state of mind, such as an opinion, a state of satisfaction or a belief. See for example *Minister for Immigration and Multicultural and Indigenous Affairs v SGLB* (2004) 78 ALJR 992; 207 ALR 12; [2004] HCA 32 at [37]: "The satisfaction of the Minister is a condition precedent to the discharge of the obligation to grant or refuse to grant the visa, and is a 'jurisdictional fact' or criterion upon which the exercise of that authority is conditioned". As Basten JA said, with the agreement of Macfarlan and Meagher JJA, in *Trives v Hornsby Shire Council* (2015) 89 NSWLR 268; 208 LGERA 361; 326 ALR 541; [2015] NSWCA 158 at [52], the term "jurisdictional fact" is a "potentially confusing label for what is better described as a precondition to the engagement of a statutory power". This debate is merely definitional. No one has denied that if the exercise of a power is preconditioned upon a state of satisfaction, then it is open to challenge the validity of the power by challenging the legal sufficiency of the state of satisfaction.

'[189] This appeal raises a separate terminological debate. It is whether "jurisdictional fact" review is available in relation to the exercise of non-statutory power. It is as arid as the first. In order to expose why, it is helpful to return to first principle.

...

'[191] ... As a matter of construction, the condition might have the legal consequence that the Secretary could not lawfully be satisfied of compliance unless the document contained certain things.

'[192] That is analogous to the "jurisdictional fact" analysis which is familiar as a matter of construction of powers conferred by legislation. The question is whether there is some objective, factual matter the existence of which is a precondition to the condition being satisfied, or whether all that matters is the subjective state of satisfaction of the Secretary.

...

'[201] In short, I see no reason why anything substantive should turn on whether the "power" is statutory or non-statutory. Indeed, the facts of this case suggest that the distinctions between "statutory" as opposed to "non-statutory", and "power" as opposed to "function", are inapt.' *Muswellbrook Shire Council v Hunter Valley Energy Coal Pty Ltd* [2019] NSWCA 216, (2019) 372 ALR 695 at [188]–[189], [191]–[192], [201], per Leeming JA

JURY
[For 61 Halsbury's Laws of England (5th Edn) (2010) paras 801–803 see now 61A Halsbury's Laws of England (5th Edn) (2010) paras 201–203.]

JUSTIFICATION
[For 32 Halsbury's Laws of England (5th Edn) (2012) para 582 see now 32 Halsbury's Laws of England (5th Edn) (2019) para 582.]

K

KNIGHT

[For 79 Halsbury's Laws of England (5th Edn) (2014) para 865 see now 79 Halsbury's Laws of England (5th Edn) (2020) para 861.]

Orders of knighthood

[For 79 Halsbury's Laws of England (5th Edn) (2014) paras 866–867 see now 79 Halsbury's Laws of England (5th Edn) (2020) paras 862–863.]

L

LAND

In mining law

[For 76 Halsbury's Laws of England (5th Edn) (2013) para 17 see now 76 Halsbury's Laws of England (5th Edn) (2019) para 17.]

LAPSE

Of testamentary gift

[For 102 Halsbury's Laws of England (5th Edn) (2010) para 160 see now 102 Halsbury's Laws of England (5th Edn) (2016) para 160.]

LAW MERCHANT

[For 32 Halsbury's Laws of England (5th Edn) (2012) para 62 see now 32 Halsbury's Laws of England (5th Edn) (2019) para 62.]

LAY DAYS

[For 7 Halsbury's Laws of England (5th Edn) (2015) para 285 see now 7 Halsbury's Laws of England (5th Edn) (2020) para 328.]

LEASE

Mining lease

[For 76 Halsbury's Laws of England (5th Edn) (2013) para 321 see now 76 Halsbury's Laws of England (5th Edn) (2019) para 318.]

LEAVE HOSPITAL

[Mental Health Act 1983, s 117.] '[5] By s 117(1):

> "This section applies to persons who are detained under section 3 above ... and then cease to be detained and (whether or not immediately after so ceasing) leave hospital."

It is the meaning of the final words of this provision which is at the centre of this dispute.

...

'[36] I also think it wholly unrealistic to suggest, as Mr Wise QC sought to do, that the expression "leave hospital" in s 117(1) necessarily applies to any absence from the hospital premises, irrespective of its length or nature. As Haddon-Cave LJ pointed out in the course of argument, there is a distinction in ordinary speech between the expressions "leave hospital" and "leave *the* hospital" (with a definite article). I agree with the judge when she said at para [40](ii) of her judgment:

> "As a matter of ordinary language, the phrase 'left hospital' is commonly used to refer to discharge from the care of a hospital, rather than simply leaving the premises for any period of time or any reason. If one person asks another 'have you left hospital yet?' they are not asking whether they have gone outside for a shopping trip. I note that, by contrast, s 17(4) refers to a patient on leave as 'absent from a hospital'. In short, a person may be 'absent from a hospital' (eg to go on a short trip outside the grounds), without having 'left hospital'."

'[37] Again, I would not go so far as to say that is impossible to use the phrase "leave hospital" in the narrow sense contended for by counsel for the claimant. But it is a perfectly ordinary and natural use of language to say that a patient who is allowed to leave the hospital in which he is detained to go on a short trip in the custody of hospital staff is not a person who has "left hospital".

'[38] As discussed, in interpreting a statutory provision it is not sufficient to consider the ordinary meanings of the words used and how the same words are used elsewhere in the Act: it is necessary to identify the purpose of the provision, read in its context. The clear purpose of s 117 is to arrange for the provision of services to a person who has been, but is not currently being, provided with treatment and care as a hospital patient. That purpose is implicit in the very expression "after-care", which is used not only in the heading but throughout the body of s 117 in the phrase "after-care services". It is further articulated by the definition of "after-care services" in s 117(6). ...

'[39] Interpreting s 117(1) in the light of this purpose, I readily accept that there will be cases in which a patient granted leave of absence from hospital under s 17 does "cease to be detained" and "leave hospital" within the meaning of s 117(1) so as to become eligible to receive after-care services during the period of their absence. I would also accept the submission made by Mr Wise QC that it is not necessary in order to trigger s 117 that the person concerned should have been "discharged" from hospital in either of the two senses, discussed in the *MM* case [*Secretary of State for Justice v MM* [2018] UKSC 60, [2019] 2 All ER 749, [2018] 3 WLR 1784] at paras [19]–[20], in which that term is used in the Act. I see no reason why s 117 should not apply to a person who is living in the community on leave of absence–either full-time or for part of the week like the claimant in the *Barking* case [*B v Barking, Havering and Brentwood Community Healthcare NHS Trust* [1999] 1 FLR 106, (1999) 47 BMLR 112]–without having been conditionally discharged from hospital under s 42(2) or 73(2) of the Act, let alone "absolutely" discharged from the liability to be detained.
...

'[44] The inescapable conclusion is that the claimant does not "cease to be detained" or "leave hospital" within the meaning of s 117(1) when he is escorted on day trips and is therefore not a person to whom s 117 applies.' *R (on the application of CXF (by his mother, his litigation friend)) v Central Bedfordshire Council* [2018] EWCA Civ 2852, [2019] 3 All ER 20 at [5], [36]–[39], [44], per Leggatt LJ

LEGACY

[For 102 Halsbury's Laws of England (5th Edn) (2010) paras 118–120 see now 102 Halsbury's Laws of England (5th Edn) (2016) paras 118–120.]

Demonstrative legacy

[For 102 Halsbury's Laws of England (5th Edn) (2010) para 120 see now 102 Halsbury's Laws of England (5th Edn) (2016) para 120.]

Specific legacy

[For 102 Halsbury's Laws of England (5th Edn) (2010) para 118 see now 102 Halsbury's Laws of England (5th Edn) (2016) para 118.]

LIBEL

[For 32 Halsbury's Laws of England (5th Edn) (2012) para 511 see now 32 Halsbury's Laws of England (5th Edn) (2019) para 510.]

LIKELY

Australia [Competition and Consumer Act 2010 (Cth), s 50: matters to be taken into account when determining whether acquisition would have the effect, or be likely to have the effect, of substantially lessening competition in a market.] '[105] The word "likely" is capable of more than one meaning. As discussed further below, it can mean more probable than not or it can mean a possibility that is real as opposed to remote. In the present case, the primary judge adopted the latter meaning. That aspect of his Honour's reasons is the subject of challenge in this appeal, and is considered below.
...

'[243] ... Strong arguments, based on the statutory text, can be made for construing the word "likely" to mean "probable". However, the word "likely" has been construed to mean a likelihood that is less than probable for 40 years (from *Tillmanns* [*Tillmanns Butcheries Pty Ltd v Australasian Meat Industry Employees' Union* (1979) 27 ALR 367; 42 FLR 331]) and there is no evidence of widespread inconvenience in the application of the law. To the contrary, the law has been amended on numerous occasions without any suggestion that the dual legal standard should be changed. ...

'[244] Similarly, if the meaning of the word "likely" was being considered for the first time, we would have been inclined to adopt the meaning probable, but there is insufficient reason to change course at this point in time. For those reasons, we reject ground 4 of Aurizon's amended notice of cross-appeal.

'[245] Nevertheless, substituting a synonym such as "real chance" for the statutory word "likely" creates the risk that the synonym may convey a different standard to the statutory language and may introduce a further element of uncertainty. As already noted, in *Tillmanns* Deane J observed that likelihood ought to be determined by reference to well-established standards of what could reasonably be expected to be the consequence of the relevant conduct in the circumstances. Similarly, in *AGL (No 3)* [*Australian Gas Light Co v Australian Competition and Consumer Commission (No 3)* (2003) 137 FCR 317; [2003] FCA 1525], French J observed (at [348]) that:

> The meaning of "likely" reflecting a "real chance or possibility" does not encompass a mere possibility. The word can offer no quantitative guidance but requires a qualitative judgment about the effects of an acquisition or proposed acquisition. The judgment it requires must not set the bar so high as effectively to expose acquiring corporations to a finding of contravention simply on the basis of possibilities, however plausible they may seem, generated by economic theory alone. On the other hand it must not set the bar so low as effectively to allow all acquisitions to proceed save those with the most obvious, direct and dramatic effects upon competition. By the language it adopts and the function thereby cast upon the Court and the regulator in their consideration of acquisitions s 50 gives effect to a kind of competition risk management policy. The application of that policy, reflected in judgments about the application of the section, must operate in the real world. The assessment of the risk or real chance of a substantial lessening of competition cannot rest upon speculation or theory. To borrow the words of the Tribunal in the Howard Smith case, the Court is concerned with "commercial likelihoods relevant to the proposed merger". The word "likely" has to be applied at a level which is commercially relevant or meaningful as must be the assessment of the substantial lessening of competition under consideration—*Rural Press Ltd v ACCC* (2003) 216 CLR 53; 203 ALR 217; [2003] HCA 75 at [41].

'[246] In the present case, the primary judge followed the authorities referred to above in construing the word "likely" as meaning "real commercial likelihood" (at [1275]), as explained by French J in *AGL (No 3)*. In our view, there is no error in his Honour's interpretation of the statutory language. We also respectfully agree with his Honour's statement of the proper approach to the application of s 50, namely:

(a) the application of s 50 requires a single evaluative judgment (at [1276]);

(b) it is a distraction (and, we would add, wrong) to ask what standards of proof apply to the primary facts which will involve predictions about the future (at [1278]);

(c) however, the degree of likelihood of any particular future fact existing or arising will be relevant to the assessment of the likely effect on competition of the acquisition (at [1279]).'

Australian Competition and Consumer Commission v Pacific National Pty Ltd [2020] FCAFC 77, (2020) 378 ALR 1 at [105], [243]–[246], per Middleton and O'bryan JJ

LIQUIDATOR
[For 16 Halsbury's Laws of England (5th Edn) (2011) para 505 see now 16 Halsbury's Laws of England (5th Edn) (2017) para 466.]

LITIGATION FRIEND
[For 10 Halsbury's Laws of England (5th Edn) (2012) paras 1314–1315 see now 10 Halsbury's Laws of England (5th Edn) (2017) paras 1400–1401.]

LOAN RELATIONSHIP
(1) For the purposes of the Corporation Tax Acts a company has a loan relationship if–

(a) the company stands in the position of a creditor or debtor as respects any money debt (whether by reference to a security or otherwise), and

(b) the debt arises from a transaction for the lending of money.

(2) References to a loan relationship and to a company being a party to a loan relationship are to be read accordingly.

...

(5) In this Part [Pt 5] 'creditor relationship', in relation to a company, means any loan relationship of the company where it stands in the position of a creditor as respects the debt in question.

(6) In this Part 'debtor relationship', in relation to a company, means any loan relationship of the company where it stands in the position of a debtor as respects the debt in question.

(Corporation Tax Act 2009, s 302)

LOOKED AFTER

[Children Act 1989, s 22(1).] '[34] Section 25(1) makes clear that s 25 [use of accommodation for restricting liberty] applies only to a child who is being looked after by the local authority. Section 22(1) of the Children Act 1989 defines being looked after as being either "in the care of" the local authority or "provided with accommodation" by the local authority. Section 105(1) of the 1989 Act provides that any reference to a child who is "in the care of" any authority means "'a child who is in their care by virtue of a care order". The court cannot make a care order in respect of a child who has reached the age of 17 years old (Children Act 1989 s 31(3)). Section 20 of the Children Act 1989 governs the provision of accommodation for children. Within the context of these proceedings, s 20(7) of the 1989 Act stipulates that a local authority may not provide accommodation under s 20 of the Act for a child if any person who has parental responsibility for that child objects.' *A City Council v LS* [2019] EWHC 1384 (Fam), [2020] 1 All ER 652 at [34], per MacDonald J

LUGGAGE

Ordinary luggage

[For 7 Halsbury's Laws of England (5th Edn) (2015) paras 53–54 see now 7 Halsbury's Laws of England (5th Edn) (2020) para 27.]

M

MAGISTRATE

[For 71 Halsbury's Laws of England (5th Edn) (2013) para 401 see now 71 Halsbury's Laws of England (5th Edn) (2020) para 401.]

MAINTENANCE (OF INFANT)

[For 98 Halsbury's Laws of England (5th Edn) (2013) para 515 see now 98 Halsbury's Laws of England (5th Edn) (2019) para 488.]

MALICE

[For 32 Halsbury's Laws of England (5th Edn) (2012) para 651 see now 32 Halsbury's Laws of England (5th Edn) (2019) para 647.]

Acting maliciously

[War risks insurance policy; cover provided for inter alia, in cl 1.5 'any terrorist or any person acting maliciously or from a political motive'. Vessel owned by the appellant was used by unknown third parties in an unsuccessful attempt to export drugs from Venezuela and was detained by Venezuelan authorities.] '[13] The present owners' case thus turns on the fact that the Institute War and Strikes Clauses identify as perils insured, not merely detainment etc under cl 1.2, but also loss or damage to the vessel caused by "any person acting maliciously" under cl 1.5. Once relied on, the specific cover against malicious acts should not, the owners submit, be undermined or cut back by an exception of "detainment ... by reason of infringement of customs ...regulations" [in cl 4.1.5] which the owners submit is most obviously addressing other situations–or which, on the owners' alternative case, is not even addressing cl 1.5 at all.

'[14] It is in the light of these submissions that the Supreme Court concluded that, despite the common ground between the parties, the necessary starting point is to examine the scope of the concept of "any person acting maliciously" in cl 1.5. This is a phrase which must be seen in context, appearing as it does in the middle of perils insured involving "loss of or damage to the Vessel caused by ... [1.5] any terrorist or any person acting maliciously or from a political motive". Its companions in that context are terrorists and persons acting from a political motive, causing loss or damage to the vessel. What the drafters appear to have had in mind are persons whose actions are aimed at causing loss of or damage to the vessel, or, it may well be, other property or persons as a by-product of which the vessel is lost or damaged. Applying a similar rationale to the central phrase "any person acting maliciously", it can be said that the present circumstances involve no such aim. Foreseeable though the risk may be that drugs being smuggled may be detected, their detection and any consequent loss or damage to the vessel were the exact opposite of the unknown smugglers' aim or, presumably, expectation.

...

'[22] In my view, therefore, the concept of "any person acting maliciously" in cl 1.5 would have been understood in 1983 and should now be understood as relating to situations where a person acts in a way which involves an element of spite or ill-will or the like in relation to the property insured or at least to other property or perhaps even a person, and consequential loss of, or damage to, the insured vessel or cargo. It is not designed to cater for situations where the state of mind of spite, ill-will or the like is absent. In the present case, foreseeable though the vessel's seizure and loss were if the smuggling attempt was discovered, the would-be smugglers cannot have had any such state of mind. They were, on the contrary, intent on avoiding detection. ...' *Atlasnavios - Navegac̦ão, Lda v Navigators Insurance Co Ltd; The B Atlantic* [2018] UKSC 26, [2018] 4 All ER 589 at [13]–[14], [22], per Lord Mance DP

MANAGED SERVICE COMPANY PROVIDER

'[6] Section 61B(1) of the ITEPA [Income Tax (Earnings and Pensions) Act 2003] defines an MSC in the following terms:

"(1) A company is a 'managed service company' if—

(a) its business consists wholly or mainly of providing (directly or indirectly) the services of an individual to other persons,

(b) payments are made (directly or indirectly) to the individual (or associates of the individual) of an amount equal to the greater part or all of the consideration for the provision of the services,

(c) the way in which those payments are made would result in the individual (or associates) receiving payments of an amount (net of tax and national insurance) exceeding that which would be received (net of tax and national insurance) if every payment in respect of the services were employment income of the individual, and

(d) a person who carries on a business of promoting or facilitating the use of companies to provide the services of individuals ('an MSC provider') is involved with the company."

'[7] For the condition in sub-s (1)(d) to be satisfied the putative MSC provider must be "involved with the company". That concept is defined in s 61B(2) ITEPA ....

'[8] Thus, an MSC is a company which (i) provides the services of an individual to others; (ii) pays that individual all or most of the fees it charges to those others; (iii) pays the individual in a way which increases the net amount received by the individual, as compared with what he would have received net if he had earned the fees as his employment income; and (iv) involves an MSC provider in its business in one of the ways then set out in s 61B(2). An MSC can be a partnership as well as a body corporate: see s 61C(3).

...

'[19] The issue before us is the issue dealt with at paras [64] onwards of the decision. It was contended before us that the definition of an MSC provider as "a person who carries on a business of promoting or facilitating the use of companies to provide the services of individuals" could either mean:

(1) HMRC's construction: that, in order for a company to be an MSC provider, the company's business must be the business of promoting or facilitating the use by individuals of companies through which the individuals will provide their services to clients; the putative MSC provider does not need also to promote or facilitate the services themselves;

(2) The Appellants' construction: that, in order to be an MSC provider, a company must promote or facilitate the services provided by the companies the use of which it has promoted or facilitated.

'[20] It was common ground that Costelloe did not promote or facilitate the services that each of the individual owners provided to the Appellants' end clients. Each Appellant arranged and negotiated its own contracts, including payment rates and terms, with the end clients, sometimes through a recruitment agency but without any control or supervision by Costelloe.

...

'[31] There is nothing either in the wording of Ch 9 ITEPA or in the external material on which the Appellants rely that supports their construction of the definition of an MSC provider in s 61B(1)(d). The business that the Government was trying to catch in the definition is precisely the business that Costelloe runs; its business is in promoting a situation in which the workers provide their services through a company instead of directly to the end client and it thereby promotes the use of companies to provide those services. Costelloe then provides the Gold Business Service to the MSC, thereby facilitating the use of the MSC by that individual in order for him or her to provide services to the end client. There is no doubt that this business is what the legislation is aimed at catching and in my judgment it succeeds in its aim.

...

'[40] I would therefore dismiss the appeal because Costelloe is, in my judgment, undoubtedly an MSC provider and the Appellants are undoubtedly MSCs.' *Christianuyi Ltd v Revenue and Customs Commissioners* [2019] EWCA Civ 474, [2019] 3 All ER 178 at [6]–[8], [19]–[20], [31], [40], per Rose LJ

MANAGEMENT

Of ship

[For 7 Halsbury's Laws of England (5th Edn) (2015) para 389 see now 7 Halsbury's Laws of England (5th Edn) (2020) para 510.]

MANDATE

[For 4 Halsbury's Laws of England (5th Edn) (2011) para 126 see now 4 Halsbury's Laws of England (5th Edn) (2020) para 126.]

MANDATORY ORDER

[For 61 Halsbury's Laws of England (5th Edn) (2010) para 703 et seq see now 61A Halsbury's Laws of England (5th Edn) (2018) para 122 et seq.]

MANIFESTLY UNFOUNDED

New Zealand [Immigration Act 2009, s 140(3): A refugee and protection officer may refuse to consider a subsequent claim for recognition as a refugee or a protected person if the officer is satisfied that the claim: (a) is manifestly unfounded or clearly abusive; or (b) repeats any claim previously made (including a subsequent claim).] '[53] Mr Pidgeon submitted the test for "manifestly unfounded" in s 140(3)(a) was high. Again, by reference to the principle of non-refoulement, he suggested a number of formulae in amplification of the words used in the section. These included that it must be shown the claim is "bound to fail", or has "no realistic prospect of success", and that a claim can only be found to be manifestly unfounded where there is no reasonable risk of refoulement "whatsoever".

'[54] Mr Pidgeon submitted that guidance could be drawn from the interpretation of s 94 of the United Kingdom's Nationality, Immigration and Asylum Act 2002 which employs the similar wording of "clearly unfounded". A claim which is considered to be "clearly unfounded" will attract a certificate precluding any appeal before an applicant can be expelled to that person's country of origin. The House of Lords has opined in relation to s 94 [*ZT (Kosovo) v Secretary of State for the Home Department* [2009] UKHL 6, [2009] 1 WLR 348 at [23] per Lord Phillips] that "[i]f any reasonable doubt exists as to whether the claim may succeed then it is not clearly unfounded".

'[55] The English Court of Appeal also emphasised the "very high threshold" that was required to be met before a claim could be characterised as "manifestly unfounded" in relation to s 72(2)(a) of the Immigration and Asylum Act 1999 (now repealed) [*R (on the application of Razgar) v Secretary of State for the Home Department* [2003] EWCA Civ 840, [2003] INLR 543 at [111]; affd *R v Secretary of State for the Home Department, ex p Razgar* [2004] UKHL 27, [2004] 2 AC 368]:

The Secretary of State cannot lawfully issue such a certificate unless the claim is *bound* to fail ... It is not sufficient that he considers that the claim is likely to fail on appeal, or even that it is very likely to fail. Moreover, as the House of Lords explained in *Yogathas*, the Court will subject the decision of the Secretary of State to "the most anxious scrutiny".

'[56] Care is required before drawing on the interpretation of the words of a statute from a different jurisdiction. However, we consider a standard whereby an officer must be sure that a claim will fail, which appears to be the approach taken by the English courts, is well within the terms of the statutory test of being "manifestly unfounded". We consider "manifestly unfounded" denotes a high standard, something which is self-evident from the particulars on which the claim relies, and is unfounded or untenable.' *WK v Refugee and Protection Officer* [2018] NZCA 258, [2019] 2 NZLR 223 at [53]–[56], per Mander J

MANOR

[For 32 Halsbury's Laws of England (5th Edn) (2012) para 95 see now 32 Halsbury's Laws of England (5th Edn) (2019) para 95.]

MANSION HOUSE

Principal mansion house

For 91 Halsbury's Laws of England (5th Edn) (2012) paras 690, 692 see now 91 Halsbury's Laws of England (5th Edn) (2019) paras 588–599.]

MARKET

[For 71 Halsbury's Laws of England (5th Edn) (2013) para 801 see now 71 Halsbury's Laws of England (5th Edn) (2020) para 701.]

MARKET OVERT

[For 71 Halsbury's Laws of England (5th Edn) (2013) para 824 see now 71 Halsbury's Laws of England (5th Edn) (2020) para 724.]

MARRIAGE

[For 72 Halsbury's Laws of England (5th Edn) (2015) paras 251, 4 see now 71 Halsbury's Laws of England (5th Edn) (2019) paras 3, 5.]

Void and voidable

[For 72 Halsbury's Laws of England (5th Edn) (2015) paras 375, 382 see now 72 Halsbury's Laws of England (5th Edn) (2019) paras 373, 379; and for 72 Halsbury's Laws of England (5th Edn) (2015) paras 387–391 see now 72 Halsbury's Laws of England (5th Edn) (2019) paras 384–389.]

MATERIAL

[For 76 Halsbury's Laws of England (5th Edn) (2013) para 773 see now 76 Halsbury's Laws of England (5th Edn) (2019) para 767.]

MATERIAL

Material consideration

[Town and Country Planning Act 1990 s 70(2): in dealing with an application for planning permission or permission in principle a local planning authority must have regard to ... '(c) any other material considerations'] '[4] The issue on the appeal is whether the promise to provide a community fund donation qualifies as a "material consideration" for the purposes of s 70(2) of the Town and Country Planning Act 1990 as amended ("the 1990 Act") and s 38(6) of the Planning and Compulsory Purchase Act 2004 ("the 2004 Act"). These are very familiar provisions in planning law. ...

'[31] Planning permission is required "for the carrying out of any development of land": s 57(1) of the 1990 Act. So far as is relevant, "development" is defined in s 55(1) to mean "the making of any material change in the use of any buildings or other land". Section 70(2) of the 1990 Act requires a planning authority to have regard to the development plan and certain other matters "so far as material to the application" and to "any other material considerations": that is to say, material to the change of use which is proposed. Similarly, in relation to an application for planning permission, the "material considerations" referred to in s 38(6) of the 2004 Act are considerations material to the change of use which is proposed.

'[32] In *Newbury [Newbury District Council v Secretary of State for the Environment]* [1980] 1 All ER 731 at 739–740, [1981] AC 578 at 599–601 Viscount Dilhorne treated the scope of the concept of "material considerations" in s 29(1) of the Town and Country Planning Act 1971 (which corresponds to what is now s 70(2) of the 1990 Act) as the same as the ambit of the power of a local planning authority (in what is now s 70(1)(a) of the 1990 Act) to impose such conditions "as they think fit" on the grant of planning permission. ...

'[37] It has long been recognised that a consequence of this approach of relying on the *Newbury* criteria to identify 'material considerations' is that planning permission cannot be bought or sold. ...

'[39] A principled approach to identifying material considerations in line with the *Newbury* criteria is important both as a protection for landowners and as a protection for the public interest. It prevents a planning authority from extracting money or other benefits from a landowner as a condition for granting permission to develop its land, when such payment or the provision of such benefits has no sufficient connection with the proposed use of the land. It also prevents a developer from offering to make payments or provide benefits which have no sufficient connection with the proposed use of the land, as a way of buying a planning permission which it would be contrary to the public interest to grant according to the merits of the development itself.

'[44] In the present case, the community benefits promised by Resilient Severndale did not satisfy the *Newbury* criteria and hence did not qualify as a material consideration within the meaning of that term in s 70(2) of the 1990 Act and s 38(6) of the 2004 Act. Dove J and the Court of Appeal were right so to hold. The benefits were not proposed as a means of pursuing any proper planning purpose, but for the ulterior purpose of providing general benefits to the community. Moreover, they did not fairly and reasonably relate to the development for which permission was sought. Resilient Severndale required planning permission for the carrying out of "development" of the land in question, as that term is defined in s 55(1) of the 1990 Act. The community benefits to be provided by Resilient Severndale did not affect the use of the land. Instead, they were proffered as a general inducement to the Council to grant planning permission and constituted a method of seeking to buy the permission sought, in breach of the principle that planning permission cannot be bought or sold. This is so whether the development scheme is regarded as commercial and profit-making in nature, as Hickinbottom LJ thought it was (para [39]), or as a purely community-run scheme to create community benefits.

'[45] For the appellants, Mr Kingston submitted that the planning statutes had to be regarded as "always speaking" so far as concerns what counts as a "material consideration", and that this meant that the meaning of this concept should be updated in line with changing government policy. I do not agree. The meaning of the term "material consideration" in s 70(2) of the 1990 Act and s 38(6) of the 2004 Act is not in doubt and updating the established meaning of the term is neither required nor appropriate. To say that the meaning of the term changes according to what is said by Ministers in policy statements would undermine the position, as explained above, that what qualifies as a "material consideration" is a question of law on which the courts have already provided authoritative rulings. The interpretation given to that statutory term by the courts provides a clear meaning which is principled and stable over time. I note that Parliament has considered it necessary to amend s 70(2) when it wishes to expand the range of factors which may be treated as material for the purposes of that provision, for instance in relation to the Welsh language: sub-para (aa).' *R (on the application of Wright) v Resilient Energy Severndale Ltd* [2019] UKSC 53, [2020] 2 All ER 1 at [4], [31]–[32], [37], [39], [44]–[45], per Lord Sales

MATRIMONIAL HOME

[For 72 Halsbury's Laws of England (5th Edn) (2015) para 269 et seq see now 72 Halsbury's Laws of England (5th Edn) (2019) para 267 et seq.]

MAY

Permissive

[For 96 Halsbury's Laws of England (5th Edn) (2012) para 615 see now 96 Halsbury's Laws of England (5th Edn) (2018) para 215.]

MEASURE (LEGISLATIVE)

[For 96 Halsbury's Laws of England (5th Edn) (2012) para 606, 606n see now 96 Halsbury's Laws of England (5th Edn) (2018) para 206, para 206 n 5.]

MINE

[For 76 Halsbury's Laws of England (5th Edn) (2013) para 3 see now 76 Halsbury's Laws of England (5th Edn) (2019) para 3.]

Open mine

[For 76 Halsbury's Laws of England (5th Edn) (2013) para 5 see now 76 Halsbury's Laws of England (5th Edn) (2019) para 5.]

MINERALS

[For 76 Halsbury's Laws of England (5th Edn) (2013) para 10 see now 76 Halsbury's Laws of England (5th Edn) (2019) para 10.]

MISCARRIAGE OF JUSTICE

'[19] Section 133 [of the Criminal Justice Act 1988] was then amended, with effect from 13 March 2014, by s 175 of the 2014 Act [Anti-social Behaviour, Crime and Policing Act 2014], so as to confine the term "miscarriage of justice" to category (1) cases. Section 133(1) remained unaltered: it continued to be necessary for the conviction to be reversed "on the ground that a new or newly discovered fact shows beyond reasonable doubt that there has been a miscarriage of justice". However, s 175 of the 2014 Act inserted s 133(1ZA) into the 1988 Act, providing a statutory definition of the term "miscarriage of justice":

"(1ZA) For the purposes of subsection (1), there has been a miscarriage of justice in relation to a person convicted of a criminal offence in England and Wales or, in a case where subsection (6H) applies, Northern Ireland, if and only if the new or newly discovered fact shows beyond reasonable doubt that the person did not commit the offence (and references in the rest of this Part to a miscarriage of justice are to be construed accordingly)."

The words "did not commit the offence" can be read as synonymous in this context with the words 'is innocent' used by this court in category (1) in *Adams* [*R (on the application of Adams) v Secretary of State for Justice* [2011] UKSC 18, [2011] 3 All ER 261, [2012] 1 AC 48]. The effect of s 133(1ZA) is therefore that there is a miscarriage of justice, for the purposes of s 133(1), only where the new or newly discovered fact shows beyond reasonable doubt that the case falls into category (1) recognised in *Adams.*' *R (on the application of Hallam) v Secretary of State for Justice; R (on the application of Nealon) v Secretary of State for Justice* [2019] UKSC 2, [2019] 2 All ER 841 at [19], per Lord Mance

Australia '[28] There was no issue between the parties as to the test to be applied in order to determine whether fresh evidence requires that a conviction be set aside and a new trial had on the basis that a miscarriage of justice has occurred. It is settled that a miscarriage of justice will be established where fresh evidence, when viewed in combination with the evidence given at trial, shows that there is a "significant possibility that the jury, acting reasonably, would have acquitted the accused" had the fresh evidence been before the jury. Nor was it in dispute that the additional evidence adduced in the Court of Appeal was fresh evidence insofar as it was evidence which was not available to or obtainable by the appellant with the exercise of reasonable diligence. That being so, a miscarriage of justice would be established if there were a significant possibility that the jury acting reasonably might have acquitted the appellant had that evidence been available to it.' *Rodi v State of Western Australia* [2018] HCA 44, (2018) 360 ALR 54 at [28], per Kiefel CJ, Bell, Keane, Nettle and Gordon JJ

MISREPRESENTATION

[For 76 Halsbury's Laws of England (5th Edn) (2013) paras 740–741 see now 76 Halsbury's Laws of England (5th Edn) (2019) paras 740–741.]

Fraudulent misrepresentation

[For 76 Halsbury's Laws of England (5th Edn) (2013) paras 755–756 see now 76 Halsbury's Laws of England (5th Edn) (2019) paras 755–756.]

Innocent misrepresentation

[For 76 Halsbury's Laws of England (5th Edn) (2013) para 761 see now 76 Halsbury's Laws of England (5th Edn) (2019) para 761.]

MOÇAMBIQUE RULE

New Zealand '[69] However, in ruling that an Irish court would be precluded from entertaining Sophie's land claims, the Judge considered himself bound to apply a common law rule known as "the Moçambique rule".

'[70] The rule is derived from a 19th century decision of the House of Lords from which it takes its name [*British South Africa Co v Companhia de Moçambique* [1893] AC 602, HL]. The House of Lords held that English courts have no jurisdiction in proceedings primarily concerned with title to or possession of immovable property situated outside England.

'[71] The land at issue in this case is of course situated in New Zealand, not outside it. However, the Associate Judge found the *Moçambique* rule "applies both ways". By that he meant it applied not only to preclude New Zealand courts from having jurisdiction to hear a proceeding involving land situated overseas, but also to preclude a foreign court (here an Irish court) having jurisdiction over land situated in New Zealand. The Judge said it was established that under New Zealand common law, New Zealand courts "will not recognise a foreign court asserting jurisdiction over land in New Zealand, particularly when questions of title are concerned".

'[72] The *Moçambique* rule is subject to two exceptions, these being the "in personam exception" and "administration of an estate exception" which we go on to discuss at [79]–[109] below, but the Judge held neither of those exceptions applied in this case.

...

'[74] In modern times, the *Moçambique* rule has been widely criticised as an anomalous historic relic. It is said to be out of step with what is now internationally acceptable, as well as being illogical and productive of injustice. There have been calls for it to be abolished in New Zealand and for proceedings relating to foreign land to be dealt with solely under the High Court Rules relating to jurisdiction and forum conveniens.

'[75] The criticisms appear to be well founded. However, we are satisfied this is not the case to decide whether the *Moçambique* rule should still be good law in New Zealand. That is because in our view, the rule has only ever applied to foreign land and not to land situated in New Zealand. To put it another way, it is not a domestic exclusive jurisdiction rule and cannot be the basis for a New Zealand court to hold that an Irish court would have no jurisdiction. None of the cases and texts cited to us by counsel support that approach.' *Christie v Foster* [2019] NZCA 623, [2020] 2 NZLR 238 at [69]–[72], [74]–[75], per French J

MOLEST

New Zealand [Wildlife Act 1953, s 2: hunting or killing in relation to any wildlife includes pursuing, disturbing, or molesting.] '[67] The verb molest is more elusive of meaning than the others. The *Oxford English Dictionary* gives the following two meanings of molest:

(a) "To cause trouble, grief, or vexation to; to vex, annoy, put to inconvenience".
(b) "To interfere or meddle with (a person) injuriously or with hostile intent. Now almost exclusively in negative contexts".

'[68] In context, we consider that molest means intentionally troubling, distressing or injuring a protected animal.' *Shark Experience Ltd v PauaMAC5 Inc* [2019] NZSC 111, [2019] 1 NZLR 791 at [67]–[68], per Winkelmann CJ

MONEY

In will

[For 102 Halsbury's Laws of England (5th Edn) (2010) para 295 see now 102 Halsbury's Laws of England (5th Edn) (2016) para 293.]

MOORING (OF VESSEL)

Moored in good safety

[For 60 Halsbury's Laws of England (5th Edn) (2011) para 307 see now 60 Halsbury's Laws of England (5th Edn) (2018) para 286.]

MORTGAGE

[For 91 Halsbury's Laws of England (5th Edn) (2012) para 2 see now 91 Halsbury's Laws of England (5th Edn) (2019) para 2.]

MOTHER

[Gender Recognition Act 2004, ss 9, 12; European Convention for the Protection of Human Rights and Fundamental Freedoms, arts 8, 14] '[1] In this case the court is required to define the term "mother" under the law of England and Wales. Down the centuries, no court has previously been required to determine the definition of "mother" under English common law and, it seems, that there have been few comparable decisions made in other courts elsewhere in the Western World. Hitherto, a person who has given birth to a child has always been regarded as that child's mother. The issue arises in modern times where an individual, who was born female, undergoes gender transition and becomes legally recognised as male before going on to conceive, carry and give birth to a child, with the result that the parent who has given birth is legally a man rather than a woman. The question posed to this court is: Is that man the "mother" or the "father" of his child?

...

'[123] The task of discerning the approach in domestic law to the issue in this case is not an easy one. The circumstances of TT, and his role, as a male, in the conception and birth of his son YY, are not expressly provided for in either the legislation governing artificial insemination or that for gender recognition. Even though the HFEA 2008 [Human Fertilisation and Embryology Act 2008] was passed four years after the GRA 2004 [Gender Recognition Act 2004], the HFEA 2008 retains the basic definitions of "mother" and "father" that appeared in the HFEA 1990 and which are expressly tied to either "a woman" or "a man", respectively. The additional concept of a second 'parent' that was introduced by the 2008 Act is, as was accepted in submissions, restricted to a second female parent in the specific circumstances of HFEA 2008, ss 42 and 43 and has no application to the facts of this case.

...

'[269] On the above analysis, the ECHR [European Convention for the Protection of Human Rights and Fundamental Freedoms] aspect of this claim turns on the same point as that which lies at the centre of the case in domestic law, namely whether the term "mother" is exclusively female or whether it is a freestanding term which, in the context of a birth applies to the person who carries a pregnancy and gives birth to a child, irrespective of their legal gender.

'[270] In the context of domestic law my conclusion at para [149] on that central point was that the latter is the case. There is no ground to support a different interpretation of the term "mother" in the context of the evaluation of proportionality under the ECHR.

...

'[279] The principal conclusion at the centre of this extensive judgment can be shortly stated. It is that there is a material difference between a person's gender and their status as a parent. Being a "mother", whilst hitherto always associated with being female, is the status afforded to a person who undergoes the physical and biological process of carrying a pregnancy and giving birth. It is now medically and legally possible for an individual, whose gender is recognised in law as male, to become pregnant and give birth to their child. Whilst that person's gender is "male", their parental status, which derives from their biological role in giving birth, is that of "mother".

'[280] At para [149], I set out my preliminary conclusions with respect to domestic law, these can now be firmly stated as:

(a) At common law a person whose egg is inseminated in their womb and who then becomes pregnant and gives birth to a child is that child's "mother";

(b) The status of being a "mother" arises from the role that a person has undertaken in the biological process of conception, pregnancy and birth;

(c) Being a "mother" or a "father" with respect to the conception, pregnancy and birth of a child is not necessarily gender specific, although until recent decades it invariably was so. It is now possible, and recognised by the law, for a "mother" to have an acquired gender of male, and for a "father" to have an acquired gender of female;

(d) GRA 2004, s 12 is both retrospective and prospective. The status of a person as the father or mother of a child is not affected by the acquisition of gender under the Act, even where the relevant birth has taken place after the issue of a GR certificate.'

R (on the application of McConnell) v Registrar General for England and Wales [2019] EWHC 2384, [2020] 2 All ER 813 at [1], [123], [269]–[270], [279]–[280], per Sir Andrew McFarlane P; affirmed [2020] EWCA Civ 559, [2020] 2 All ER 813

(1) The woman who is carrying or has carried a child as a result of the placing in her of an embryo or of sperm and eggs, and no other woman, is to be treated as the mother of the child.

(2) Subsection (1) does not apply to any child to the extent that the child is treated by virtue of adoption as not being the woman's child.

(Human Fertilisation and Embryology Act 2008, s 33)

N

NAME

[For 88 Halsbury's Laws of England (5th Edn) (2012) paras 326–329 see now 88 Halsbury's Laws of England (5th Edn) (2019) paras 329–332.]

NATIONALITY

[For 4 Halsbury's Laws of England (5th Edn) (2011) para 401 et seq see now 4 Halsbury's Laws of England (5th Edn) (2020) para 401 et seq.]

NECESSARIES

Of child

[For 9 Halsbury's Laws of England (5th Edn) (2012) paras 18–19 see now 9 Halsbury's Laws of England (5th Edn) (2017) paras 18–19; and for 91 Halsbury's Laws of England (5th Edn) (2012) para 38 see now 91 Halsbury's Laws of England (5th Edn) (2019) para 37.]

Of wife

[For 72 Halsbury's Laws of England (5th Edn) (2015) para 262 see now 72 Halsbury's Laws of England (5th Edn) (2019) para 260.]

NEW INFORMATION

Australia [Migration Act 1958 (Cth), s 473DC(1).] '[16] The meaning given to "new information" by s 473DC(1) for the purposes of Pt 7AA is "any documents or information" that satisfy two conditions. The first condition, specified in s 473DC(1)(a), requires that the documents or information not have been before the Minister or delegate at the time of the making of the decision under review. The second condition, specified in s 473DC(1)(b), re-quires that the Authority consider that the documents or information "may be relevant".

…

'[20] The fundamental difficulty with the notion that the Certificate [that disclosure of information or matter contained in the Identity Assessment Form would be contrary to the public interest] met the definition of "new information" in s 473DC(1) is essentially that captured in the central argument of the Minister in the appeal to this Court that the Certificate was incapable of satisfying the description of "information".

…

'[22] Interpreted in accordance with the authority of *Plaintiff M174/2016* [*Plaintiff M174/2016 v Minister for Immigration and Border Protection* (2018) 264 CLR 217; 353 ALR 600; [2018] HCA 16] and *SZMTA* [*Minister for Immigration and Border Protection v SZMTA* (2019) 264 CLR 421; 363 ALR 599; 163 ALD 1; [2019] HCA 3], the reference to "any documents or information" in the definition of "new information" in s 473DC(1) has no application to a certificate issued or purporting to be issued under s 473GB(5) for the purpose of s 473GB(1)(a), just as the definition has no application to a written notification made or purporting to be made under s 473GB(2)(a). A certificate or notification of that nature is an instrument which, if valid, has statutory consequences under s 473GB(3)(a) and (b). It is not a document which communicates knowledge of facts or circumstances of an evidentiary nature.

'[23] Consistently with the confinement of s 473DC(1)'s reference to "any documents or information" to documentation or information of an evidentiary nature, the word "relevant" in s 473DC(1)(b) can only sensibly be read as having the same meaning that the word "relevant" has in s 473CB(1)(c). Documentation or information of an evidentiary nature that the Authority considers may be "relevant" is documentation or information of an evidentiary nature that the Authority considers "capable directly or indirectly of rationally affecting assessment of the probability of the existence of some fact about which the Authority might be required to make a finding in the conduct of its review of the referred decision".

'[24] The Certificate was therefore not a "document" nor did it contain "information" within the reference to "any documents or information" in the definition of "new information" in s 473DC(1). Moreover, even if the Authority had treated the Certificate as valid to enliven the powers conferred by s 473GB(3)(a) and (b), and even if the Authority had gone on to exercise the power conferred by s 473GB(3)(a) to take the Identity Assessment Form into account in making some finding of fact in the review, the Authority cannot thereby be taken to have considered that the Certificate "may be relevant" within the meaning of s 473DC(1)(b).

...

'[30] In light of the context in which "new information" appears in s 473DB(1)(a), I agree with the joint judgment that these words should not be interpreted to mean all information which is new. The words must mean only new information of an evidentiary nature. This restriction upon the ordinary meaning of "new information" in Pt 7AA can be most directly seen in the "definition" of "new information" in s 473DC(1), which provides that subject to Pt 7AA the Authority "may, in relation to a fast track decision, get any documents or information (*new information*) that: (a) were not before the Minister when the Minister made the decision under section 65; and (b) the Authority considers may be relevant". The relevance to which s 473DC(1) refers is relevance to the Authority's decision. The documents or information which comprise "new information" must therefore be documents or information that are capable of being considered by the Authority to be relevant to its decision. That class of documents concerns material or documentation of an evidentiary nature.' *Minister for Immigration and Border Protection v CED16* [2020] HCA 24, (2020) 380 ALR 216 at [16], [20], [22]–[23], per Gageler, Keane, Nettle and Gordon JJ and at [30], per Edelman J

NEXT

Australia [Migration Act 1958 (Cth), s 494AA(4): ineligibility period means the period from the time of the offshore entry until the time when the person next ceases to be an unlawful non-citizen.] '[95] The function of the word "next" in the definition of "ineligibility period" appears curious, until it is recalled that an individual may move in and out of the status of an unlawful non-citizen, depending on whether an individual holds a visa or not. The function of the word "next" is, in my opinion, to indicate that the period which is defined as the "ineligibility period" runs from the time a person enters Australia until that person is granted a visa *for the first time* after the unauthorised entry. The word "next" relates back to the time of unauthorised entry and is used to signify the end point of the ineligibility period. That is, it is not a recurring period of time, it is a fixed period of time which will expire when an individual is first granted a visa after her or his unauthorised entry.

'[96] Therefore, hypothetically, if an individual who is an unauthorised maritime arrival is granted a visa, this visa is then cancelled, and the person becomes an unlawful non-citizen again, the "ineligibility period" will not apply to that person again. That period has expired for that particular individual. Indeed, consistently with my observation above, it may be that it is also no longer correct to assign to such a person the status of an unauthorised maritime arrival.' *DBE17 (by his litigation guardian Arthur) v Commonwealth* [2018] FCA 1307, (2018) 361 ALR 423 at [95]–[96], per Mortimer J

NEXT OF KIN

[For 102 Halsbury's Laws of England (5th Edn) (2010) paras 344–345 see now 102 Halsbury's Laws of England (5th Edn) (2016) paras 343–344.]

NON EST FACTUM

[For 32 Halsbury's Laws of England (5th Edn) (2012) para 269 see now 32 Halsbury's Laws of England (5th Edn) (2019) para 269.]

NOTICE

Of intended prosecution

[For 90 Halsbury's Laws of England (5th Edn) (2011) para 785 see now 90 Halsbury's Laws of England (5th Edn) (2018) para 799.]

NOTORIETY

[For 32 Halsbury's Laws of England (5th Edn) (2012) para 57 see now 32 Halsbury's Laws of England (5th Edn) (2019) para 57.]

NOVATION

[For 22 Halsbury's Laws of England (5th Edn) (2012) para 598 see now 22 Halsbury's Laws of England (5th Edn) (2019) para 389.]

NUISANCE

To highway

[For 55 Halsbury's Laws of England (5th Edn) (2012) para 325 see now 55 Halsbury's Laws of England (5th Edn) (2019) para 354.]

NULLITY

[For 72 Halsbury's Laws of England (5th Edn) (2015) paras 375–376 see now 72 Halsbury's Laws of England (5th Edn) (2019) paras 373–374.]

NUPTIAL AGREEMENT

[For 22 Halsbury's Laws of England (5th Edn) (2012) para 441 see now 22 Halsbury's Laws of England (5th Edn) (2019) para 232.]

O

OBLIGATION
[For 32 Halsbury's Laws of England (5th Edn) (2012) para 291 see now 32 Halsbury's Laws of England (5th Edn) (2019) para 291.]

OBLIGEE—OBLIGOR
[For 32 Halsbury's Laws of England (5th Edn) (2012) para 289 see now 32 Halsbury's Laws of England (5th Edn) (2019) para 289.]

OBLITERATION
[For 103 Halsbury's Laws of England (5th Edn) (2010) para 735 see now 103 Halsbury's Laws of England (5th Edn) (2016) para 735.]

OCCUPATION (OF PROPERTY)

Australia [Native Title Act 1993 (Cth), ss 47A, 47B.] '[418] The primary judge stated that whether activity amounted to occupation is a question of fact and degree to be determined on the evidence before the Court in each case (at [270]–[272]). His Honour referred to a series of general propositions drawn from [215] of *Moses* [*Moses v Western Australia* (2007) 160 FCR 148; 241 ALR 268; [2007] FCAFC 78]:

It is largely a matter of common sense, but is founded upon the words of ss 47A and 47B in their context and as considered in the authorities:
(1) to "occupy" an area for the purposes of ss 47A and 47B of the NTA involves the exercise of some physical activity or activities in relation to the area;
(2) to "occupy" an area does not require the performance of an activity or activities on every part of the land;
(3) to "occupy" an area does not necessarily involve consistently or repeatedly performing the activity or activities over part of the area;
(4) to "occupy" an area does not require constant performance of the activity or activities over parts of the area; it is possible to conclude that an area is occupied where there are spasmodic or occasional physical activities carried on over the area;
(5) to occupy an area at a particular time does not necessarily require contemporaneous activity on that area at the particular time; it is possible to conclude that an area of land is occupied in circumstances where at the time the application is made there is no immediately contemporaneous activity being carried on in the area;
(6) the fact of occupation does not necessarily entail a frequent physical presence in the area; for example, the storage of sacred objects on the area or the holding, from time to time, of traditional ceremonies on the area may constitute occupation for the purposes of the NTA: see, eg *Rubibi Community v Western Australia* (2001) 112 FCR 409; [2001] FCA 607 at [182];
(7) evidence to establish occupation need not necessarily be confined to evidence of activities occurring on the particular area; it may be possible to establish that a particular area is occupied by reference to occupation of a wider area which includes the particular area: *Risk (on behalf of the Larrakia Peoples) v Northern Territory* [2006] FCA 404 at [890];
(8) occupation need not be "traditional": Rubibi Community v Western Australia (No 7) [2006] FCA 459 at [84];
(9) whether occupation has been made out in a particular case is always a question of fact and degree.

'[419] The primary judge said that at common law a person may be in occupation of a large expanse of land without physically exercising their rights over every part of it (at [271]). He referred to the well-known example of a person residing in a homestead as nevertheless being in occupation of an entire farm or pastoral station despite the fact that he or she may not have physically exercised their rights over every part of it.

...

'[442] The authorities make clear that the question of "occupy" in s 47B(1)(c) is distinct from the question of connection to country under s 223(1)(c): *Moses* at [210]; *Risk (on behalf of the Larrakia Peoples) v Northern Territory* [2006] FCA 404 (*Risk*) at [890]–[891]; *Rubibi (No 7)* [83]; *Sebastian* at [288]; *Narrier v Western Australia* [2016] FCA 1519 at [1223] (*Narrier (No 1)*). Although the contrary view in *Daniel* at [938] had been referred to without adverse comment in *Alyawarr* at [194], *Moses* cleared away any remaining ambiguity.

...

'[462] It is clear that "occupy" is a term of long ancestry within the common law and that it describes a particular relationship to land and that "occupy" in s 47B(1)(c) means "actual occupation" or "occupation in fact". However, contrary to FMG's position, this does not mean that it is appropriate to derive from *Wagga Wagga Motor Registry Claim* [*Daruk; Minister Administering Crown Lands Act v New South Wales Aboriginal Land Council* (2008) 237 CLR 285; 249 ALR 602; [2008] HCA 48] and *Berrima Gaol* [*New South Wales Aboriginal Land Council v Minister Administering the Crown Lands Act* (2016) 260 CLR 232; 339 ALR 367; [2016] HCA 50] a specific standard or threshold that "requires a particular nature and degree of presence on the land" or is limited to what FMG described as "indigenous presence on the land ... in a concrete real world sense, not simply in the sense of spiritual beliefs in respect of that land". Similarly, we do not see these authorities as requiring a particular type of physical presence or intensity of use before there can be a conclusion of occupation in fact. While intensity of use may be one way of establishing that one or more persons treat the land as their own, it is not the only way to establish occupation.

'[463] In our view, to derive and impose a requirement by transplanting statements and conclusions made in the context of s 36(1)(b) of the ALR Act [Aboriginal Land Rights Act 1983 (NSW)] into the different context of s 47B(1)(c) of the Native Title Act would be to commit the very error repeatedly warned against. Whereas the enquiry under the ALR Act is concerned with determining whether the State is in occupation of the land, the enquiry under the Native Title Act is concerned with determining whether

one or members of the claim group occupy the relevant area over which native title would otherwise be extinguished.

'[464] The proper approach, and the one outlined in *Alyawarr* [*Northern Territory v Alyawarr, Kaytetye, Warumungu, Wakaya Native Title Claim Group* (2005) 145 FCR 442; 220 ALR 431; [2005] FCAFC 135], *Moses and Banjima* [*Tucker (on behalf of the Banjima People) v Western Australia* (2015) 231 FCR 456; 322 ALR 199; [2015] FCAFC 84]], to which we now turn, is one that is sensitive to the traditions of Aboriginal people and their unique relationship with their country. In that context, it is important that taxonomical categories of relationship, right or interest developed in an Anglo-Australian context (eg possession, use and occupation) are applied in a manner sensitive to the full complexity of the relationship between Indigenous peoples and their land. This does not mean they are devoid of content, only that the application of these concepts will necessarily be different in the context of the Native Title Act.

...

'[473] In our view, there is nothing unsound in the primary judge's analysis as a question of principle. FMG's complaints are in substance challenges to the primary judge's findings of fact. To the extent FMG submits that evidence of a spiritual, cultural or social kind can **never** be relevant to an enquiry into occupation, or contribute to a factual finding of occupation, we reject that contention.' *Fortescue Metals Group Ltd v Warrie (on behalf of the Yindjibarndi People)* [2019] FCAFC 177, (2019) 374 ALR 448 at [418]–[419], [442], [462]–[464], [473], per Robertson and Griffiths JJ

OFFENCE

Motoring offence

[For 90 Halsbury's Laws of England (5th Edn) (2011) para 815 see now 90 Halsbury's Laws of England (5th Edn) (2018) para 829.]

OFFER

[For 22 Halsbury's Laws of England (5th Edn) (2012) para 234 see now 22 Halsbury's Laws of England (5th Edn) (2019) para 34.]

OFFICIAL RECEIVER

[For 5 Halsbury's Laws of England (5th Edn) (2013) para 35 see now 5 Halsbury's Laws of England (5th Edn) (2020) para 34.]

OFFSPRING
[For 102 Halsbury's Laws of England (5th Edn) (2010) para 336 see now 102 Halsbury's Laws of England (5th Edn) (2016) para 335.]

ON THE FAITH OF

New Zealand [Securities Act 1978, s 56(1).] '[93] The liability imposed on issuers, directors and promoters under s 56(1) is a liability to compensate investors who invested "on the faith of [the prospectus]" for any loss or damage they may have sustained "by reason of such untrue statement". The positions of the parties as to the interpretation of s 56(1) were starkly contrasting. Mr Houghton's position was that all he needed to prove was that there had been an untrue statement in the prospectus, upon which he would be entitled to compensation equal to the total amount of his investment. On this view, no element of materiality is required. The respondents argued in the High Court that an investor had to prove they had read the untrue statement in the prospectus and had relied on it explicitly, in the same way as for a claim for negligent misstatement. They argued that, if the investor could prove such reliance, their loss would be the difference between the price they paid for their Feltex shares and the fair value of the shares had accurate disclosure been made.
...
'[121] The phrase "on the faith of" has a long statutory pedigree, beginning with the Directors Liability Act 1890 (UK). In New Zealand, it has appeared in provisions relating to prospectuses since 1891. In all instances, it has been used in the context of a provision referring to a prospectus that constitutes the offer document for the securities being offered for subscription and the subscription is made on the terms of the prospectus. In that context, the phrase can be seen as broadly synonymous with "in reliance on", as the Court of Appeal noted.
'[122] There are also other statutory references to "on the faith of" in different contexts that indicate it is intended to be broadly synonymous with "in reliance on".
...
'[127] We consider that "on the faith of" means in reliance on the truth of the publicly registered document, which informs the market, but does not require that investors have seen or read the prospectus. Investors rely on the accuracy of the prospectus in the sense that they assume it contains no untrue statements and that the advice they receive or the market commentary they observe is founded on accurate and complete disclosure of the information included in the prospectus. So, to adapt the approach taken by Lord Halsbury in *Arnison v Smith* [(1889) 41 ChD 365] to which the Court of Appeal referred to when discussing the present statutory context, it can be inferred that if a prospectus contained a misleading statement, the investor who subscribed for shares invested on the faith of the prospectus assuming the statement was true. This inference would be displaced if the investor knew the truth and invested anyway. We leave open whether there may be other circumstances where the inference may be displaced.
'[128] We recognise that this means that the "on the faith of" aspect of s 56(1) will not be difficult for an investor to satisfy in the event that a prospectus contains an untrue statement. We see that as consistent with the investor protection objective of the Securities Act. ...'
Houghton v Saunders [2018] NZSC 74, [2019] 1 NZLR 1 at [93], [121]–[122], [127]–[128], per Elias CJ, Glazebrook, O'Regan, Arnold and Kós JJ

OPENNESS
'[1] The short point in this appeal is whether the appellant county council, as local planning authority, correctly understood the meaning of the word "openness" in the national planning policies applying to mineral working in the Green Belt, as expressed in the National Planning Policy Framework ("NPPF"). ...
'[22] The concept of "openness" in para 90 of the NPPF seems to me a good example of such a broad policy concept. It is naturally read as referring back to the underlying aim of Green Belt policy, stated at the beginning of this section "to prevent urban sprawl by keeping land permanently open". Openness is the counterpart of urban sprawl and is also linked to the purposes to be served by the Green Belt. As PPG2 [Planning Policy Guidance 2: Green Belts] made clear, it is not necessarily a statement about the visual qualities of the land, though in some cases this may be an aspect of the planning judgement involved in applying this broad policy concept. Nor does it imply freedom from any form of development. Paragraph 90 shows that some forms of development, including mineral extraction, may in principle be appropriate, and compatible with the

concept of openness. A large quarry may not be visually attractive while it lasts, but the minerals can only be extracted where they are found, and the impact is temporary and subject to restoration. Further, as a barrier to urban sprawl a quarry may be regarded in Green Belt policy terms as no less effective than a stretch of agricultural land.' *R (on the application of Samuel Smith Old Brewery (Tadcaster)) v North Yorkshire County Council* [2020] UKSC 3, [2020] 3 All ER 527 at [1], [22], per Lord Carnwath

OPTION
[For 22 Halsbury's Laws of England (5th Edn) (2012) para 241 see now 22 Halsbury's Laws of England (5th Edn) (2019) para 41.]

ORDER IN COUNCIL
[For 96 Halsbury's Laws of England (5th Edn) (2012) para 1031 see now 96 Halsbury's Laws of England (5th Edn) (2018) para 638.]

ORDER OF COUNCIL
[For 96 Halsbury's Laws of England (5th Edn) (2012) para 1031 see now 96 Halsbury's Laws of England (5th Edn) (2018) para 638.]

ORGANISATION
[Ministry of Housing and Local Government Provisional Order Confirmation (Greater London Parks and Open Spaces) Act 1967, Sch 1, art 7(1)(a)(vi): power for local authority in any open space to provide and maintain 'centres and other facilities (whether indoor or open air) for use of clubs, societies or organisations whose objects or activities are wholly or mainly of a recreational, social or educational character'; whether this included a day nursery for pre-school children.] '[29] I am prepared to assume in Mr Giffin's favour, without deciding, that para (vi) does not impose a hard-edged requirement that the organisation be not-for-profit. Nevertheless I consider that the interested party is not the type of "club, society or organisation" with which sub-para (vi) is concerned.

'[30] It is common ground that the interested party is not a club or society. The term "organisation" in sub-para (vi) is, in my judg-ment, there to sweep up organisations which are not strictly or properly described as clubs or societies, but which nevertheless share their principal characteristic of being run for the benefit of members sharing a common interest. The interested party does not operate on this basis, but is a limited company providing services for clients or customers. If Wandsworth's construction were correct, it is difficult to see why the words "clubs" and "societies" were used in sub-para (vi) when the words "any organisation" would have had the effect for which they contend.' *R (on the application of Muir) v Wandsworth Borough Council (Smart Pre-Schools Ltd, interested party)* [2018] EWCA Civ 1035, [2018] 4 All ER 422 at [29]–[30], per Floyd LJ

OTHER SUITABLE PERSON
[Children Act 1989, Sch 2, para 19(4): where the court is satisfied that a child does not have sufficient understanding to give or withhold his consent to living in a country other than England and Wales, it may disregard the requirement for consent and give approval if the child is to live in the country concerned with a parent, guardian, special guardian, or 'other suitable person'.] '[40] On the first issue, (i), para 19(4) applies only if the child is "to live ... with a parent, guardian, special guardian or other suitable person". As Floyd LJ observed during the hearing it is not easy to see how a child could live with a company or an unincorporated "body of persons". For example, while a child can live in a residential home which might be owned by a company it would be difficult to argue that, as a result, the child was living with a person. Further, when this is added to the fact that the words "other suitable person" follow a list comprising natural persons, I do not consider it is possible to interpret this provision as meaning other than that it is confined, as decided by Sir James Munby P, to natural persons. Whilst I recognise that there might well be a practical need, as submitted by Mr Howling, this cannot counter the factors referred to above and such a need alone would not provide a legitimate basis for the proposed statutory interpretation.

'[41] The result of this conclusion is that, when a child does not consent, and regardless of whether they do or do not have sufficient understanding, the court is not permitted to approve their placement in Scotland other than with a natural person. The consequence is that a local authority cannot "arrange for, or assist in arranging for, any child in their care", who does not consent, to live in a residential home in Scotland (or, indeed, anywhere else outside England and Wales).

'[42] Given the limited submissions we heard on the history which might lie behind this particular provision and on the broader potential ramifications, I do not propose to address Ms Irving's additional submission as to whether the term "other suitable person" might be further confined. All I would say is that a court would clearly need to establish who would have parental responsibility or, in broader terms, legal responsibility, for a child before that child could be placed outside England and Wales. ...' *Re C (a child)* [2019] EWCA Civ 1714, [2020] 3 All ER 634 at [40]–[42], per Moylan LJ

OUTSTANDING BENEFIT

[Patents Act 1977, s 40: employee entitled to compensation where he has made an invention belonging to the employer for which a patent has been granted and the patent is (having regard among other things to the size and nature of the employer's undertaking) of outstanding benefit to the employer.] '[30] An employee who makes an invention which belongs to his employer from the outset and for which a patent has been granted is therefore entitled to compensation if he or she establishes: first, that the patent is, having regard among other things to the size and nature of the employer's undertaking, of outstanding benefit to the employer; and secondly, that, by reason of these matters, it is just that he or she be awarded compensation.

...

'[39] In my view these cases are all helpful to a point as illustrations of circumstances which were found to fall each side of the line. But at the end of the day they provide no substitute for the statutory test which requires the benefit to be outstanding. This is an ordinary English word meaning exceptional or such as to stand out and it refers here to the benefit (in terms of money or money's worth) of the patent to the employer rather than the degree of inventiveness of the employee. It is, however, both a relative and qualitative term and so I must now consider the context in which the question is to be asked and answered. Put another way, in relation to what must the benefit from the patent be outstanding? Which factors may be taken into account in making that assessment?

'[40] Here the 1977 Act provides some guidance. It says that the court must have regard

among other things to the size and nature of the employer's undertaking. But this gives rise to two further questions which were the subject of a good deal of argument before us. What is the employer's undertaking for this purpose? And what is the relevance of that undertaking's size and nature?

...

'[52] In some cases it may be possible to see that a patent has been of outstanding benefit to an employer by looking at the size and profitability of the whole business. In the *Kelly* case [*Kelly v GE Healthcare Ltd* [2009] EWHC 181 (Pat), [2009] IP & T 927, [2009] RPC 363] ..., for example, the benefits of patent protection went far beyond anything which one would normally expect to arise from the sort of work the employees were doing. The patents protected Amersham's business from generic competition and allowed it to make major deals; and sales of the patented product accounted for a large proportion of its profits. In short, the patents transformed its business. Similarly, as Patten LJ explained at para [28], a straightforward comparison of profitability may be sufficient, in the case of a smaller company, to show an outstanding benefit without recourse to wider considerations of the scope of an employee's duties or the expectations the employer may have had about the anticipated level of return.

'[53] I also recognise that a large undertaking may be able to exert greater leverage than a smaller undertaking when negotiating licence fees. This was a matter to which the hearing officer referred in para [207] of his judgment. There he explained and I agree that a particular sum might represent an excellent return for a small undertaking but might not be so regarded by a large undertaking which was in a position to spend substantial sums on litigation to enforce its rights. Much the same might apply to sales of a patented product. A large undertaking might be able to harness its goodwill and sales force in a way that a smaller undertaking could not do. These would be appropriate matters to take into account.

'[54] On the other hand, I think a tribunal should be very cautious before accepting a submission that a patent has not been of outstanding benefit to an employer simply because it has had no significant impact on its overall profitability or the value of all of its sales. Those profits and sales may have been generated by a range of different products which have nothing to do with the technology the subject of the

patent; the parts of the business responsible for them may not have contributed to any commercial success of the patented invention; and they may be a very poor guide to whether the benefit the employer has derived from the patent is out of the ordinary. Indeed, I find it very hard to see how a failure materially to affect the aggregated sales value or overall profitability of the business could, in and of itself, justify a finding that the benefit of a patent has not been outstanding.'
Shanks v Unilever plc [2019] UKSC 45, [2020] 2 All ER 733 at [30], [39]–[40], [52]–[54], per Lord Kitchin

P

PARLIAMENTARY PRIVILEGE

Canada '19. Parliamentary privilege is defined as "the sum of the privileges, immunities and powers enjoyed by the Senate, the House of Commons and provincial legislative assemblies, and by each member individually, without which they could not discharge their functions" (*Vaid [Canada (House of Commons) v Vaid* 2005 SCC 30, [2005] 1 SCR 667], at para 29(2)). These privileges, immunities, and powers exceed those afforded to the general population (*Erskine May's Treatise on The Law, Privileges, Proceedings and Usage of Parliament* (24th ed 2011), by M Jack, at p 203). Therefore, parliamentary privilege "is an exemption from some duty, burden, attendance or liability to which others are subject" (Maingot [Maingot, J P Joseph: *Parliamentary Immunity in Canada*, Toronto: LexisNexis, 2016], at p 13). Decisions falling within the scope of parliamentary privilege cannot be reviewed by an external body, including a court (*Stockdale v Hansard* (1839) 9 Ad & E 1, 112 ER 1112 (QB), at p 1168; *New Brunswick Broadcasting [New Brunswick Broadcasting Co v Nova Scotia (Speaker of the House of Assembly)* [1993] 1 SCR 319], at pp 350 and 382–384; *Vaid*, at para 29(9)).' *Chagnon v Syndicat de la fonction publique et parapublique du Québec* [2018] 2 SCR 687, [2018] SCJ No 39, at para 19, per Karakatsanis J

PARTICULAR

Canada [Tobacco Damages and Health Care Costs Recovery Act, SBC 2000, c 30, s 2(5).] '2. … This appeal requires the Court to interpret one of those procedural provisions— specifically, s 2(5)(b), which governs the compellability of health care documents where the Province has sued to recover the cost of health care benefits "on an aggregate basis" (that is, for a population of insured persons, as opposed to for particular individual insured persons). Section 2(5)(b) provides, generally, that "the health care records and documents of particular individual insured persons or the documents relating to the provision of health care benefits for particular individual insured persons <u>are not</u> <u>compellable</u>".

…

'31. The ordinary meaning of the word "particular" is *distinct* or *specific*. This is consistent with the *Oxford English Dictionary* (online) which defines "particular" as meaning "one among a number … single; <u>distinct</u>, individual, <u>specific</u>" (emphasis added). This definition supports the view that the databases—even once anonymized—fall within s 2(5)(b)'s scope as comprising the "health care records and documents of", and the "documents relating to the provision of health care benefits for", each *distinct* and *specific* individual in British Columbia.

…

'36. It follows from the foregoing that I agree with the Province that the databases constitute "health care records and documents of particular individual insured persons or … documents relating to the provision of health care benefits for particular individual insured persons". As such, by operation of s 2(5)(b) the databases are not compellable. To be clear, the databases will be compellable once "relied on by an expert witness": s 2(5)(b). A "statistically meaningful sample" of the databases, once anonymized, may also be compelled on a successful application under ss 2(5)(d) and 2(5)(e).' *British Columbia v Philip Morris International Inc* [2018] SCJ No 36, [2018] 2 SCR 595 at paras 2, 31, 36, per Brown J

PARTNERSHIP

[For 79 Halsbury's Laws of England (5th Edn) (2014) para 4 see now 79 Halsbury's Laws of England (5th Edn) (2020) para 4.]

PARTY-WALL

[For 4 Halsbury's Laws of England (5th Edn) (2011) para 365 see now 4 Halsbury's Laws of England (5th Edn) (2020) para 364.]

PATENT

[For 79 Halsbury's Laws of England (5th Edn) (2014) para 303 see now 79 Halsbury's Laws of England (5th Edn) (2020) para 304.]

PAWN

[For 4 Halsbury's Laws of England (5th Edn) (2011) paras 189–190 see now 4 Halsbury's Laws of England (5th Edn) (2020) paras 188–189.]

PAWNBROKER

[For 4 Halsbury's Laws of England (5th Edn) (2011) para 189 see now 4 Halsbury's Laws of England (5th Edn) (2020) para 188.]

PEDLAR

[For 71 Halsbury's Laws of England (5th Edn) (2013) para 907 et seq see now 71 Halsbury's Laws of England (5th Edn) (2020) para 809 et seq.]

PEERAGE

[For 79 Halsbury's Laws of England (5th Edn) (2014) paras 803–806 see now 79 Halsbury's Laws of England (5th Edn) (2020) paras 803–806.]

PENALTY

New Zealand '[51] With the assistance of the foregoing, I consider that the following factors are relevant to whether a measure may qualify as a penalty:
(a) The measure is imposed following a conviction.
(b) The measure forms part of an arsenal of sanctions imposed in furtherance of sentencing purposes and principles and/or has a significant impact on the liberty of the person.

(c) The measure forms part of an arsenal of sanctions imposed in furtherance of sentencing purposes and principles and/or has a significant impact on the liberty of the person.
(d) The process used to impose the measure is a criminal process.
(e) The measure is given effect to in a prison or a prison-like institution or may result in imprisonment.
(f) The measure is non-therapeutic or not implemented in a therapeutic way.
(g) The severity of the conditions of the measure.
...

'[160] I answer the questions as follows:
(c) Is an ESO [extended supervision order] a penalty?
For present purposes, there are two types of ESO, a retrospective ESO and a prospective ESO. A retrospective ESO is an ESO imposed on an offender who committed their qualifying offending before the ESO regime came into force in respect of that offending. A prospective ESO is an ESO imposed on an offender who committed their qualifying offending after the ESO regime came into force in respect of that offending. Both types of ESO are penalties....
(e) Is a PPO [public protection order] a penalty?
No, but elements of the PPO regime appear to be punitive, and a PPO may be imposed with punitive effect. ...'

[The ESO regime is set out in the Parole Act 2002 at ss 107A–107Z. The PPO regime is set out in the Public Safety (Public Protection Orders) Act 2014.] *Chief Executive of the Department of Corrections v Chisnall* [2019] NZHC 3126, [2020] 2 NZLR 110 at [51], [160], per Whata J

PERAMBULATION

[For 32 Halsbury's Laws of England (5th Edn) (2012) para 40 see now 32 Halsbury's Laws of England (5th Edn) (2019) para 40.]

PERIOD OF OWNERSHIP

[Taxation of Chargeable Gains Act 1992, ss 222, 223.] '[13] The FTT [First-tier Tribunal] concluded that principal private residence relief relieved Mr Higgins from any liability to CGT on his sale of the Apartment. In the FTT's view (see para [6](10) of its decision):

"The period of ownership for the purpose of ss 222 and 223 began when Mr Higgins owned the legal and equitable interest in the lease of the Apartment and owned the legal right to occupy the Apartment. That was the date of legal completion of the purchase of the lease on 5 January 2010. The period of ownership ended on 5 January 2012 when the contract for sale (entered into on 15 December 2011) was completed."

...

'[15] The central question on this appeal is as to the meaning of the words "period of ownership" in s 223 of the TCGA. If in Mr Higgins' case that period did not begin until 5 January 2010, then the Apartment was his main residence "throughout the period of ownership" and no CGT can be payable. If, on the other hand, Mr Higgins' "period of ownership" began when contracts for the purchase were exchanged, s 223(2) will be in point and he will enjoy relief from CGT as to only part of the gain he made on the Apartment.

...

'[21] HMRC's case also, as it seems to me, runs counter to the ordinary meaning of the words 'period of ownership'. The expression would not naturally, I think, be taken to extend to the interval between contract and completion. A purchaser would, as a matter of ordinary language, be described as 'owner' only once the purchase had been completed. ... The mere fact that someone has contracted to buy a property will not give him "ownership" such as could allow him to possess, occupy or even use the property, let alone to make it his "only or main residence".

'[22] It would anyway be hard to see how Mr Higgins' "period of ownership" of the Apartment could have begun before late 2009. When contracts were exchanged in 2006, the Apartment was just a "space in the tower". The present case is thus distinguishable from one in which someone contracts to buy a plot of land on which a house is to be built. The plot of land will, of course, already exist. In contrast, the Apartment did not come into existence until November/December 2009.

...

'[29] In all the circumstances, I agree with Miss Shaw QC that the FTT was right about how the legislation should be interpreted and,

hence, that Mr Higgins' "period of ownership" of the Apartment for the purpose of s 223 of the TCGA did not begin until his purchase was completed.' *Higgins v Revenue and Customs Commissioners* [2019] EWCA Civ 1860, [2020] 2 All ER 451 at [13], [15], [21]–[22], [29], per Newey LJ

PERILS OF THE SEAS

[For 60 Halsbury's Laws of England (5th Edn) (2011) para 323 see now 60 Halsbury's Laws of England (5th Edn) (2018) para 302.]

[For 7 Halsbury's Laws of England (5th Edn) (2015) para 272 see now 7 Halsbury's Laws of England (5th Edn) (2020) para 315.]

PERSON ACTING IN AN OFFICIAL CAPACITY

[Criminal Justice Act 1988, s 134: offence of torture committed by a 'public official or person acting in an official capacity'.] '[23] Section 134 CJA was intended to give effect to UNCAT [the United Nations Convention against Torture and Other Cruel, Inhuman or Degrading Treatment or Punishment 1984] in domestic law. As a result, the words "person acting in an official capacity" must bear the same meaning in s 134 as in art 1, UNCAT. (See *R v Bow Street Metropolitan Stipendiary Magistrate, ex p Pinochet Ugarte (Amnesty International intervening) (No 3)* [1999] 2 All ER 97 at 109, [2000] 1 AC 147 at 200 per Lord Browne-Wilkinson.)
...

...

'[76] First, I am persuaded that the prosecution is correct in its interpretation of art 1 UNCAT and s 134 CJA. I consider that the words of those provisions in their ordinary meaning support this reading. They are sufficiently wide to include conduct by a person acting in an official capacity on behalf of an entity exercising governmental control over a civilian population in a territory over which it exercises de facto control. In particular, I can see no justification for imposing the limitation on those words for which the appellant contends, which would require the conduct to be on behalf of the government of the State concerned. On the contrary, the words in their ordinary meaning are apt to include conduct on behalf of a de facto authority which seeks to overthrow the government of the State. This reading also conforms with the object and purpose of the provisions. Here I attach particular significance to the purpose of the Convention in seeking to establish a regime for the international regulation of "official" torture as opposed to private acts of individuals. Torture perpetrated on behalf of a de facto governmental authority is clearly a matter of proper concern to the international community and within the rationale of the scheme. In addition, some support for this conclusion can be found in the decisions of the CAT under art 22(7), UNCAT and it is favoured by the preponderant weight of academic comment. I would express the principle in the following terms.

" 'A person acting in an official capacity' in section 134(1) of the Criminal Justice Act 1988 includes a person who acts or purports to act, otherwise than in a private and individual capacity, for or on behalf of an organisation or body which exercises, in the territory controlled by that organisation or body and in which the relevant conduct occurs, functions normally exer-cised by governments over their civilian populations. Furthermore, it covers any such person whether acting in peace time or in a situation of armed conflict."

R v Reeves Taylor [2019] UKSC 51, [2020] 3 All ER 177 at [23], [76], per Lord Lloyd-Jones

PERSON IMPOSING
THE REQUIREMENT
[Financial Services and Markets Act 2000, s 177(1).] '[12] Section 177(1) provides:

"If a person other than the investigator ('the defaulter') fails to comply with a requirement imposed on him under this Part the person imposing the requirement may certify that fact in writing to the court."

'[13] The principal point raised by Neville relies on the phrase in s 177(1): "the person imposing the requirement". Neville's argument is that the person imposing the requirement of 18 October 2018 was Mr Cawser and so the subsection required Mr Cawser to certify the fact that Neville had not complied with the requirement. The same point would arise in relation to the requirement of 18 April 2018 where the investigator was Mr Craddock. ...
'[14] Although the FCA [Financial Conduct Authority] has not put its case in these terms, it

would seem that it proceeds on the basis that it was the FCA which imposed the requirement of 18 October 2018 and therefore it was open to the FCA to certify non-compliance for the purposes of s 177(1).
...
'[27] Having regard to the material and the considerations set out above, I hold that it was open to the FCA to certify for the purposes of s 177(1) that Neville had failed to comply with a requirement imposed on it. For this purpose, the FCA can say that it was "the person imposing the requirement" when the requirement was imposed by an investigator acting "on its behalf".' *Financial Conduct Authority v Neville Registrars Ltd* [2019] EWHC 1611 (Ch), [2020] 1 All ER 78 at [12]–[14], [27], per Morgan J

PERSONAL REPRESENTATIVE
[For 103 Halsbury's Laws of England (5th Edn) (2010) para 608 see now 103 Halsbury's Laws of England (5th Edn) (2016) para 608.]

PIN MONEY
[For 91 Halsbury's Laws of England (5th Edn) (2012) para 625 see now 91 Halsbury's Laws of England (5th Edn) (2019) para 523.]

PIRACY
[For 61 Halsbury's Laws of England (5th Edn) (2010) para 156 see now 61 Halsbury's Laws of England (5th Edn) (2018) para 168.]
[For 60 Halsbury's Laws of England (5th Edn) (2011) para 331 see now 60 Halsbury's Laws of England (5th Edn) (2018) para 310.]

PIT
[For 76 Halsbury's Laws of England (5th Edn) (2013) para 16 see now 76 Halsbury's Laws of England (5th Edn) (2019) para 16.]

PLACE OF ABODE

Australia [Income Tax Assessment Act 1936 (Cth), s 6(i): a 'resident of Australia' includes a person whose domicile is in Australia, unless the commissioner is satisfied that the person's permanent place of abode is outside Australia.] '[40] In the context of the legislative history, in our view, the phrase "place of abode" is not a reference, as one might have thought, only to a person's specific house or flat or other dwelling. If that had been Parliament's intention it would have used the phrase "permanent abode" rather than "permanent place of abode". The word "place" in the context of the phrase "outside Australia" in subpara (i) invites a consideration of the town or country in which a person is physically residing "permanently". So long as the taxpayer has "definitely abandoned" his or her residence in Australia, it does not serve the function or purpose of the exception to subpara (i) to require that the taxpayer be permanently located at a particular house or flat in a particular town within a foreign country. Nor, indeed, does it serve the functional purpose of the exception to require the person to live in one particular town, suburb or village within a given country. In our view, drawing a distinction between someone who buys a singular flat in a foreign country as against someone who lives in a series of temporary flats in that same country does not promote the rationale of the exception in subpara (i). That rationale is that a person domiciled in Australia is not to be made subject to federal income tax when they have abandoned in a permanent way their Australian residence. For the promotion of that rationale, it is unnecessary for the taxpayer to live outside of Australia in any particular way. It follows that the word "place" should accordingly be read as including a reference to a country or state. Having said that, we do not favour the proposition that it does not matter if the taxpayer is not permanently in one country, but moves between foreign countries. In our view, the words "permanent place" require the identification of a country in which the taxpayer is living permanently. We shall return to the concept of permanence.' *Harding v Commissioner of Taxation* [2019] FCAFC 29, (2019) 365 ALR 286 at [40], per Davies and Steward JJ

PLAINLY WRONG

'[30] Thus, it is a long settled principle, stated and restated in domestic and wider common law jurisprudence, that an appellate court should not interfere with the trial judge's conclusions on primary facts unless it is satisfied that he was plainly wrong: *McGraddie v McGraddie* [2013] UKSC 58, [2013] 1 WLR 2477, 2013 SLT 1212. What does "plainly wrong" mean? The Supreme Court explained in *Henderson v*

Foxworth Investments Ltd [2014] UKSC 41, 2014 SC (UKSC) 203, [2014] 1 WLR 2600 (at [62]):

"Given that the Extra Division correctly identified that an appellate court can interfere where it is satisfied that the trial judge has gone 'plainly wrong', and considered that that criterion was met in the present case, there may be some value in considering the meaning of that phrase. There is a risk that it may be misunderstood. The adverb 'plainly' does not refer to the degree of confidence felt by the appellate court that it would not have reached the same conclusion as the trial judge. It does not matter, with whatever degree of certainty, that the appellate court considers that it would have reached a different conclusion. What matters is whether the decision under appeal is one that no reasonable judge could have reached."

'[31] The mere fact that a trial judge has not expressly mentioned some piece of evidence does not lead to the conclusion that he overlooked it. That point, too, was made in *Henderson* at [48]:

"An appellate court is bound, unless there is compelling reason to the contrary, to assume that the trial judge has taken the whole of the evidence into his consideration …"

'[32] At [57] Lord Reed added:

"I would add that, in any event, the validity of the findings of fact made by a trial judge is not aptly tested by considering whether the judgment presents a balanced account of the evidence. The trial judge must of course consider all the material evidence (although, as I have explained, it need not all be discussed in his judgment). The weight which he gives to it is however preeminently a matter for him, subject only to the requirement, as I shall shortly explain, that his findings be such as might reasonably be made. An appellate court could therefore set aside a judgment on the basis that the judge failed to give the evidence a balanced consideration *only if the judge's conclusion was rationally insupportable*." (Emphasis added.)'

ACLBDD Holdings Ltd v Staechelin; Note [2019] EWCA Civ 817, [2019] 3 All ER 429 at [30]–[32], per Lewison LJ

POLICY OF INSURANCE

[For 60 Halsbury's Laws of England (5th Edn) (2011) paras 96–97 see now 60 Halsbury's Laws of England (5th Edn) (2018) paras 73–74.]

POLITICALLY EXPOSED PERSON

In subsection (4)(a), 'politically exposed person' means a person who is—
(a) an individual who is, or has been, entrusted with prominent public functions by an international organisation or by a State other than the United Kingdom or another EEA State,
(b) a family member of a person within paragraph (a),
(c) known to be a close associate of a person within that paragraph, or
(d) otherwise connected with a person within that paragraph.

(Proceeds of Crime Act 2002, ss 326B(7), 396B(7) (inserted by the Criminal Finances Act 2017, ss 1, 4))

PORT

[For 60 Halsbury's Laws of England (5th Edn) (2011) para 305 see now 60 Halsbury's Laws of England (5th Edn) (2018) para 284.]

[For 85 Halsbury's Laws of England (5th Edn) (2013) para 8 see now 85 Halsbury's Laws of England (5th Edn) (2020) para 8.]

Dockyard port

[For 85 Halsbury's Laws of England (5th Edn) (2013) para 11 see now 85 Halsbury's Laws of England (5th Edn) (2020) para 11.]

Franchise port

[For 85 Halsbury's Laws of England (5th Edn) (2013) para 5 see now 85 Halsbury's Laws of England (5th Edn) (2020) para 5.]

PORTION

[For 91 Halsbury's Laws of England (5th Edn) (2012) para 628 see now 91 Halsbury's Laws of England (5th Edn) (2019) para 528.]

POST OBIT

[For 32 Halsbury's Laws of England (5th Edn) (2012) para 297 see now 32 Halsbury's Laws of England (5th Edn) (2019) para 297.]

POWER

[For 98 Halsbury's Laws of England (5th Edn) (2013) para 43 see now 98 Halsbury's Laws of England (5th Edn) (2019) paras 1, 39–43.]

PRACTICAL INJUSTICE

Australia [Migration Act 1958 (Cth), s 438: if the Secretary of the Department of Immigration and Border Protection gives to the Administrative Appeals Tribunal a document or information to which s 438 applies, the Secretary must notify the Tribunal in writing that s 438 applies in relation to the document or information.] '[38] Because procedural fairness requires disclosure of the fact of notification, non-disclosure of the fact of notification constitutes, without more, a breach of the Tribunal's implied obligation of procedural fairness. For such a breach to constitute jurisdictional error on the part of the Tribunal, however, the breach must give rise to a "practical injustice": the breach must result in a denial of an opportunity to make submissions and that denial must be material to the Tribunal's decision.' *Minister for Immigration and Border Protection v SZMTA (Matter No S36 of 2018)* [2019] HCA 3, (2019) 363 ALR 599 at [38], per Bell, Gageler and Keane JJ

PREAMBLE

[For 96 Halsbury's Laws of England (5th Edn) (2012) para 671 see now 96 Halsbury's Laws of England (5th Edn) (2018) para 272.]

PRECARIOUS

[Nationality, Immigration and Asylum Act 2002, s 117B(5).] '[1] The Home Secretary determines to exercise his power to remove a foreign national from the UK. The foreign national contends that the determination is unlawful on the ground that her removal would violate her right to respect for her private life under art 8 of the European Convention on Human Rights and s 6(1) of the Human Rights Act 1998 ("the 1998 Act"). Section 117B(5) of the Nationality, Immigration and Asylum Act 2002 ("the 2002 Act") provides that little weight should be given to a private life which she established at a time when her immigration status was "precarious". What does the word "precarious" mean in this context? This is the primary question posed by the present appeal.

...

'[42] The provisional view of Sales LJ, set out in para [25] above, was that leave to remain short of indefinite leave might sometimes confer on a person a status not properly to be described as precarious; and that the concept of precariousness might fall to be applied having regard to the person's overall circumstances. The view of Sales LJ is entitled to great respect. In para [36] above I have recognised the need for a degree, no doubt limited, of flexibility in the application of Pt 5A of the 2002 Act. But I will shortly explain how, elsewhere, the statute does permit a limited degree of it. I do not consider that the ordinary meaning of the word "precarious" requires, or that in its context Parliament must have intended the word to require, that its application to the facts of a case should depend upon a subtle evaluation of the overall circumstances such as Sales LJ had in mind.

'[43] The bright-line interpretation of the word "precarious" in s 117B(5), commended by the specialist tribunal with the maximum weight of its authority, is linguistically and teleologically legitimate; and, for that matter, it is consistent with the way in which the ECtHR expressed itself in the *Jeunesse* case [*Jeunesse v Netherlands* (App no 12738/10) (2014) 60 EHRR 789, [2014] ECHR 12738/10] (see para [34] above) and in which this court expressed itself in the *Agyarko* case [*R (on the application of Agyarko) v Secretary of State for the Home Dept, R (on the application of Ikuga) v Secretary of State for the Home Dept* [2017] UKSC 11, [2017] 4 All ER 575, [2017] 1 WLR 823] (see para [35] above).

'[44] The answer to the primary question posed by the present appeal is therefore that everyone who, not being a UK citizen, is present in the UK and who has leave to reside here other than to do so indefinitely has a precarious immigration status for the purposes of s 117B(5).' *Rhuppiah v Secretary of State for the Home Department* [2018] UKSC 58, [2019] 1 All ER 1007 at [1], [42]–[44], per Lord Wilson JSC

PREMIUM

Insurance

[For 60 Halsbury's Laws of England (5th Edn) (2011) para 150 see now 60 Halsbury's Laws of England (5th Edn) (2018) para 128.]

PRESENTED TO THE COURT

[Matrimonial Causes Act 1973, s 3(1).] [28] In the light of *Butler v Butler (Queen's Proctor Intervening)* [1990] 1 FLR 114, [1990] FCR 336, the case admits of no possible argument. District Judge Simmonds was correct to treat the petition as having been "presented to the court" within the meaning of s 3(1) on the day when it was received by the court, namely on 22 June 2015. The petition was therefore presented in breach of s 3(1), with the inevitable consequences spelt out by Sir Stephen Brown P. ...' *Baron v Baron* [2019] EWFC 26, [2020] 1 All ER 272 at [28], per Sir James Munby

PRIVILEGE

Australia [Native Title Act 1993 (Cth), s 253.] '[55] In ascertaining the meaning of the word "privilege" in s 253 of the Native Title Act, it is also necessary to bear steadily in mind that the task is one of statutory construction, not Hohfeldian claim right analysis. The nature of the right, interest, obligation or liberty described by the word is not "disposed of by nomenclature" and it is by no means unprecedented to find the terms "right" and "privilege" used in the "wider and laxer sense" in legislation. "Privilege", being a protean term, takes its meaning from its context.

'[56] If the definition of "interest" in s 253 of the Native Title Act stood alone, it might be that "privilege" would be taken to mean some advantage in relation to land that is peculiar to an individual or group of individuals as opposed to members of the public generally. But s 253 of the Native Title Act does not stand alone, and it is not to be construed as if it did. Although a definitional provision, it is part of the Native Title Act, and, like all other provisions of an Act, it is to be construed in the context of the Act as a whole. Just as the definition of "interest" and, therefore, the meaning of "privilege" in s 253 informs the meaning of the other provisions of the Native Title Act that refer to "interest" or "interests", such other provisions, bearing in mind their purpose and the mischief to which they are directed, inform the meaning of "interest" and, therefore, the meaning of "privilege" in s 253. As McHugh J noticed in *Kelly v R* [(2004) 218 CLR 216; 205 ALR 274; [2004] HCA 12], "[n]othing is more likely to defeat the intention of the legislature than to give a definition a narrow, literal meaning and then use that meaning to negate the evident policy or purpose of a substantive enactment".

'[57] If "privilege" in the definition of "interest" in s 253 were confined to a privilege in the sense of some right, advantage or immunity enjoyed by some beyond the usual rights or advantages of others, it would exclude the ability of the public to access and enjoy the foreshore which exists as a result of the lack of legal prohibition from entering upon unallocated Crown land, validly confirmed by s 14 of the Titles Validation Act in accordance with s 212(2) of the Native Title Act.65 In that event, the confirmed ability would not be within the description of "any other interests" in s 225(c), and so would not be recorded in the native title determinations to which it relates despite impairing the relevant native title rights. That this is so provides a strong indication that "other interests" in s 225(c) is a sufficiently broad concept to include the confirmed ability of the public to access and enjoy the foreshore. And in turn, that provides a strong indication that the confirmed ability is within the notion of a "privilege" in the definition of "interest" in s 253.

'[58] Given, then, that it is the duty of the Court to avoid, so far as the text of the Act permits, a construction inconsistent with the purpose of a provision and instead "look to see whether any other meaning produces a more reasonable result",66 and, as has been seen, that one available, and not inapposite, meaning of "privilege" is of a liberty that the law tolerates but does not support by imposing a duty on anyone else, it should be concluded that "privilege" in the definition of "interest" in s 253 includes the confirmed ability of the public to access and enjoy the foreshore which exists as a result of the lack of legal prohibition on entering upon unallocated Crown land.' *Western Australia v Manado (on behalf of the Bindunbur Native Title Claim Group)* [2020] HCA 9, (2020) 376 ALR 427 at [55]–[58], per Nettle J

Absolute privilege

[For 32 Halsbury's Laws of England (5th Edn) (2012) paras 595–596 see now 32 Halsbury's Laws of England (5th Edn) (2019) paras 594–595.]

Qualified privilege

[For 32 Halsbury's Laws of England (5th Edn) (2012) paras 595, 609 see now 32 Halsbury's Laws of England (5th Edn) (2019) paras 594, 607.]

PRIZE

Admiralty

[For 85 Halsbury's Laws of England (5th Edn) (2012) paras 601–603 see now 85 Halsbury's Laws of England (5th Edn) (2020) paras 701–703.]

PRO-MUTUUM

[For 4 Halsbury's Laws of England (5th Edn) (2011) para 142 see now 4 Halsbury's Laws of England (5th Edn) (2020) para 142.]

PROCEEDINGS

Proceedings in a criminal cause or matter

[Justice and Security Act 2013, s 6: whether judicial review proceedings were 'proceedings in a criminal cause or matter'.] '[4] The issue on this appeal is whether on the hearing of the application for judicial review, it would be open to the Court to receive closed material disclosed only to the court and a special advocate but not to the Appellants. As will appear, this depends on whether the judicial review proceedings are "proceedings in a criminal cause or matter".

...
'[15] In my opinion, the Appellants are entitled to succeed on this appeal because in its ordinary and natural meaning "proceedings in a criminal cause or matter" include proceedings by way of judicial review of a decision made in a criminal cause, and nothing in the context or purpose of the legislation suggests a different meaning.' *R (on the application of Belhaj) v Director of Public Prosecutions* [2018] UKSC 33, [2018] 4 All ER 561 at [4], [15], per Lord Sumption

PROFIT À PRENDRE

[For 76 Halsbury's Laws of England (5th Edn) (2013) para 21 see now 76 Halsbury's Laws of England (5th Edn) (2019) para 21.]

PROHIBITING ORDER

[For 61 Halsbury's Laws of England (5th Edn) (2010) para 689 see now 61A Halsbury's Laws of England (5th Edn) (2019) para 106.]

PROPERTY OF THE COMMONWEALTH

Australia [Archives Act 1983 (Cth), ss 3(1), 70, Pt V; whether archived correspondence between former Governor-General and HM the Queen was property of the Commonwealth.] '[6] We would allow Professor Hocking's appeal from the judgment of the Full Court, declare the deposited correspondence to be Commonwealth records within the meaning of the Archives Act and order that a writ of mandamus issue to compel the Director-General to reconsider Professor Hocking's request for access. ...

...

'[40] The critical expression "Commonwealth record" is in relevant part defined [in the Archives Act 1983, s 3(1)(a)] to mean "a record that is the property of the Commonwealth or of a Commonwealth institution" other than a record of that description which is "exempt material" because it is included in a collection maintained by another custodial institution, such as the National Library of Australia. The cognate expression "current Commonwealth record" is defined to mean "a Commonwealth record that is required to be readily available for the purposes of a Commonwealth institution".

...

'[89] Property is not "a monolithic notion of standard content and invariable intensity"; it is not "a term of art with one specific and precise meaning". It is "a term that can be, and is, applied to many different kinds of relationship with a subject matter". The relationship with a subject matter is in some contexts best understood in terms of a "bundle of rights". In other contexts, it is best understood in terms of a "legally endorsed concentration of power".

...

'[92] The question, however, is not as to the content of the common law concepts of "possession" or "possessory title" but as to the meaning of "property" within the context of the Archives Act. The two are not the same.

'[93] Within the definition of "Commonwealth record", "property" obviously connotes a relationship between a record — a tangible thing — on the one hand and either the Commonwealth as a body politic or a Commonwealth institution as a functional unit of government on the other hand. The nature and intensity of the requisite relationship is a question of statutory construction the resolution of which is informed by the statutory context.

...

'[95] Purposively construed in the context of the Archives Act, the relationship between a record and either the Commonwealth as a body politic or a Commonwealth institution as a functional unit of government connoted by "property" is best understood as a legally endorsed concentration of power to control the physical custody of the record. The power might arise from a capacity to exercise a common law or statutory right arising from ownership or possession. But it need not so arise. The power might be exclusive. But it need not be.' *Hocking v Director-General of the National Archives of Australia* [2020] HCA 19, (2020) 379 ALR 395 at [6], [40], [89], [92]–[93], per Kiefel CJ, Bell, Gageler, Keane JJ

PROPERTY OF THE COMPANY

Australia [Corporations Act 2001 (Cth), s 433: whether the insolvent corporate trustee's right of indemnity is 'property of the company' within the meaning of s 433.] '[269] The primary judge's conclusion that the corporate trustee's right of indemnity by way of exoneration was not "property of the company" cannot be sustained in the light of relevant High Court authority.

'[270] The primary judge emphasised from the outset of his analysis that the character of the relevant assets would never change. Money used by a trustee in exercise of the right of exoneration "remained trust money", in the primary judge's view. The assets "remain trust assets". The right of indemnity was "property held in trust", rather than "the corporate trustee's own beneficial 'personal property".

'[271] It is inconsistent, in our opinion, with High Court authority to hold that the right of indemnity is not property of the corporate trustee because the assets are trust assets. In *Octavo* [*Octavo Investments Pty Ltd v Knight* (1979) 144 CLR 360; 27 ALR 129; 4 ACLR 575] the High Court held the trustee's interest "amounts to a proprietary interest". In *Buckle* [*Chief Commissioner of Stamp Duties (NSW) v Buckle* (1998) 192 CLR 226; 151 ALR 1; [1998] HCA 4] the High Court held that once a right of indemnity (including for exoneration) arose "there exist the respective proprietary rights, in order of priority, of the trustee and the beneficiaries". In both *Buckle* and *CPT* [*CPT Custodian Pty Ltd v Commissioner of State Revenue* (2005) 224 CLR 98; 221 ALR 196; [2005] HCA 53] the High Court said that it was not possible to identify the trust fund until account was taken of the right of exoneration. In *Bruton [Bruton Holdings Pty Ltd (in liq) v Commissioner of Taxation* (2009) 239 CLR 346; 258 ALR 612; 73 ACSR 241; [2009] HCA 32] the High Court reiterated that the trustee's right "amounted to a proprietary interest".' *Commonwealth v Byrnes (in their capacity as joint and several Recs and Mgrs of Amerind Pty Ltd (recs and mgrs apptd) (in liq))* [2018] VSCA 41, (2018) 354 ALR 789 at [269]–[271], per Ferguson CJ, Whelan, Kyrou, McLeish and Dodds-Streeton JJA

PROROGATION

'[2] Parliamentary sittings are normally divided into sessions, usually lasting for about a year, but sometimes less and sometimes, as with the current session, much longer. Prorogation of Parliament brings the current session to an end. The next session begins, usually a short time later, with the Queen's Speech. While Parliament is prorogued, neither House can meet, debate and pass legislation. Neither House can debate Government policy. Nor may members of either House ask written or oral questions of Ministers. They may not meet and take evidence in committees. In general, Bills which have not yet completed all their stages are lost and will have to start again from scratch in the next session of Parliament. In certain circumstances, individual Bills may be "carried over" into the next session and pick up where they left off. The Government remains in office and can exercise its powers to make delegated legislation and bring it into force. It may also exercise all the other powers which the law permits. It cannot procure the passing of Acts of Parliament or obtain Parliamentary approval for further spending.

'[3] Parliament does not decide when it should be prorogued. This is a prerogative power exercised by the Crown on the advice of the Privy Council. In practice, as noted in the House of Commons Library Briefing Paper (No 8589, 11 June 2019), "this process has been a formality in the UK for more than a century: the Government of the day advises the Crown to prorogue and that request is acquiesced to". In theory the monarch could attend Parliament and make the proclamation proroguing it in person, but the last monarch to do this was Queen Victoria in 1854. Under current practice, a proclamation is made by Order in Council a few days before the actual prorogation, specifying a range of days within which Parliament may be prorogued and the date on which the prorogation would end. The Lord Chancellor prepares a commission under the great seal instructing the Commissioners accordingly. On the day chosen for the prorogation, the Commissioners enter the House of Lords; the House of Commons is summoned; the command of the monarch appointing the Commission is read; and Parliament is formally prorogued.

'[4] Prorogation must be distinguished from the dissolution of Parliament. The dissolution of Parliament brings the current Parliament to an end. Members of the House of Commons cease to be Members of Parliament. A general election is then held to elect a new House of Commons. The Government remains in office but there are conventional constraints on what it can do during that period. These days, dissolution is usually preceded by a short period of prorogation.

'[5] Dissolution used also to be a prerogative power of the Crown but is now governed by the Fixed-term Parliaments Act 2011. This provides for general elections to be held every five years and for an earlier election to be held in only two circumstances: either the House of Commons votes, by a majority of at least two-thirds of the number of seats (including vacant seats) in the House, to hold an early election; or the House of Commons votes that it has no confidence in Her Majesty's Government and no-one is able to form a Government in which the House does have confidence within 14 days. Parliament is dissolved 25 days before polling day and cannot otherwise be dissolved. The Act expressly provides that it does not affect Her Majesty's power to prorogue Parliament (s 6(1)).

'[6] Prorogation must also be distinguished from the House adjourning or going into recess. This is decided, not by the Crown acting on the advice of the Prime Minister, but by each House passing a motion to that effect. The Houses might go into recess at different times from one another. In the House of Commons, the motion is moved by the Prime Minister. In the House of Lords, it is moved by the Lord Speaker. During a recess, the House does not sit but Parliamentary business can otherwise continue as usual. Committees may meet, written Parliamentary questions can be asked and must be answered.' *R (on the application of Miller) v Prime Minister; Cherry v Advocate General for Scotland* [2019] UKSC 41, [2019] 4 All ER 299 at [2]–[6], per Lady Hale P and Lord Reed DP

PROTECTED NEW ZEALAND OBJECT

New Zealand [Protected Objects Act 1975, s 2(1)(a).] '[89] The purpose of the Protected Objects Act is to protect certain objects of particular national value to New Zealand. The focus is therefore on individual items that, as individual items, have significance for one or more of the reasons set out in s 2(1)(a). The Act is not designed, as the Courts below held, to protect natural materials such as swamp kauri in bulk. It is true that protected New Zealand object is defined to include a collection or assemblage of objects but these terms imply that the collection or assemblage is in one place or in the hands of one owner. That does not apply to swamp kauri.

'[90] Further, to require all pieces of a bulk natural material, such as swamp kauri, to be subject to an application process before export would create a major administrative burden, both on the Ministry and the public. This cannot have been the intention of the Act. It is true that an exemption could be granted if there are sufficient examples of swamp kauri in public ownership but, if swamp kauri generally had been intended to be covered by the Act, this then raises the question, given the finite nature of the resource, as to what would be a sufficient amount in public ownership in order for it to satisfy the criteria for an exemption.' *Northland Environmental Protection Society Inc v Chief Executive of the Ministry for Primary Industries* [2018] NZSC 105, [2019] 1 NZLR 257 at [89]–[90], per Glazebrook J

PROXIMATE CAUSE

[For 60 Halsbury's Laws of England (5th Edn) (2011) para 347 see now 60 Halsbury's Laws of England (5th Edn) (2018) para 326.]

PUBLIC BODY

New Zealand [Subsidies and Countervailing Measures Agreement ('SCM Agreement') annexed to the World Trade Organisation ('WTO') Agreement. Whether the Ministry of Business, Innovation and Employment ('MBIE') interpreted the "public body" test correctly before advising the Minister that state-owned commercial banks in China ('SOCB's) and state-invested enterprises ('SIE's) were not public bodies.] '[82] Article 1.1(a) of the SCM Agreement deems subsidies to exist where financial contributions of certain kinds (as set out in (i) to (iv)) are made by a "government or any public body". Consistent with this, the DCD Act [Dumping and Countervailing Duties Act 1988] defines "subsidy" as including a financial contribution provided by a "foreign Government" and, also consistently, "foreign Government" is defined as including "a person, agency, or institution acting for, or on behalf of, a Government".

'[83] The proper test to be applied for determining whether an entity is a "public body" is relevant to two of the alleged subsidy programmes: (1) whether Chinese producers of the subject goods received benefits by way of policy loans from SOCBs; and (2) whether Chinese producers of the subject goods received benefits because SIEs provided inputs to them at LTAR ['less than adequate remuneration']. MBIE's Final Report rejected these claims on the basis it was not established that SOCBs and the SIEs were public bodies.

'[118] In my view the quoted paragraphs are not entirely clear on this point. MBIE is correct that the test for whether an entity is a public body is not whether it is meaningfully controlled by government. The test is whether an entity possesses, exercises or is vested with government authority. In DS436 the WTO Appellate Body held that formal indicia of control (the ability to appoint shareholders and directors) were not sufficient to determine if an entity possessed, exercised or was vested with government functions. The WTO Appellate Body also held that the entity did not need to have the power to regulate, control, or supervise individuals or otherwise restrain their conduct.

[119] It is not clear in the above quoted paragraphs that MBIE appreciated that ADRP 2013 (Gal) had concluded that the "material did not show that the control amounted to meaningful control in the sense intended by the WTO Appellate Body [in DS379]" on an erroneous basis: namely, that there was no material to demonstrate there had been "a delegation of governmental authority to SIEs to impose state-mandated policies on participants in the iron and steel industry". The correct position, as clarified in DS436, is that SIEs could potentially possess, exercise or be vested with government authority even if they did not have a power of control over third parties.' *New Zealand Steel Ltd v Minister of Commerce and Consumer Affairs* [2018] NZHC 2454,

[2019] 2 NZLR 525 at [82]–[83], [118]–[119], per Malton J

PUBLIC POLICY

[For 22 Halsbury's Laws of England (5th Edn) (2012) paras 429–431 see now 22 Halsbury's Laws of England (5th Edn) (2020) paras 220–222.]

PUBLICATION—PUBLISH

Defamation

[For 32 Halsbury's Laws of England (5th Edn) (2012) paras 562, 579 see now 32 Halsbury's Laws of England (5th Edn) (2019) paras 562, 579.]

PUFFING

[For 76 Halsbury's Laws of England (5th Edn) (2013) paras 713–714 see now 76 Halsbury's Laws of England (5th Edn) (2019) paras 713–714.]

PURSUE

New Zealand [Wildlife Act 1953, s 2: hunting or killing in relation to any wildlife includes pursuing, disturbing, or molesting.] '[63] The dictionary meaning of the word "pursue" includes to follow with intent to overtake for some purpose — usually capturing in some way. It is implicit in the act of "pursuing" that the defendant intends to chase the animal. Travelling the same path through water as a marine species as a matter of chance is not pursuing it if there is no intention to follow. In the context of this Act, we are satisfied that "pursuing" is to be construed as to mean intentionally chasing. We use the word "chase" because we do not consider the term was intended to capture merely following an animal at a safe distance.

'[64] The Court of Appeal has given "pursue" a broader meaning than intentionally chasing to include, as a prohibited action, luring a protected animal. On its analysis, the use of baits and berley to attract sharks amounts to pursuit. Shark Experience argues that the Court of Appeal erred in this as "pursue" does not naturally bear this meaning. It argues that if such activity was intended to be prohibited, the language of luring or attracting would have been used.

'[65] We agree that the meaning the Court of Appeal gave to the word "pursue" is neither consistent with the natural and ordinary meaning of the word pursue, nor with the statutory purpose. Pursuing something normally entails following it or chasing it. Luring an animal with the use of attractants is not normally spoken of as pursuing it, although if the purpose for which attractants are used is catching or killing the animal, it is likely to be prohibited as the act of hunting.

'[66] The purpose of the Act is to protect wildlife. Pursuing an animal in the sense of chasing it for whatever reason can be stressful for the animal, and so prohibiting pursuit of an animal is consistent with that purpose. But attracting an animal to food, or to scent, thereby allowing the animal to be observed is not necessarily, on its own, obviously harmful. We accept Shark Experience's submission that adopting the broader interpretation of "pursue" favoured by the Court of Appeal would over criminalise conduct. The Court of Appeal attempted to manage this risk by adding the "risk of harm" gloss to both this and the prohibited act of disturbing protected wildlife. On our interpretation of "pursue", the addition of that gloss is not necessary.

...

'[93] ... In the s 2(1) definition of "hunt or kill": "pursuing" means to intentionally chase but does not include luring or attracting or merely following the animal at a safe distance.' *Shark Experience Ltd v PauaMAC5 Inc* [2019] NZSC 111, [2019] 1 NZLR 791 at [63]–[66], [93], per Winkelmann CJ

Q

QUANTUM MERUIT

[For 88 Halsbury's Laws of England (5th Edn) (2012) para 408 see now 88 Halsbury's Laws of England (5th Edn) (2019) para 408.]

QUARRY

[For 76 Halsbury's Laws of England (5th Edn) (2013) para 4 see now 76 Halsbury's Laws of England (5th Edn) (2019) para 4.]

QUASHING ORDER

[For 61 Halsbury's Laws of England (5th Edn) (2010) para 689 see now 61A Halsbury's Laws of England (5th Edn) (2018) para 106.]

QUASI CONTRACT

[For 88 Halsbury's Laws of England (5th Edn) (2012) para 401 see now 88 Halsbury's Laws of England (5th Edn) (2019) para 401.]

QUASI EASEMENT

[For 32 Halsbury's Laws of England (5th Edn) (2012) para 29 see now 32 Halsbury's Laws of England (5th Edn) (2019) para 29.]

R

REALISABLE PROPERTY

[Criminal Justice Act 1988, s 80: confiscation order; provision for a receiver to be appointed in respect of 'realisable property'.] '[7] This appeal relates to an order made by Jay J on 29 June 2017. The order provided, among other things, for the schedule to the receivership order of 13 January 2016 to be amended to include certain pension policies in Mr Ahmed's name.

'[8] Mr Ahmed challenges that part of Jay J's order. His case is that the pension policies have as yet no realisable value and that they will continue to have none for a number of years. That being so, he said, they cannot represent "realisable property". In contrast, Mr Jonathan Kinnear QC, who appeared for the CPS with Mr Michael Newbold, submitted that the policies are "realisable property" within the meaning of the 1988 Act and, hence, that Jay J was right to include them in the schedule to the receivership order.

'[9] Mitting J was empowered to appoint a receiver by s 80 of the 1988 Act. That provided for a receiver to be appointed "in respect of realisable property" (s 80(2)) and to be granted power "to realise any realisable property in such manner as the court may direct" (s 80(5)). The term "realisable property" was defined in s 74 of the Act to include "any property held by the defendant", and s 102 explained that "Property is held by any person if he holds any interest in it" (s 102(7)) and that " 'interest', in relation to property, includes right" (s 102(1)).

'[10] Mr Ahmed does not dispute that he has an interest in each of the pension policies that Jay J decided should be added to the schedule to the receivership order. It inevitably follows, having regard to the provisions of the 1988 Act quoted in the previous paragraph, that the policies are "realisable property" within the meaning of the Act. Equally, they must form part of the "realisable property of the Defendants" of which Mr Long was appointed receiver. That being so, there can, as I see it, be no valid objection to the policies being included in the schedule to the receivership order.' *Ahmed v Crown Prosecution Service* [2018] EWCA Civ 2543, [2019] 1 All ER 1003 at [7]–[10], per Newey LJ

REASONABLE

[Data Protection Act 1988, s 7(4)(b): data controller not required to comply with a request for personal data where it would entail disclosing information relating to another individual who can be identified from that information, unless it is reasonable in all the circumstances to comply with the request without the consent of the other individual.] '[105] It is therefore in my judgment significant that Parliament has used the word "reasonable" and not some other word such as "appropriate". The word "reasonable" conveys that there may be one or more courses open to the data controller and that his choice, if within sub-s (4), will prevail. In that sense, I agree with Sales LJ that the court should defer to the data controller and not substitute the court's own opinion.' *DB v General Medical Council* [2018] EWCA Civ 1497, [2019] 2 All ER 219 at [105], per Arden LJ

REBUILD

[For 91 Halsbury's Laws of England (5th Edn) (2012) para 716 et seq see now 91 Halsbury's Laws of England (5th Edn) (2019) para 613 et seq.]

RECEIVER

[For 88 Halsbury's Laws of England (5th Edn) (2012) para 1 see now 88 Halsbury's Laws of England (5th Edn) (2019) para 1.]

RECORDS OF THE COURT

[CPR 5.4C: copies from court records for a person not a party to proceedings.] '[22] The

Master considered that the "records of the court" comprised all documents filed with the court and that this included trial bundles and documents, such as skeleton arguments and transcripts, held with them.

'[23] CIH [Cape Intermediate Holdings Ltd] contended that none of these documents, other than statements of case, are properly to be regarded as being part of the "records of the court" and that the Master had no jurisdiction to make the order she did.

...

'[36] The critical issue in relation to the court's jurisdiction under CPR 5.4C(2) is the meaning of the "records of the court". This is not a defined term under the CPR.

...

'[40] In my judgment CIH's core submission is correct. The "records of the court" are essentially documents kept by the court office as a record of the proceedings, many of which will be of a formal nature. The principal documents which are likely to fall within that description are those set out in para 4.2A of CPR 5APD.4, together with "communication between the court and a party or another person", as CPR 5.4C(2) makes clear. In some cases there will be documents held by the court office additional to those listed in para 4.2A of CPR 5APD.4, but they will only be "records of the court" if they are of an analogous nature.

'[41] This will include a list of documents, but not the disclosed documents themselves. It may include witness statements and exhibits filed in relation to an application notice or Pt 8 proceedings (see CPR 8.5), but not usually witness statements or expert reports exchanged by the parties in relation to a trial. Such statements and reports are not generally required to be filed with the court and they will typically be provided to the court only as part of the trial bundles.

'[42] The receipt document for the trial bundles may be a record of the court, but not the trial bundles themselves. ...

...

'[49] The Master's finding that the trial bundles were "records of the court" was the essential basis upon which she ordered copying of the documents listed in the Order. The Order in fact went further and also treated skeleton arguments and trial transcripts as being part of the "records of the court".

...

'[54] The Order made in this case was of unprecedented scope and went far beyond the relatively narrow confines of CPR 5.4C(2). For the avoidance of doubt, I consider that it should be made clear that the "records of the court" for the purpose of that rule do not generally include:

(1) The trial bundles.
(2) The trial witness statements.
(3) The trial expert reports.
(4) The trial skeleton arguments or opening or closing notes or submissions.
(5) The trial transcripts.'

Dring (on behalf of the Asbestos Victims Support Groups Forum UK) v Cape Intermediate Holdings Ltd [2018] EWCA Civ 1795, [2019] 1 All ER 804 at [22]–[23], [36], [40]–[42], [49], [54], per Hamblen LJ

REFERENDUM EXPENSES

[Political Parties, Elections and Referendums Act 2000, s 111(2): offence if total 'referendum expenses' incurred by or on behalf of any individual or body during the referendum period exceeded £10,000, unless the individual was a 'permitted participant'.] '[1] The issue in this case is whether the Electoral Commission (the statutory body responsible for overseeing elections and referendums in the UK) has correctly interpreted the law which limited spending by participants in connection with the referendum held in June 2016 on whether or not the UK should remain a member of the European Union. More particularly, the issue is whether the Electoral Commission was correct to conclude that, on the proper interpretation of the legislation, certain payments made by Vote Leave Ltd were not "referendum expenses" incurred by Vote Leave but only donations made by Vote Leave to meet expenses incurred by another campaigner for a "leave" outcome of the referendum called Mr Darren Grimes.

...

'[94] For the reasons given, we conclude that the Electoral Commission has misinterpreted the definition of" 'referendum expenses" in s 111(2) of PPERA. The source of its error is a mistaken assumption that an individual or body which makes a donation to a permitted participant cannot thereby incur referendum expenses. As a result of this error, the Electoral Commission has interpreted the definition in a way that is inconsistent with both the language and the purpose of the legislation.

'[95] The email communications which we summarised at paras [13]–[20] above show that Vote Leave made each of the AIQ Payments (totalling £620,000) at the request of Mr Grimes for the agreed purpose of paying for advertising which Mr Grimes ordered from AIQ [AggregateIQ Data Services Ltd]. We see no reason to doubt that the payments were, as they were said to be, donations made by Vote Leave to Mr Grimes to meet referendum expenses which he incurred by purchasing advertising services from AIQ. But it is also clear that, on the proper interpretation of the statutory provisions as we have analysed them, Vote Leave "incurred expenses" by making the payments, that those expenses were incurred "in respect of" advertising (one of the matters listed in Pt I of Sch 13 to PPERA) and that the expenses were incurred "for referendum purposes" within the meaning of s 111(3) of PPERA. They were therefore "referendum expenses" as defined in s 111(2) of PPERA irrespective of whether they were also "common plan expenses" within the meaning of para 22 of Sch 1 to EURA, as the Electoral Commission has now found.

'[96]   It was suggested on behalf of the Electoral Commission that this is not a rational conclusion because Vote Leave could equally well have sent the money to Mr Grimes to enable him to pay AIQ instead of paying AIQ itself directly and that, even on the claimant's case, Vote Leave would then have avoided the regulatory control on referendum expenses because the expenses would not then have been qualifying expenses falling within Pt I of Sch 13 to PPERA. It was suggested that it is not reasonable to adopt an interpretation which leads to such an arbitrary difference in result.

'[97]   However, if Vote Leave had sent the money to Mr Grimes on the agreed basis that he would use it to pay for services ordered from AIQ, the result would not have been different. In that case too, as we interpret the statutory test, the payments would also have been referendum expenses incurred by Vote Leave.' *R (on the application of the Good Law Project) v Electoral Commission (Vote Leave Ltd and another, interested parties)* [2018] EWHC 2414 (Admin), [2019] 1 All ER 365 at [1], [94]–[97], per Leggatt LJ

RELATIONS

[For 102 Halsbury's Laws of England (5th Edn) (2010) para 350 see now 102 Halsbury's Laws of England (5th Edn) (2016) para 349.]

RELEVANT

Relevant criminal activity

Australia [Australian Crime Commission Act 2002 (Cth), s 7C: power of the board of the ACC to authorise, in writing, the ACC to undertake intelligence operations or to investigate matters relating to federally relevant criminal activity.] '[100]   The defined phrase "relevant criminal activity" indicates that the subject matter of an investigation need not concern or respond to a particular allegation that a relevant offence has been committed, is being committed or may be committed by a person or class of persons. The concept is wider than that. It includes any *circumstances implying that* (for present purposes) serious and organised crime may have been, may be being, or may in future be, committed against a law of the Commonwealth, of a State or of a Territory. Where circumstances imply that serious and organised crime is being committed, it may be that the Board will not, at the time of an authorisation or determination, have in its possession information identifying or tending to identify the persons responsible for engaging in or organising the criminal activity, the particular offences that might sanction the activity, the scale of the activity, the place of its commission or other particulars. The discovery of as yet unknown particular information of that kind may permissibly form a part of the investigatory purpose.' *CXXXVIII v Commonwealth of Australia* [2019] FCAFC 54, (2019) 366 ALR 436 at [100], per Charlesworth J

RELIGIOUS PURPOSES

[For 8 Halsbury's Laws of England (5th Edn) (2015) para 27 et seq see now 8 Halsbury's Laws of England (5th Edn) (2019) para 28 et seq.]

REPRESENTATION

[Delete the reference to 60 Halsbury's Laws of England (5th Edn) (2011) para 36.]

[For 76 Halsbury's Laws of England (5th Edn) (2013) paras 702, 715–716 see now 76 Halsbury's Laws of England (5th Edn) (2019) paras 702, 715–716.]

REPRESENTATIVES

In will

[For 102 Halsbury's Laws of England (5th Edn) (2010) para 365 see now 102 Halsbury's Laws of England (5th Edn) (2016) para 364.]

RESERVATION

[For 32 Halsbury's Laws of England (5th Edn) (2012) para 440 see now 32 Halsbury's Laws of England (5th Edn) (2019) para 440.]

RESIDE—RESIDENCE

'[46] I accept entirely that there is a difference between residence and habitual residence. Unlike with habitual residence, a person can be resident in two countries at the same time (see *Marinos* [*Marinos v Marinos* [2007] EWHC 2047 (Fam), [2007] 2 FLR 1018] at para [48] and *V v V* [*V v V (Divorce: Jurisdiction)* [2011] EWHC 1190 (Fam), [2011] 2 FLR 778] at paras [50] and [51]). The obvious example would be the wife in *Marinos* who had homes in Greece (where her husband and children lived) and in England (where she worked and lived with her parents). In that case, she divided her time roughly equally between the two, but I accept Mr Howard's submission that it does not have to be equal. He postulated the case of a barrister who lives and works in London from Monday to Friday and goes home to his/her family in Dorset (per Mr Howard) or France every weekend.

'[47] Mr Marks is, however, correct that residence has to be something more than just a place where you or your spouse own a property. It has to be somewhere where you reside as opposed to where you visit. The most obvious example would be a holiday home which would not amount to residence, but another example might be the super-rich who own numerous homes all around the world. They visit these homes. They do not reside in each and every one of them.' *Pierburg v Pierburg* [2019] EWFC 24, [2019] 3 All ER 551 at [46]–[47], per Moor J

[European Parliament and Council Directive 2004/38/EC ('the Citizens Directive'), art 17(1)(a); Immigration (European Economic Area) Regulations 2006, SI 2006/1003, reg 5(2): entitlement to state pension credit conditional on having a right of residence in the UK.] '[81] … The reference in Recital (19) to the Citizens Directive to rights of permanent residence acquired under Regulation 1251/70 is a strong indication that the EU legislature intended the concept of continuous residence as used in art 17(1)(a) of the Directive to reflect the concept of continuous residence as used in art 2(1)(a) of the Regulation. Accordingly, both in its text, which contrasts with the text of recital (17), and by reason of its reference back

to rights acquired under Regulation 1251/70, Recital (19) indicates that the concept of residence as referred to in art 17(1)(a) is factual residence, as the respondent contends.

'[82] We consider that recital (3) to the Citizens Directive reinforces this interpretation of art 17(1)(a). It explains that the EU legislature intended to codify and review the existing EU instruments dealing with workers and others "in order to simplify and strengthen the right of free movement and residence of all Union citizens". Thus, it was part of the purpose of the Directive to enhance existing rights of free movement and residence, such as those which had arisen under Regulation 1251/70, and not to subject them to new restrictive conditions. The same point emerges from recital (1) to Regulation 635/2006, which repealed Regulation 1251/70, as follows:

> "[The Citizens Directive] consolidated in a single text the legislation on the free movement of citizens of the Union. Article 17 thereof includes the main elements of [Regulation 1251/70] and amends them by granting beneficiaries of the right to remain a more privileged status, namely that of the right of permanent residence."

…

'[88] In the *Alarape* case [Alarape v Secretary of State for the Home Dept (AIRE Centre intervening) (Case C-529/11) EU:C:2013:290, [2014] All ER (EC) 470, [2013] 1 WLR 2883, ECJ] the CJEU addressed the question whether periods of residence completed pursuant to art 12 of Regulation 1612/68, which provides a right for the child of a worker to be admitted to educational courses in the host member state, could count towards the five years of "legal residence" required for acquisition of a right of permanent residence under art 16(1) of the Citizens Directive. The CJEU applied its ruling in the *Ziolkowski* judgment [*Ziolkowski v Land Berlin* (Joined cases C-424/10 and C-425/10) [2014] All ER (EC) 314, [2013] 3 CMLR 1013, ECJ] regarding the meaning of "legal residence" in art 16(1) and held that residence pursuant to art 12 of Regulation 1612/68, but which did not comply with art 7 of the Citizens Directive, did not count for the purposes of art 16(1). In our view, this does not support Mr Chamberlain's interpretation of art 17(1) of the Citizens Directive. If anything, it tends to support Judge Ward's interpretation of that provision. That is because, following the guidance in the judgments in *Ziolkowski* and *Alarape*, residence in a host member state pursuant to rights under Regulation 1251/70 and Directive 75/34/EEC likewise would not count as "legal residence" for the purpose of art 16(1) of the Citizens Directive; but it is rights acquired by residence pursuant to Regulation 1251/70 and Directive 75/34/EEC which are intended to be respected and protected by art 17 of the Citizens Directive: see recital (19) to that Directive.

...

'[92] For the reasons set out above, in our judgment the Court of Appeal erred in its interpretation of art 17(1). Judge Ward arrived at a correct interpretation of that provision, in holding that residence in art 17(1) refers to factual residence rather than "legal residence" as required under art 16(1), as interpreted by the CJEU in the *Ziolkowski* judgment.' *Gubeladze v Secretary of State for Work and Pensions* [2019] UKSC 31, [2019] 4 All ER 389 at [81]–[82], [88], [92], per Lord Lloyd-Jones and Lord Sales

Habitual residence

[Council Regulation 2201/2003/EC, art 3: jurisdiction in relation to divorce.] '[43] There is no dispute that, for these purposes, you can only have one habitual residence. Habitual residence is defined as the place where the person has established, on a fixed basis, his or her permanent or habitual centre of interests. All relevant facts will be taken into account in determining that. There is no specific timeframe for having established habitual residence. In some cases, it can be done very quickly. In others, it will take longer. If there is a planned, purposeful and permanent relocation to another country, habitual residence can be acquired contemporaneously (or virtually contemporaneously) with the loss of a previous habitual residence. For example, in *Z v Z (Divorce: Jurisdiction)* [2009] EWHC 2626 (Fam), [2010] 1 FLR 694, Ryder J found that a wife had established habitual residence in England "at or shortly after" the family moved to London.

'[44] There was some debate as to whether a person could ever be without a habitual residence. It seems that you can be for a brief period but only whilst you establish your new centre of interests. The example given by Munby J in *Marinos* [*Marinos v Marinos* [2007] EWHC 2047 (Fam), [2007] 2 FLR 1018] is that of a wife who lost her habitual residence in Greece as the aircraft on which she and the children were travelling to London took off. She

then acquired a new habitual residence in this country as the aircraft touched down at Heathrow.

'[45] The test is qualitative not quantitative. In other words, it is not simply a head-count of days and nights, although time spent in a particular location will be a relevant factor in most cases.' *Pierburg v Pierburg* [2019] EWFC 24, [2019] 3 All ER 551 at [43]–[45], per Moor J

Canada [Convention on the Civil Aspects of International Child Abduction ('Hague Convention'), art 3.] '5. For the reasons that follow, I conclude that this Court should adopt the hybrid approach to determining habitual residence under Article 3 of the *Hague Convention*, and a non-technical approach to considering a child's objection to removal under Article 13(2).

...

'43. On the hybrid approach to habitual residence, the application judge determines the focal point of the child's life – "the family and social environment in which its life has developed" – immediately prior to the removal or retention: Pérez-Vera, at p 428; see also *Jackson v Graczyk* (2006) 45 RFL (6th) 43 (Ont SCJ), at para 33. The judge considers all relevant links and circumstances – the child's links to and circumstances in country A; the circumstances of the child's move from country A to country B; and the child's links to and circumstances in country B.

...

'47. The hybrid approach is "fact-bound, practical, and unencumbered with rigid rules, formulas, or presumptions": *Redmond v Redmond*, 724 F 3d 729 (7th Cir 2013), at p 746. It requires the application judge to look to the entirety of the child's situation. While courts allude to factors or considerations that tend to recur, there is no legal test for habitual residence and the list of potentially relevant factors is not closed. The temptation "to overlay the factual concept of habitual residence with legal constructs" must be resisted: *A v A [A v A (Children: Habitual Residence)* [2013] UKSC 60, [2014] AC 1] at paras 37–39.' *Office of the Children's Lawyer v Balev* [2018] SCJ No 16, [2018] 1 SCR 398 at paras 5, 43, 47, per McLachlin CJ

RESTITUTIO IN INTEGRUM

[For 29 Halsbury's Laws of England (5th Edn) (2014) para 440 see now 29 Halsbury's Laws of England (5th Edn) (2019) para 440.]

RESTRAINT OF PRINCES
[For 60 Halsbury's Laws of England (5th Edn) (2011) para 323 see now 60 Halsbury's Laws of England (5th Edn) (2018) para 410.]

RETAINED DIRECT EU LEGISLATION
'Retained direct EU legislation' means any direct EU legislation which forms part of domestic law by virtue of section 3 (as modified by or under this Act or by other domestic law from time to time, and including any instruments made under it on or after IP completion day). (European Union (Withdrawal) Act 2018, s 20(1) (definition amended by the European Union (Withdrawal Agreement) Act 2020, s 41(4), Sch 5, Pt 2, paras 38, 44(1), (2)(f)))

RETROSPECTIVE
[For 96 Halsbury's Laws of England (5th Edn) (2012) paras 1185–1186 see now 96 Halsbury's Laws of England (5th Edn) (2018) paras 801–802.]

RIGHT

Enjoyment as of right
[For 32 Halsbury's Laws of England (5th Edn) (2012) para 23 see now 32 Halsbury's Laws of England (5th Edn) (2019) para 23.]

RIGHT OF WAY
[For 32 Halsbury's Laws of England (5th Edn) (2012) para 36 see now 32 Halsbury's Laws of England (5th Edn) (2019) para 36.]

RIGHT TO BEAR ARMS

New Zealand '[13] Underpinning almost all aspects of the Kiwi Party's case is the claim that New Zealand citizens have a constitutional right to bear arms and in particular, weapons, magazines and gun parts that have been prohibited by the Amendment Act [the Arms (Prohibited Firearms, Magazines, and Parts) Amendment Act 2019].

'[14] This so-called constitutional right is said to be derived from ancient custom, which evolved into a common law right and was affirmed by Magna Carta, the Bill of Rights 1688 and the Treaty of Waitangi. In his supplementary submissions filed on 20 March Mr Minchin, counsel for the Kiwi Party, maintained "the right to bear arms is the practical application of the legal principles that 'no power is unfettered' and is the mark of a free society".

...
'[17] An examination of the constitutional instruments relied upon by Mr Minchin quickly exposes the fallacy of his argument that New Zealanders have a constitutional right to bear arms.

...
'[26] It is striking that the so-called right to bear arms is not referred to in any international human rights instrument, such as the International Covenant on Civil and Political Rights or the European Convention on Human Rights. Of the 190 countries that have a written constitution, only the constitutions of Guatemala, Mexico and the United States refer to a right to bear arms. The relevant parts of the constitutions of Guatemala and Mexico are modelled on the Second Amendment of the United States Constitution but expressly provide for limits according to law. Thus, it can be fairly said that the right to bear arms is an example of American constitutional exceptionalism. Even in the United States, the ability of a citizen to possess and use firearms may be subject to legislative control. Thus, assault weapons have been banned by seven State legislatures, including those in California and New York.

'[27] Our examination of the arguments advanced by Mr Minchin leads to the following conclusions:
(a) The so-called right to bear arms is not supported by any constitutional instruments that apply in New Zealand.
(b) In this country, as in almost all countries, a citizen's ability to possess, own and use firearms is regulated by legislation.
(c) There are only three countries which have some form of constitutional right to bear arms.
(d) There is no constitutional right to bear arms in New Zealand let alone the arms that are prohibited by the Amendment Act.'

Kiwi Party Inc v Attorney-General [2020] NZCA 80, [2020] 2 NZLR 224 at [13]–[14], [17], [26]–[27], per Collins J

ROYAL ASSENT

[For 96 Halsbury's Laws of England (5th Edn) (2012) paras 871–873 see now 96 Halsbury's Laws of England (5th Edn) (2018) paras 488–490.]

ROYALTY

[For 76 Halsbury's Laws of England (5th Edn) (2013) para 334 see now 76 Halsbury's Laws of England (5th Edn) (2019) para 331.]

S

SAFE PORT

[For 7 Halsbury's Laws of England (5th Edn) (2015) para 519 see now 7 Halsbury's Laws of England (5th Edn) (2020) para 201.]

SALE OF GOODS

[For 91 Halsbury's Laws of England (5th Edn) (2012) para 1 see now 91 Halsbury's Laws of England (5th Edn) (2019) para 1.]

By description

[For 91 Halsbury's Laws of England (5th Edn) (2012) para 73 see now 91 Halsbury's Laws of England (5th Edn) (2019) para 75.]

By sample

[For 91 Halsbury's Laws of England (5th Edn) (2012) para 94 see now 91 Halsbury's Laws of England (5th Edn) (2019) para 96.]

SALIENT FEATURES

Australia '[210] The recognition of duties of care despite such problems [tending to hinder the recognition, or qualify the scope, of duties of care] has come to depend on the presence of "salient features" in the relationship between the alleged tortfeasor and victim, such as the former's control, assumption of responsibility or knowledge and the latter's vulnerability or reliance: *Caltex Oil (Australia) Pty Ltd v The Dredge "Willemstad"* (1976) 136 CLR 529 at 576–577, 11 ALR 227 at 261–262 (Stephen J); *Perre* [*Perre v Apand Pty Ltd* (1999) 198 CLR 180, 164 ALR 606, [1999] HCA 36] at [198]–[201] (Gummow J); *Caltex v Stavar* [*Caltex Refineries (Qld) Pty Ltd v Stavar* (2009) 259 ALR 616, 75 NSWLR 649, [2009] NSWCA 258] at [102]–[104] (Allsop P). Those expressions have, however, acquired restricted

meanings from the cases in which they are applied: see, for example, the authorities collected in *Ku-ring-gai Council v Chan* (2017) 224 LGERA 330, [2017] NSWCA 226 at [69], [71], [81] as to "vulnerability" and "reliance". Such restrictions prevent each salient feature from becoming, like "proximity", a statement of conclusion without practical content, and they ensure that consideration of salient features is undertaken to facilitate, not supplant, analogical reasoning: see *Brookfield* [*Brookfield Multiplex v Owners—Corporation Strata Plan 61288* (2014) 254 CLR 185, [2014] HCA 36] at [20]–[25] (French CJ).' *Ibrahimi v Commonwealth of Australia* [2018] NSWCA 321, (2018) 366 ALR 341 at [210], per Payne JA

SALVAGE

Salvage charges

[For 60 Halsbury's Laws of England (5th Edn) (2011) para 400 see now 60 Halsbury's Laws of England (5th Edn) (2018) para 378.]

SAME

Same interest

[CPR 19.6(1).] '[83] The procedural rule is clear: a representative action may only be started, and the court may only order that a claim be continued as a representative action, if the representative party and those whom that party represents, have "the same interest in" the claim. ...

...

'[85] ... Mr Tomlinson makes four central submissions:

(1) Persons have the "same interest" if they have a common interest and a common grievance.

(2) Persons may have the same interest in a claim even if there are disagreements between them and even if the quantum of damages that they have suffered is different.

(3) A representative claimant may represent a class, even if the members of that class have been affected by the defendant's actions in different ways.

(4) There is no limit to the number of persons that can be within the class to be represented.

'[86] The first three of these propositions give rise to dispute. Google submits that the existence of a common grievance against the same defendant is not enough to satisfy the "same interest" condition. In particular, where the defendant is alleged to have damaged individual rights and interests, the representative action will be unavailable unless every member of the class has suffered the same damage (or their share of a readily ascertainable aggregate amount is clear). Further, and in any event, the procedure will be unavailable where different potential defences are available in respect of claims by different members of the class. I accept Google's submissions, and in my judgment these principles apply to the facts of this case, so as to disqualify this claim.' *Lloyd v Google LLC* [2018] EWHC 2599 (QB), [2019] 1 All ER 740 at [83], [85], per Warby J

SCOPE

[Coroners and Justice Act 2009, s 5: scope of inquest.] '[20] In two important paragraphs 18 and 19 of the ruling, the Coroner said:

"18. The word 'scope' has no special meaning of its own. By 'scope' all that is generally meant is a list of the topics upon which the coroner, in the coroner's discretion, will call relevant evidence so as to be able to answer the four key statutory questions: Who died? How, when and where did they come by their death?

"19. These questions and the answers to them, known as the determination, are provided by statute in Sections 5 and 10 of the Coroners and Justice Act 2009. They are the four central questions in every inquest. When decided the answers to them are recorded by the coroner or the jury, if there is one, in the statutory Record of Inquest."

...

'[57] In our judgment the Coroner's statement of "the meaning of scope", in paras 18 and following of his ruling (see [20] above) was correct. Moreover, however the test is formulated, his decision in the present case to exclude

the Perpetrator Issue from the scope of this inquest was not, in our view, unlawful in the public law sense.' *R (on the application of Hambleton and others) v Coroner for the Birmingham Inquests (1974)* [2018] EWCA Civ 2081, [2019] 2 All ER 251 at [20], [57], per Lord Burnett CJ, Hallett VP and McCombe LJ

SEAWORTHY

[For 60 Halsbury's Laws of England (5th Edn) (2011) paras 257–258 see now 60 Halsbury's Laws of England (5th Edn) (2018) paras 236–237.]

[For 7 Halsbury's Laws of England (5th Edn) (2015) para 419 et seq see now 7 Halsbury's Laws of England (5th Edn) (2020) para 223 et seq.]

SECURE ACCOMMODATION

[Children Act 1989, s 25.] '[46] The phrase "secure accommodation" is defined in s 25(1) as meaning "accommodation ... provided for the purpose of restricting liberty". The same definition appears in [the Children (Secure Accommodation) Regulations 1991, SI 1991/1505,] reg 2 ("accommodation which is provided for the purpose of restricting the liberty of children to whom section 25 ... applies"). At first sight, this looks like a relatively straightforward definition, although, as will become clear, it is by no means necessarily easy to apply.

'[47] The ALC [Association of Lawyers for Children] argues that the effect of s 25(7)(d) and reg 3 of the 1991 Regulations is to incorporate into the definition of "secure accommodation" for the purposes of s 25 the qualification that, if the accommodation is a children's home, it must be approved by the Secretary of State for that use. But there is nothing in s 25 itself to suggest that the meaning of the words "secure accommodation" is qualified by reference to s 25(7)(d) or reg 3. A close examination of the words of the section and the Regulation demonstrates that this is not so. Section 25(7)(d) provides that "the Secretary of State may by regulations provide that ... a child may only be placed in secure accommodation that is of a description specified in the regulations ...". Adopting a straightforward construction of s 25(7)(d), the phrase "secure accommodation that is of a description specified in the regulations" describes a subset, not a prerequisite, of "secure accommodation". Similarly, a straightforward

construction of reg 3(1) ("accommodation in a children's home shall not be used as secure accommodation unless ... approved by the Secretary of State for that use") is that it excludes certain accommodation from being used as secure accommodation, but does not alter the definition of "secure accommodation" itself. Although reg 3(1) (as reg 3 in the original form of the Regulations made pursuant to powers granted in the original Sch 2 to the 1989 Act) has been in force since the early days of the Children Act 1989, s 25(7)(d) was only inserted by amendment introduced in the Children and Social Work Act 2017. Thus, if the ALC's submission is correct, the definition of "secure accommodation" was changed by this amendment. If it had been Parliament's intention to change the meaning of "secure accommodation", it would surely have done so in much clearer terms.

'[48] A straightforward construction of the words of s 25 therefore leads to the conclusion that "secure accommodation" means nothing more or less than accommodation provided for the purpose of restricting liberty.' *Re B (a child) (Association of Lawyers for Children intervening)* [2019] EWCA Civ 2025, [2020] 3 All ER 375 at [46]–[48], per Baker LJ

SECURED CREDITOR

[For 5 Halsbury's Laws of England (5th Edn) (2013) para 574 see now 5 Halsbury's Laws of England (5th Edn) (2020) para 555.]

SECURITIES

In will

[For 102 Halsbury's Laws of England (5th Edn) (2010) para 296 see now 102 Halsbury's Laws of England (5th Edn) (2016) para 294.]

SEDITION

[Note that 11(1) Halsbury's Laws (4th Edn 2006 Reissue) para 371 is not reproduced in 25 and 26 Halsbury's Laws of England (5th Edn) (2016).]

SEISED

[European Parliament and Council Regulation 1215/2012/EU, art 29: where proceedings in-

volving the same cause of action and between the same parties are brought in the courts of different member states, any court other than the court first seised must of its own motion stay its proceedings until such time as the jurisdiction of the court first seised is established.] '[17] I will take first the issue whether the Cypriot court is now seised of the Cypriot proceedings. The immediate effect of the order made on 22 May 2018 was that there were no longer any proceedings pending before the Cypriot court. But, at that time, the appellants had the right to file an appeal against that order, which they did within the time permitted for doing so. The effect of filing an appeal did not stay or suspend the effect of the order but, I assume (although the court does not have evidence on the point), a successful appeal will set aside the order with effect from the time it was made. It was not suggested to us that the effect would be different from this but Ms Wickenden, on behalf of the respondent, submitted that the correct position currently was that the Cypriot court had ceased to be seised on 22 May 2018 and that the Supreme Court of Cyprus became seised on the filing of the appeal, but it was for the purposes of art 29 the court second seised. I am unable to accept this analysis. The Supreme Court is seised only of an appeal. The choice, as it seems to me, must be between the Cypriot court not being currently seised as a result of the order of 22 May 2018 (and only becoming seised again if an appeal succeeds, at which time it will be the court second seised) and the Cypriot court still being seised by reason of filing the appeal and remaining so at least until the appeal is determined.

...

'[20] ... I would hold ... that the Cypriot court remains seised of the Cypriot proceedings until the appeal against the order of 22 May 2018 is determined. It is true that, because of the particular circumstances prevailing in the Supreme Court of Cyprus, it will probably be a long time until the appeal is finally disposed of, but the autonomous meaning of "seised" in art 29 cannot depend on factors of this sort which will vary greatly among member states.' *Easy Rent a Car Ltd v Easygroup Ltd* [2019] EWCA Civ 477, [2019] 4 All ER 1087 at [17], [20], per David Richards LJ

SEIZURE

Of ship

[For 60 Halsbury's Laws of England (5th Edn) (2011) para 328 see now 60 Halsbury's Laws of England (5th Edn) (2018) para 307.]

SEND

Sent to the parties

[Employment Appeal Tribunal Rules 1993, SI 1993/2854, r 3(3): an appeal must be brought within '42 days from the date on which the written reasons were sent to the parties'.]

'[24] The issue is whether a judgment is "sent to the parties" where in the case of one of the parties it is sent to a person other than that party or his or her representative. I should make two points by way of preliminary.

'[25] First, it was common ground before us, and is plainly right, that it is irrelevant for the purpose of r 3(3) when or whether the judgment is *received* by any party: what matters is when they were *sent*. ...

'[26] Secondly, although what happened in this case was that the judgment was sent to a former representative, that is not the only kind of error that could occur. It will be important to test any proposed answer as it would apply to other kinds of "mis-sending". ...

...

'[35] The starting-point must be the words of the rule itself. I see the force of Mr Margo's submission that as a matter of ordinary English it is hard to describe a document as having been "sent to the parties" when in the case of one of them it has been sent neither to the party himself or herself nor to their nominated representative. I also agree with him that the reasoning at para 52 of Judge Hand's judgment in *Carroll* [*Carroll v Mayor's Office for Policing and Crime* [2015] ICR 835, [2015] All ER (D) 209 (Feb)] (see para [27](4) above) is unconvincing: to say that a document is "sent to the parties" even where it is sent to someone who is not a party only asserts what it is necessary to prove, and Mr Margo's submission does not require any words to be read in (at least as regards "category (1) cases"). However, I also see force in Mr Moretto's point that the language of the rule refers to a single date, which is difficult to reconcile with a construction under which different dates would apply in the event of the mis-sending of the judgment to one of the parties. That being so, a strictly literal

approach may not be appropriate: the phrase "sent to the parties" could reasonably be read as connoting the act of promulgation—perhaps equivalent to "sent out" or "published"—rather than the mechanics of despatch to each of the parties. I am not to be taking as saying that, as a matter of language, Mr Moretto's construction is to be preferred to Mr Margo's—only that both are reasonably possible. But once that point is reached it is necessary to consider which produces the more sensible result in practice.

'[36] As to that, I prefer Mr Moretto's contention. In my view there is an obvious practical advantage in having a single, contemporaneously recorded, date from which time for appealing runs for both parties, so that everyone knows where they stand from the moment that the judgment is promulgated; and I think it very likely that that is what the rule-maker intended. Even though there appears to be no formal obligation on the tribunal to include the standard-form endorsement recording the date at which the judgment is sent to the parties, the EAT Practice Direction clearly shows that that was the practice at the time that the Rules were made, and it can safely be assumed that the rule-maker was aware of it (and even if he was not he would certainly have assumed that the date of sending would appear in the covering letter).

'[37] Of course justice requires that where the judgment is mis-sent the party affected should not be unfairly prejudiced by the tribunal's mistake; but construing the rule so that time will not run until whatever date the mistake is corrected is a rigid solution which goes further than is necessary to correct the problem. ...

'[38] In my view a just outcome in mis-sending cases can be achieved more flexibly and sensibly, as Judge Hand held in *Carroll*, by the appropriate use of the EAT's discretion to extend time under r 37. I do not agree with Mr Margo that having to rely on the discretion causes any substantial prejudice to the party in question, at least if the principles governing its exercise are clear. ...

...

'[92] For the reasons given by Underhill LJ at paras [35]–[36] of his judgment I agree that it is possible to construe "sent to the parties" as meaning "promulgated" (even if the tribunal then fails to send the document to one party at the correct address). I agree that this construction of r 3(3), when coupled with the discretion to extend time conferred by r 37, produces the

more sensible result in practice; and therefore it seems to me that it was the result which the draftsman was seeking to achieve. I also agree with all that Underhill LJ says about the way in which the r 37 discretion should be exercised in cases of this kind where the tribunal has made an error.' *Rana v Ealing London Borough Council; Bonnie v Department for Work and Pensions* [2018] EWCA Civ 2074, [2019] 1 All ER 1078 at [24]–[26], [35]–[38], per Underhill VP and at [92], per Bean LJ

SEQUESTRATION

Writ of sequestration

[For 22 Halsbury's Laws of England (5th Edn) (2012) para 97 see now 24 Halsbury's Laws of England (5th Edn) (2019) para 95.]

SERVANT

Household servant

[For 102 Halsbury's Laws of England (5th Edn) (2010) para 367 see now 102 Halsbury's Laws of England (5th Edn) (2016) para 366.]

SERVICES

Canada [Canadian Human Rights Act, RSC 1985, c H-6, s 5.] '92. This case is about the scope of s 5 of the *CHRA*, which reads as follows:

5 It is a discriminatory practice in the provision of goods, services, facilities or accommodation customarily available to the general public:

    (a) to deny, or to deny access to, any such good, service, facility or accommodation to any individual, or

    (b) to differentiate adversely in relation to any individual,

on a prohibited ground of discrimination.

'93. Do the present complaints allege a discriminatory practice in the provision of a service customarily available to the general public? Before the Tribunal, the complainants sought to challenge the registration provisions of the *Indian Act* as making discriminatory distinctions on the basis of race, national or ethnic origin, sex and family status …. They did not challenge the actions of the Registrar in processing their applications. At their core,

these complaints are about Parliament's decision not to extend "Indian" status to persons in similar circumstances. This was properly characterized by the Tribunal as a bare challenge to legislation.

…

'95. What, then, is encompassed in s 5? The wording of this section focuses on the *provision* of services. The French version of the *CHRA* says that it is a discriminatory practice for the *service provider* ("*le fournisseur … de services*") to deny or differentiate adversely in relation to an individual. The use of this language suggests that s 5 is geared towards discrimination perpetrated by service providers.

'96. In our view, Parliament is not a service provider, and was not providing a service when it enacted the registration provisions of the *Indian Act*. Moreover, law-making is unlike any of the other terms listed in s 5; it does not resemble a good, facility or accommodation (see *Forward* [*Forward v Canada (Citizenship and Immigration)* 2008 CHRT 5], at para 42 (CanLII)). As observed by the Tribunal in *Andrews*, the legislative process is unique ….

'97. Parliament can be distinguished from the administrative decision makers that operate under legislative authority. These individuals and statutory bodies, which include the Registrar, may be "service providers", or entities that "provi[de] … services … customarily available to the general public". If they use their statutory discretion in a manner that effectively denies access to a service or makes an adverse differentiation on the basis of a prohibited ground, s 5 will be engaged. But, when their job is simply to apply legislated criteria, the challenge is not to the provision of services, but to the legislation itself (*Murphy* [*Public Service Alliance of Canada v Canada Revenue Agency*, 2012 FCA 7, 428 NR 240], at para 6).

'98. Furthermore, the relevant jurisprudence suggests that the enactment of legislation is not a service. This Court has defined a service as (1) something of benefit (2) that is held out or offered to the public (*Gould* [*Gould v Yukon Order of Pioneers* [1996] 1 SCR 571]; see also *Watkin* [*Canada (Attorney General) v Watkin* 2008 FCA 170, 378 NR 268], at para 31). In *Gould*, La Forest J (concurring) said, at para 55:

There is a transitive connotation from the language employed by the various provisions; it is not until the service, accommodation, facility, etc, passes from the service provider and has been held out to the public that it attracts the anti-discrimination prohibition.

Again, La Forest J's definition in *Gould* focuses on the service provider. When Parliament crafts statutory eligibility criteria, there is no "transitive connotation". Nothing is being held out by Parliament to the public. It is only when the service provider itself discriminates that s 5 is engaged.

...

'104. In sum, we agree with the Tribunal and the courts below that bare challenges to legislation cannot be brought under s 5 of the *CHRA*. The act of legislating is not a service. ...' *Canada (Canadian Human Rights Commission) v Canada (Attorney General)* [2018] SCJ No 31, [2018] 2 SCR 230 at paras 92–93, 95–98, 104, per Côté and Rowe JJ

SETTLEMENT

[For 91 Halsbury's Laws of England (5th Edn) (2012) para 501 see now 91 Halsbury's Laws of England (5th Edn) (2019) para 401.]

Compound settlement

[For 91 Halsbury's Laws of England (5th Edn) (2012) para 501 see now 91 Halsbury's Laws of England (5th Edn) (2019) para 401.]

Marriage settlement

[For 91 Halsbury's Laws of England (5th Edn) (2012) para 503 see now 91 Halsbury's Laws of England (5th Edn) (2019) para 403.]

Post-nuptial settlement

[For 91 Halsbury's Laws of England (5th Edn) (2012) para 504 see now 91 Halsbury's Laws of England (5th Edn) (2019) para 404.]

Protective settlement

[For 91 Halsbury's Laws of England (5th Edn) (2012) para 507 see now 91 Halsbury's Laws of England (5th Edn) (2019) para 407.]

Strict settlement

[For 91 Halsbury's Laws of England (5th Edn) (2012) para 506 see now 91 Halsbury's Laws of England (5th Edn) (2019) para 406.]

SHIPMENT

[For 91 Halsbury's Laws of England (5th Edn) (2012) para 341 see now 7 Halsbury's Laws of England (5th Edn) (2020) para 394.]

SKINNY LABEL

'[2] The essence of the problem is fairly simply stated, although the details are more complicated. The patentee markets a prescription-only drug for three different indications under a single registered trade mark. Patent protection for the drug itself has now expired, but the patentee still has a second medical use patent for one of the three indications. A supplier of generic pharmaceuticals wishes to enter the market for the drug for the two non-patented indications, as it is lawfully entitled to do. To that end, the generic supplier obtains a marketing authorisation for a generic version of the drug limited to those two indications (a so-called "skinny label"), and it only identifies those indications in its summary of product characteristics ("SmPC") and patient information leaflet ("PIL").' *Warner-Lambert Co LLC v Actavis Group PTC EHF* [2015] EWHC 72 (Pat) at [2], per Arnold J

'[9] Actavis' product is marketed under the trade mark Lecaent. Actavis have now obtained a marketing authorisation for Lecaent on the basis that Lecaent and Lyrica are bioequivalent. So there can be no doubt that Lecaent is in fact suitable for treating neuropathic pain. However, the summary of product characteristics ("SmPC") and patient information leaflet ("PIL") for Lecaent only identify the medicine as suitable for epilepsy and GAD, ie the non-patented indications. It is important to understand that neither the SmPC nor the PIL contains any warning or injunction against using the medicine for other indications or indeed for the patented indication. The same is true of the packaging of the product. A marketing authorisation which is restricted in this way is described in the industry as a "skinny label" to reflect the narrowness of the indications compared with another authorisation with a wider range of indications. Another expression which is used is that the patented indication has been "carved out".' *Warner Lambert Co LLC v Actavis Group PTC EHF* [2015] EWCA Civ 556, [2015] IP & T 875 at [9], per Floyd LJ

'[8] Lecaent is marketed under a "skinny label", ie for the treatment of some indications only. The Summary of Product Characteristics prepared for the purpose of obtaining marketing authorisation and the Patient Information Leaflet included in the packet state that the conditions for which Lecaent is indicated are epilepsy and GAD, for which patent protection has expired.

…

'[66] Because doctors commonly prescribe generically and the pharmacist generally does not usually know what indication is being treated, the use of "skinny labels" specifying the purpose of the generic product cannot reliably prevent the pharmacist from dispensing the generic product for a patent-protected use. Dispensing pharmacists know that Lyrica and Lecaent are identical, and the same dosage regime can be used for all indications for which pregabalin has received marketing authorisation.' *Warner-Lambert Co LLC v Generics (UK) Ltd (t/a Mylan) (Secretary of State for Health and others intervening)* [2018] UKSC 56, [2019] 3 All ER 95 at [8], [66], per Lord Sumption

SLANDER

[For 32 Halsbury's Laws of England (5th Edn) (2012) para 512 see now 32 Halsbury's Laws of England (5th Edn) (2019) para 511.]

Slander of goods or title

[For 32 Halsbury's Laws of England (5th Edn) (2012) para 778 see now 32 Halsbury's Laws of England (5th Edn) (2019) para 776.]

SLIP RULE

The court may at any time correct an accidental slip or omission in a judgment or order. (CPR 40.12(1))

The court may at any time correct an accidental slip or omission in a judgment or order (the 'slip rule'). Where good practice has not been followed and, as a result the court has been misled, it is appropriate to correct or vary the order. However, the slip rule is limited to accidental slips or omissions and the court should be very cautious before going behind an apparent agreement between counsel. The slip rule cannot be used to enable the court to have second thoughts or to add to its original order but it can be used to amend an order to give effect to the court's intentions at the relevant time. (12A Halsbury's Laws of England (5th Edn) (2015) para 1226)

[Tribunal Procedure (Upper Tribunal) Rules 2008, SI 2008/2698, r 42: tribunal may 'at any time correct any clerical mistake or other accidental slip or omission in a decision or record of a decision'.] '[18] … It was common ground before us that that rule, in common with slip rules applying to other jurisdictions, applies only to what I have above called "errors of expression". If the error was substantial the rule has no application. …

…

'[29] I accept, nevertheless, that there is a conceptual difference between the formal decision and the reasons for that decision, even if it is not always reflected in the form of the decision. The real question is whether Parliament in enacting the provision empowering the TPC [Tribunal Procedure Committee], or the TPC in making the rule, intended that the Upper Tribunal (and, in the case of the statute, the First-tier Tribunal) should only have the power to correct slips in its formal decision and not the reasons. I start with the language itself, ignoring at this stage any consideration of the scope of the slip rule in the CPR. As to that, the language is not explicit, and I think there are two possible approaches to the formula "a decision or record of a decision"; but on neither approach do I think that there can be detected a clear intention to limit the power of correction to the formal decision. I take the two approaches in turn.

'[30] A strict approach would be that it was necessary to give some different content to the two different elements—"decision" and "record of a decision". That can be done by treating the former as referring to the reasons and the latter as referring to the formal decision. I accept that if that were the intention the language is not very apt; but it is not impossible, and I am unable to see any other way of differentiating between them.

'[31] The alternative approach, which I would favour, is that the strict approach attributes to the draftsman a greater degree of precision than was intended, and that the two elements in the phrase can be taken as a composite. On that approach it seems to me more in accordance with ordinary legal usage to read the reference to a "decision" as being to the totality of the decision, comprising both the formal decision and the reasons. It is true that that would render the reference to the "record of the decision" redundant, but if we are not taking a strict approach it would be enough to recognise that that sometimes happens.

'[32] My reading, on either approach, of the effect of the language used is reinforced by considering the purpose of a slip rule of this kind. It is not only in the case of a formal decision that it may be desirable for a court or tribunal to be able to correct accidental errors. Most obviously, such an error in its reasons might lead to further error, or in any event difficulty, on an appeal or in further proceedings in the same litigation, or in other cases where the decision was followed. The present case would, if the Tribunal's figure could be established to be an accidental error, be a good example of that; and clearly the applicant in *Hazeltine* thought that the missing "not" might create difficulties in understanding Whitford J's reasoning on the pending appeal. There may be other circumstances in which the impossibility of correcting an error could lead to other kinds of injustice or undesirable consequences. I can see no sufficient reason why the draftsman should have intended to frame a slip rule in terms that allowed correction in the one situation but not the other.

'[33] I note in this connection that r 31 of the Tribunal Procedure (First-tier Tribunal) (Immigration and Asylum Chamber) Rules 2014, SI 2014/2604 permits the correction of "any ... accidental slip or omission in a decision, direction *or any document produced by it*" (emphasis added). Whatever "decision" might cover if it stood alone, the italicised words appear to put it beyond doubt that the power extends to the written reasons for any decision. The TPC thus regarded it as desirable in that context that the slip rule should not be limited to formal decisions. It would be odd, to put it no higher, if we were to give r 42 a construction which produced a different result in the Upper Tribunal.

'[34] Of course adopting such a construction means that r 42 would be wider in its scope than r 40.12(1) of the Civil Procedure Rules, as construed in *A (a child) [Re A (a child) (appeal: jurisdiction)* [2014] EWCA Civ 871, [2014] 1 WLR 4453]. That may be untidy, but I do not regard it as unacceptable. The reasoning in *A (a Child)* depended on the established meaning of the phrase "judgment or order" and not on any view taken by the Court that a wider construction would be undesirable on grounds of policy or principle. Nor is there any reason to suppose that the drafters of the CPR themselves made a deliberate choice in favour of a narrow construction. It appears that they simply adopted the familiar formulation used in the RSC. Indeed if *Hazeltine [Hazeltine Corp v International Computers Ltd* [1980] FSR 521, Pat Ct] is correctly decided, any inconveniences caused by a narrow construction of the slip

rule in the CPR itself are removed by the fact that there is an inherent jurisdiction to correct the reasons for a judgment or order.

'[35] I would for those reasons hold that the Upper Tribunal has power under r 42 to correct clerical mistakes and other accidental slips or omissions not only in its formal decisions but in its reasons for those decisions.

...

'[39] ... The purpose of the slip rule is to allow the court or tribunal to correct errors of expression so as to express what it actually meant to say. Only it can say whether a particular error is indeed an error of expression and, if so, how it should be corrected. It follows that there would normally be no role for this Court. ...' *AS (Afghanistan) v Secretary of State for the Home Department* [2019] EWCA Civ 208, [2019] 3 All ER 36 at [18], [29]–[35], [39], per Underhill VP

Australia [Uniform Civil Procedure Rules 2005, r 36.17.] '[255] On the slip rule ground, Al Maha submitted that the power under the slip rule is contingent on there being "a clerical mistake, or an error arising from an accidental slip or omission, in a judgment or order" and the exercise of the power under the slip rule is to "correct the mistake or error". Al Maha contended that the amendments made by the Commissioner to the conditions of consent and to approve an amended plan did not correct a "clerical mistake" or "an error arising from an accidental slip or omission", but rather were substantive amendments to the conditions of consent and the approved plans.

'[256] Al Maha submitted that the power to correct an error arising from accidental slip or omission directs attention to what the Court whose record is to be corrected did or intended to do, however "[i]t does not permit reconsideration, let alone alteration, of the substance of the result that was reached and recorded" (*Burrell v R* (2008) 238 CLR 218; 248 ALR 428; [2008] HCA 34 at [21]; *Achurch v R* (2015) 253 CLR 141; 306 ALR 566; 143 ALD 1; [2014] HCA 10 at [18]). Al Maha submitted that the application of the slip rule to correct an error would only be appropriate if the solution to the error does not involve controversy or depend on evaluative or discretionary judgment (*Newmont Yandal Operations Pty Ltd v J Aron Corporation* (2007) 70 NSWLR 411; [2007] NSWCA 195 (*Newmont Yandal*) at [129], citing *Storey & Keers Pty Ltd v Johnstone* (1987) 9 NSWLR 446 at 453). The slip rule cannot be used to "cloak the court with jurisdiction" which it otherwise would not have, or for the purpose of expanding the court's jurisdiction (*Tonab Investments Pty Ltd v Optima Developments Pty Ltd* (2015) 90 NSWLR 268; [2015] NSWCA 287 (*Tonab Investments*) at [61], [67] and [113]).

...

'[266] The slip rule decision was outside the power of the slip rule. The slip rule decision purported to amend order 3 made on 26 February 2018 to grant development consent to the development application on the conditions in Annexure A to the orders. As I have found earlier, the development for which consent was sought in the further amended development application and to which consent was granted included construction of the driveway connection to Hilts Road on Al Maha's land. The slip rule decision purported to modify the development consent so as to no longer authorise the carrying out of this development on Al Maha's land. It sought to achieve this modification of the consent by amending certain conditions of consent and substituting an amended plan. None of these modifications, however, could be described as corrections of "a clerical mistake" or "an error arising from an accidental slip or omission" in order 3 of the Commissioner's orders or in the annexed conditions of consent. The order and the annexed conditions of consent did not contain any mistake or error in granting consent to the construction of the driveway connection to Hilts Road.

'[267] The power under the slip rule could be exercised to correct mistakes or errors in the decision or orders of the Commissioner in order to carry into effect the intention of the Commissioner making the order: *Newmont Yandal* at [116]. The relevant intention of the Commissioner is the objective intention, not the subjective intention, of the Commissioner at the time the decision and orders were made: *Newmont Yandal* at [91], [102] and see *Tonab Investments* at [65]. The Commissioner's ex post facto observation in making the slip rule amendments, that "these amendments confirm that the consent and approved plans do not authorise the carrying out of any development on 36 Leicester Avenue, Strathfield", is at best "no more than evidentiary and may not even be admissible over objection": *Newmont Yandal* at [95].

'[268]   Where the order sought to be amended under the slip rule is an order of the Court granting development consent, the intention of the Commissioner (or Judge) who

made the order is to be discerned from the reasons for judgment (if there are reasons) and a construction of the development consent granted by the Commissioner (or Judge). ...' *Al Maha Pty Ltd v Huajun Investments Pty Ltd* [2018] NSWCA 245, (2018) 365 ALR 86 at [255]–[256], [266]–[268], per Preston CJ of LEC

SOLIDARITY

Canada [Civil Code of Québec, art 1526.] '1. This appeal illustrates the apparent conflict that sometimes exists between two core principles of extracontractual liability in Quebec civil law. The first of these principles is that of full compensation for injury. The second is the principle that, unless an exception applies, a person is liable for reparation only of injuries caused by his or her own fault.

'2. The *Civil Code of Québec* ("*CCQ*" or "*Code*") establishes a scheme that strikes a balance between these principles. Article 1457 of the *Code* provides for full compensation for injury caused by a fault. Article 1525 para 1 provides that solidarity between debtors is not presumed. Articles 1480 and 1526 set out the circumstances in which there is a solidary obligation to make reparation for injury caused by an extracontractual fault. The *Code* thus lays down the general principle that a person is liable only for damage he or she causes, but qualifies this principle to favour full compensation of a victim who suffers a single injury as a result of extracontractual faults committed by two or more persons. However, because solidarity represents a deviation from the general principle, it must be applied strictly (see D Lluelles and B Moore, *Droit des obligations* (2nd ed 2012), at No 2581).

...

'74. Article 1526 *CCQ* provides for solidarity in the case of persons who have, by committing a common fault or contributory faults, caused one and the same injury to another person (Baudouin, Deslauriers and Moore, at Nos 1–720 to 1–722; *Code civil du Québec: Annotations—Commentaires 2017–2018*, at p 1287; Lluelles and Moore, at No 2578). It is of the very essence of extracontractual solidarity that the debtors be obligated to the creditor for "the same thing" (art 1523 *CCQ*; Lluelles and Moore, at No 2577; see also M Tancelin, *Des obligations en droit mixte du Québec* (7th ed 2009), at No 1388). The injury contemplated in art 1526 *CCQ* is therefore subject to the require-ment that there be a single injury.' *Montréal (Ville) v Lonardi* [2018] SCJ No 29, [2018] 1 SCR 104 at paras 1, 2, 74, per Gascon J

STALLAGE

[For 71 Halsbury's Laws of England (5th Edn) (2013) para 834 see now 71 Halsbury's Laws of England (5th Edn) (2020) para 737.]

STATUTE

[For 96 Halsbury's Laws of England (5th Edn) (2012) paras 606, 619–624, 625–633 see now 96 Halsbury's Laws of England (5th Edn) (2018) paras 206, 219–224, 225–233.]

Codifying statute

[For 96 Halsbury's Laws of England (5th Edn) (2012) para 639 see now 96 Halsbury's Laws of England (5th Edn) (2018) para 239.]

Consolidating statute

[For 96 Halsbury's Laws of England (5th Edn) (2012) para 638 see now 96 Halsbury's Laws of England (5th Edn) (2018) para 238.]

Penal statute

[For 96 Halsbury's Laws of England (5th Edn) (2012) para 617 see now 96 Halsbury's Laws of England (5th Edn) (2018) para 217.]

STATUTORY INSTRUMENT

[For 96 Halsbury's Laws of England (5th Edn) (2012) para 1045 see now 96 Halsbury's Laws of England (5th Edn) (2018) para 656.]
[See also the Statutory Instruments Act 1946, s 1(1A) (inserted by the Government of Wales Act 1998, s 125, Sch 12 para 2; and substituted by the Government of Wales Act 2006, s 160(1), Sch 10 paras 1, 2); and the Deregulation Act 2015, s 105.]

STRANDING

[For 60 Halsbury's Laws of England (5th Edn) (2011) para 340 see now 60 Halsbury's Laws of England (5th Edn) (2018) para 319.]

STREET

[For 55 Halsbury's Laws of England (5th Edn) (2012) para 9 see now 55 Halsbury's Laws of England (5th Edn) (2019) para 9.]

Private street

[For 55 Halsbury's Laws of England (5th Edn) (2012) para 10 see now 55 Halsbury's Laws of England (5th Edn) (2019) para 10.]

STRIKE (STOPPAGE OF WORK)

[For 41 Halsbury's Laws of England (5th Edn) (2009) para 1304 see now 41A Halsbury's Laws of England (5th Edn) (2014) para 1340.]

SUBORDINATE LEGISLATION

[For 96 Halsbury's Laws of England (5th Edn) (2012) paras 1030–1031 see now 96 Halsbury's Laws of England (5th Edn) (2012) paras 637–638.]

SUBROGATION

[For 60 Halsbury's Laws of England (5th Edn) (2011) para 216 see now 60 Halsbury's Laws of England (5th Edn) (2018) para 195.]

SUFFICIENT

Sufficiently influenced

Australia [Income Tax Assessment Act 1936 (Cth), s 318(2), (6).] '[48] The central issue in this appeal from a decision of the Administrative Appeals Tribunal is the correct construction of s 318(2) and (6) of the Income Tax Assessment Act 1936 (Cth) (ITAA 1936). These provisions are found in Pt X of the ITAA 1936. Section 318(6) describes the meaning of "sufficiently influenced" which, relevantly for present purposes, is a phrase used in s 318(2) to identify the "associates" of a company.
...
'[80] Section 318(6) gives content to the test in s 318(2)(d)(i) and (e)(i) to be applied to identify whether an entity is to be regarded as an "associate" of another as either a "controlling entity" or "controlled company". The terms of s 318(2)(d) and (e) indicate that, whatever else "sufficiently influenced" means, it is more than legal control through majority voting power:

(1) An entity can be a "controlling entity" under s 318(2)(d) without having legal control through a majority voting interest, where the connection between the acts of "the company, or its directors" and the "directions, instructions or wishes" of the "controlling entity" are such that there the "primary entity" is "sufficiently influenced" by the "controlling entity", within the meaning of s 318(6)(b).

(2) An entity can be a "controlled entity" under s 318(2)(e) without the "primary entity" having legal control through a majority voting interest, where the connection between the acts of the "controlled entity" or its directors and the directions, instructions or wishes of the "primary entity" are such that the "controlled entity" is "sufficiently influenced" by the "primary entity", within the meaning of s 318(6)(b).

'[81] Whilst "sufficiently influenced" means something more than legal control through majority voting power, the concept of "control" is relevant to s 318(2)(d) and (e). Unlike paras (a)–(c), paras (d) and (e) are not describing relationships in which an entity might be expected to benefit, absent any consideration of "control". This is perhaps indicated by the use of the terms "controlling entity" and "controlled entity", and is certainly indicated by the text of the provisions, which look to legal control (in the sense of a majority voting interest) or something which is not legal control but attracts the description "sufficiently influenced" in the sense of acting "in accordance with" the "directions, instructions or wishes" of another. The s 318(6)(b) description of "sufficiently influenced" may be seen to describe a species of control or influence, or expected control or influence, which falls short of legal control. The critical issue in the proceedings is how far short it falls.

'[82] A number of observations should also be made concerning the description supplied by s 318(6)(b) of when "a company is sufficiently influenced" for the purposes of s 318(2).

'[83] First, the paragraph directs attention to the position of the company *and* the position of its directors: it is sufficient if either "the company, or its directors" are caught by the terms of the paragraph. The respondent submitted that the reference to "the company" in the phrase "the company, or its directors" was not a reference to the company in general meeting but merely recognised that a company acts through

natural persons. This submission is rejected for the reasons given at paragraphs [131]–[134] below.

'[84] Secondly, s 318(6)(b) turns on whether either the company or its directors are:
(1) accustomed;
(2) under an obligation (whether formal or informal); or
(3) might reasonably be expected, to act in accordance with the directions, instructions of wishes of the entity or entities.

[85] These three matters are not a composite phrase denoting a single test (cf: *Sea Shepherd Australia Ltd v Commissioner of Taxation* (2013) 212 FCR 252; [2013] FCAFC 68 at [34] (Gordon J)); whilst each matter must be interpreted having regard to all of the words in s 318(6)(b) and in the context of the whole statute, the three matters comprise different considerations, each of which is independently sufficient to attract the conclusion that a company or its directors are "sufficiently influenced":
(1) The first matter—whether a company or its directors are "accustomed" to act in accordance with another's instructions or wishes—depends upon past facts.
(2) The second matter—whether there is an "obligation" to act in accordance with another's directions, instructions or wishes—depends upon a presently existing (or existing at the time the question is relevantly asked) formal or informal obligation.
(3) The third matter—whether a company or its directors "might reasonably be expected" to act in accordance with another's directions, instructions or wishes—requires a prediction as to future events and a consideration as to the objective likelihood of those future events occurring.

'[86] Thirdly, the terms of s 318(6)(b) do not require that there be a legal ability to require the company (or its directors) to act in accordance with the directions, instructions or wishes conveyed. It is enough if, as a matter of past or present fact or future expectation, the company or its directors are accustomed, or under a formal or informal obligation, or might reasonably be expected, to act in accordance with the directions, instructions or wishes of the primary entity.

'[87] Fourthly, s 318(6)(b) is satisfied only where the act is "in accordance with" the relevant directions, instructions or wishes. This is not established by the mere coincidence that the relevant act accorded with the relevant directions, instructions or wishes. There must be something more. This is because s 318(6)(b) is concerned with when "a company is sufficiently influenced", indicating that something more is required than mere coincidence between: (a) an action by the company or its directors; and (b) the directions, instructions or wishes of another. The parties were agreed that "in accordance with" imports considerations of causation. The level of causation required by the words "in accordance with" when used in a statute is informed by the statutory context in which the words are used.

'[88] Fifthly, there is nothing in s 318(6)(b) which expressly specifies how many, or what types of, acts must be "in accordance with" the directions, instructions or wishes of another.' *Commissioner of Taxation v BHP Billiton Ltd* [2019] FCAFC 4, (2019) 366 ALR 206 at [48], [80]–[88], perThawley J

SUPPORT

Easement of

[For 76 Halsbury's Laws of England (5th Edn) (2013) paras 117, 119 see now 76 Halsbury's Laws of England (5th Edn) (2019) paras 114, 116.]

SURFACE

[For 76 Halsbury's Laws of England (5th Edn) (2013) para 17 see now 76 Halsbury's Laws of England (5th Edn) (2019) para 17.]

SURVIVE–SURVIVOR

[For 102 Halsbury's Laws of England (5th Edn) (2010) paras 317–318 see now 102 Halsbury's Laws of England (5th Edn) (2016) paras 315–316.]

SUSPECT (VERB)

Has reasonable cause to suspect

[Terrorism Act 2000, s 17: offence of making money or property available to another when the donor knows or 'has reasonable cause to suspect' that it will or may be used for the purposes of terrorism.] '[4] The question which arises on this appeal concerns the correct mean-

ing of the expression "has reasonable cause to suspect" in s 17(b). Does it mean that the accused must actually suspect, and for reasonable cause, that the money may be used for the purposes of terrorism? Or is it sufficient that on the information known to him there exists, assessed objectively, reasonable cause to suspect that that may be the use to which it is put?

...

'[6] ... Both the trial judge and the Court of Appeal (Criminal Division) concluded that the correct answer was that the words used in the statute plainly mean that it is sufficient that on the information known to the accused, there exists, assessed objectively, reasonable cause to suspect that the money may be used for the purposes of terrorism.

...

'[24] In the present case it would be an error to suppose that the form of offence-creating words adopted by Parliament result in an offence of strict liability. It is certainly true that because objectively assessed reasonable cause for suspicion is sufficient, an accused can commit this offence without knowledge or actual suspicion that the money might be used for terrorist purposes. But the accused's state of mind is not, as it is in offences which are truly of strict liability, irrelevant. The requirement that there exist objectively assessed cause for suspicion focuses attention on what information the accused had. As the Crown agreed before this court, that requirement is satisfied when, on the information available to the accused, a reasonable person would (not might or could) suspect that the money might be used for terrorism. The state of mind of such a person is, whilst clearly less culpable than that of a person who knows that the money may be used for that purpose, not accurately described as in no way blameworthy. It was for Parliament to decide whether the gravity of the threat of terrorism justified attaching criminal responsibility to such a person, but it was clearly entitled to conclude that it did. It is normal, not unusual, for a single offence to be committed by persons exhibiting different levels of culpability. The difference in culpability can, absent other aggravating features of the case, be expected to be reflected in any sentence imposed if conviction results.

'[25] For these reasons it is clear that the conclusions arrived at by the trial judge and the Court of Appeal were correct. ...' *R v Lane* [2018] UKSC 36, [2019] 1 All ER 299 at [4], [6], [24]–[25], per Lord Hughes

SUSPENSION

Grounds of suspension ... of limitation periods

[Athens Convention relating to the Carriage of Passengers and their Luggage by Sea 1974, art 16(3): the law of the court seised of the case governs the 'grounds of suspension and interruption of limitation periods'.] '[30] In my view, the words in art 16(3) of the Athens Convention, 'the grounds of suspension ... of limitation periods' are sufficiently wide to cover domestic rules which postpone the start of a limitation period as well as those which stop the clock after the limitation period has begun. I therefore agree with Lord Glennie in the judgment of the Inner House (para [17]): 'The word "suspension" ... is also apt to include the deferment or suspension of something which has not yet started.

...

'[33] ... Hirst LJ observed (obiter) [in *Higham v Stena Sealink Ltd* [1996] 3 All ER 660, [1996] 1 WLR 1107] that there were other sections in the Limitation Act 1980, such as s 32, which postpones the limitation period in the case of fraud, concealment or mistake, which might at first sight be eligible to qualify under art 16(3) of the Convention. But he went on to express the tentative view that the fact that in each case the section postponed the periods of limitation "prescribed by this Act" or words to that effect might disqualify them ([1996] 3 All ER 660 at 664, [1996] 1 WLR 1107at 1111). If in expressing that view he meant that the grounds of suspension in the lex fori were to apply under art 16(3) of the Convention only if they were framed to extend beyond the scope of the domestic limitation regime of the lex fori so as to cover limitation periods in conventions such as the Athens Convention, I must respectfully disagree. In my view, where art 16(3) speaks of the law of the court seised governing "the grounds of suspension ... of limitation *periods*" (in the plural) it was applying the grounds—such as minority or mental incapacity—which the lex fori would apply to domestic claims for personal injury, or death or loss or damage to property. Thus, the existence of a ground in a domestic limitation statute which suspended the limitation periods set out in that statute, such as s 32 of the Limitation Act 1980 (fraud, concealment or mistake) or in this appeal s 18 of the [Prescription and Limitation (Scotland) Act 1973] (legal disability by reason of non-age or unsoundness of mind) is sufficient

to bring art 16(3) into operation and extend the art 16 time bar by one year.' *Warner v Scapa Flow Charters* [2018] UKSC 52, [2019] 2 All ER 1042 at [30], [33], per Lord Hodge

SWAMP KAURI

New Zealand '[1] This appeal concerns the export of swamp kauri and products made from swamp kauri. Swamp kauri is kauri that has been buried and preserved in swamps for anywhere between 800 and 60,000 years. It is found largely in Northland in areas that were, but usually are no longer, wetlands. It is extracted almost exclusively from privately owned scrub or farm land and is of high commercial value, given its age and the size of the timber pieces that can be milled. Exports of swamp kauri increased significantly from 2010 to 2015.' *Northland Environmental Protection Society Inc v Chief Executive of the Ministry for Primary Industries* [2018] NZSC 105, [2019] 1 NZLR 257 at [1], per Glazebrook J

SYSTEMIC MĀORI DEPRIVATION

New Zealand '[40] The effects of colonisation on Māori communities are well documented. Loss of land and other tribal resources together with the destruction of traditional social structures, tikanga, culture and language preceded widescale migration from tribal rohe to urban areas. For every generation since, Māori have been disproportionately represented among the poorest, most illiterate and most criminalised in New Zealand. The entrenched asymmetry of Māori in prisons is only one of many indicators of the systemic nature of this social disadvantage. For ease of reference I will refer to this pervasive and persistent social disadvantage affecting Māori as systemic Māori deprivation.

...

'[43] Relevantly, the normative basis for recognition of systemic Māori deprivation as a mitigating sentencing factor is not dependent on racial or ethnic classification. Rather, it is the presence of systemic deprivation in the lives of Māori offenders and their whānau that may trigger the potential for a differential sentencing response. ...' *Solicitor-General v Heta* [2018] NZHC 2453, [2019] 2 NZLR 241 at [40], [43], per Whata J

T

TERM CERTAIN

[Housing Act 1988, s 21(1A)(a).] '[53] Given the foregoing discussion, it is not strictly necessary for us to decide whether Mr Grundy is right that a fixed term tenancy with a break clause allowing it to be terminated during the first year is not a tenancy for a "term certain" within the meaning of s 21(1A)(a). But, having heard argument on the point, I propose to set out my views.

'[54] The words "term certain" are not defined in either HA [Housing Act] 1985 or HA 1988 but they were used as part of the definition of a secure tenancy in HA 1985 prior to the introduction of the provisions dealing with flexible tenancies. Given that a flexible tenancy is a species of secure tenancy (see s 107A(1)), it seems reasonable to suppose that the draftsman of the amendments introduced by the Localism Act adopted that definition for the purposes of the changes made to both HA 1985 and HA 1988.

...

'[56] My reading of [the HA 1985 s 82(1)–(3)] is that a secure tenancy which is not a periodic tenancy is treated as granted for a term certain even if it can be terminated by the landlord during the term. This is made clear by the opening words of s 82(3).

'[57] Such a conclusion would accord with principle. "Term certain" is not, of course, terminology exclusive to the Housing Acts. The requirement that a tenancy should be granted for a term certain has been part of the common law for centuries. ...

...

'[59] A tenancy granted for a fixed term of, say, two years is limited by grant to a term certain of that duration notwithstanding that it may be brought to an end sooner by forfeiture or by the operation of a break clause. The word "certain" does not mean certain to last for the duration of the term. It means that the lease was granted for a term expressed to expire on a certain as opposed to an uncertain date. A lease granted for two years but with a break clause is nonetheless granted for a term certain of two years. It will end with certainty on that date regardless of any other circumstances.

...

'[65] I do not therefore accept Mr Grundy's submission that the words "term certain" are otiose in the context of s 21(1A) HA 1988. Certainty of term is a condition of every valid tenancy and the reference to a "tenancy for a term certain" in s 82(1)(a) HA 1985 was no more than the use of well-established nomenclature to describe a tenancy granted for a term of years. In formulating the provisions of s 107A(2)(a) HA 1985 and s 21(1A)(a) HA 1988 the draftsman has merely added the requirement for a two year minimum period to that definition.' *Livewest Homes Ltd v Bamber* [2019] EWCA Civ 1174, [2020] 2 All ER 181 at [53]–[54], [56]–[57], [59], [65], per Patten LJ

TESTAMENT

[For 102 Halsbury's Laws of England (5th Edn) (2010) para 1 see now 102 Halsbury's Laws of England (5th Edn) (2016) para 1.]

TESTAMENTARY

Testamentary expenses

[For 103 Halsbury's Laws of England (5th Edn) (2010) paras 1012–1013 see now 103 Halsbury's Laws of England (5th Edn) (2016) paras 1013–1014.]

THOSE IN THE LOCALITY

[Anti-social Behaviour, Crime and Policing Act 2014, s 59: public spaces protection order ('PSPO').] '[41] It is clear from the terms of the 2014 Act itself that Parliament deliberately decided not to limit, by way of a statutory definition or statutory guidance, the expression "those in the locality". The looseness of that expression is to be contrasted with the express limitation of an "interested person" who may apply under s 66 of the 2014 Act to the High Court to challenge the validity of PSPO or its variation. "Interested person" is defined in s 66(1) as "an individual who lives in the restricted area or who regularly works in or visits that area". Similarly, the obligation on a local authority under s 72 of the 2014 Act to consult before making, extending the duration of, varying or discharging a PSPO, is limited to certain persons representing the police and the community and (under s 72(4)(c)) to "the owner or occupier of land within the restricted area". Parliament plainly decided not to limit s 59(2)(a) in either of those ways.

'[42] Accordingly, while we agree with May J in *Summers* [*Summers v Richmond upon Thames London Borough Council* [2018] EWHC 782 (Admin), [2018] 1 WLR 4729, [2018] LLR 624] that the expression "those in the locality" in s 59 includes those who regularly visit or work in the locality, in addition to residents, it will depend on the precise local circumstances whether or not it extends to others.

...

'[47] We agree with May J in *Summers* at [25] that the 2014 Act gives local authorities a wide discretion to decide what behaviours are troublesome and require to be addressed within their local area. Equally, in deciding who is "in the locality" for the purpose of protection from such activities by way of a PSPO a local authority will (applying the words of May J to that issue) use its local knowledge, taking into account local conditions on the ground.

'[48] We do not consider there is any scope for narrowing the proper interpretation of the expression "those in the locality" in s 59(2)(a) on the ground that it is a criminal offence to breach a PSPO or because s 72(1) requires a local authority, in deciding whether to make, extend or vary a PSPO, to have particular regard to rights of freedom of expression and freedom of assembly in arts 10 and 11 ECHR [European Convention on Human Rights]. Any general presumption in relation to statutory provisions which criminalise conduct or activity (which was not explored in any detail before us) must be subject to the particular statutory provisions and framework in question. As regards s 72(1), its provisions are neutral on the issue of the proper interpretation of s 59(2)(a) as they pre-suppose that it is indeed lawful, where the

statutory conditions for a PSPO are satisfied, for the PSPO to interfere with rights under arts 10 and 11 ECHR.

'[49] We conclude that Ealing was correct to interpret the expression "those in the locality" in s 52(2)(a) as capable of embracing occasional visitors, and were entitled to decide on the facts that the women, their family members and supporters visiting the Centre, in addition to staff and local residents, fell within that section.' *Dulgheriu v Ealing London Borough Council (National Council for Civil Liberties (trading as Liberty) intervening)* [2019] EWCA Civ 1490, [2020] 3 All ER 545 at [41]–[42], [47]–[49], per Sir Terence Etherton MR, King and Nicola Davies LJJ

THREAT

Of legal proceedings

[For 79 Halsbury's Laws of England (5th Edn) (2014) para 557 see now 79 Halsbury's Laws of England (5th Edn) (2020) para 577.]

TOLL

Market toll

[For 71 Halsbury's Laws of England (5th Edn) (2013) paras 826–827 see now 71 Halsbury's Laws of England (5th Edn) (2020) paras 730–731.]

Toll thorough

[55 Halsbury's Laws of England (5th Edn) (2012) para 213 see now 55 Halsbury's Laws of England (5th Edn) (2019) para 241.]

Toll traverse

[55 Halsbury's Laws of England (5th Edn) (2012) para 213 see now 55 Halsbury's Laws of England (5th Edn) (2019) para 241.]

TIME IMMEMORIAL

[For 32 Halsbury's Laws of England (5th Edn) (2012) para 7 see now 32 Halsbury's Laws of England (5th Edn) (2019) para 7.]

TOTAL LOSS (MARINE INSURANCE)

[For 60 Halsbury's Laws of England (5th Edn) (2011) para 424 see now 60 Halsbury's Laws of England (5th Edn) (2018) para 402.]

TRADE EFFLUENT

[Water Industry Act 1991, s 141(1)] '[9] As the judge correctly said, the question on this issue is whether a liquid which contains a mixture of the product of trade or industry and surface water constitutes trade effluent within the meaning of the statutory definition. At [53] the judge set out the approach he would adopt to the interpretation of the statute. Mr Davies-Jones QC, on behalf of Boots, did not criticise anything that the judge had said in that respect; although he showed additional materials which would support the judge's distillation of principle. Since it is common ground that the judge was correct in setting out the principles, it is not necessary to do more than to repeat the relevant parts of his summary:

"(1) In construing the definition, the Court must strive to give it a *fully informed construction*. (2) That requires the Court to have regard to the *'context'* of the statutory provision as well as to its terms. (3) The *'context'* of a statutory provision includes its legislative history, its statutory purpose and other Acts *in pari materia*. (4) The Court must also have regard to the consequences of rival constructions. (5) The Court should presume that the legislator did <u>not</u> intend a construction which would operate unjustly or anomalously and <u>did</u> intend one which promotes consistency in the law."

...

'[13] The consequences of the judge's interpretation, [counsel for Boots] submitted, were unjust. Boots had been charged both for the drainage of surface water by reference to the area of the site; and again for part of that surface water at trade effluent rates in so far as it formed part of the mixed liquid discharged into the foul sewer.

'[14] In my judgment this involves a misreading of the definition. First, the definition in s 141 does not expressly exclude surface or storm water, whereas it does expressly exclude domestic sewage. So the threefold classification [domestic sewage, surface water and trade effluent] is not reproduced in the definition. Second, s 106 refers to at least three (and possibly four) different types of sewer. Three are expressly mentioned: a foul water sewer, a surface water sewer and a storm-water overflow sewer. The fourth is a combined sewer which is implicit in the provision in s 106(2)(b) which applies "where separate public sewers are provided for foul water and surface water". If there are no separate sewers, then necessarily there must be a combined sewer. So that classification does not replicate the threefold division. Third, the definition expressly includes liquid partly produced in the course of trade. That part of the definition which contemplates a liquid partly produced in the course of trade thus contemplates a mixture. Moreover, the definition also contemplates a different kind of mixture, viz a mixture of liquid and suspended particles of matter.' *Boots UK Ltd v Severn Trent Water Ltd* [2018] EWCA Civ 2795, [2019] 3 All ER 371 at [9], [13]–[14], per Lewison LJ

TRADE UNION

[For 40 Halsbury's Laws of England (5th Edn) (2009) para 846 et seq see now 41 Halsbury's Laws of England (5th Edn) (2014) para 891 et seq.]

TRANSIT

[For 91 Halsbury's Laws of England (5th Edn) (2012) para 257 see now 91 Halsbury's Laws of England (5th Edn) (2019) para 258.]

TREASURE TROVE

[For 29 Halsbury's Laws of England (5th Edn) (2014) para 297 see now 29 Halsbury's Laws of England (5th Edn) (2019) para 292.]

TRIBUNAL

The word 'tribunal' is ... used in a wide variety of circumstances. The term 'tribunal' originally meant the raised platform provided for a magistrate's seat, from the Latin 'tribunus' or head of a tribe. The term developed to mean a body established to settle certain types of dispute or a court of justice. (24A Halsbury's Laws of England (5th Edn) (2019) para 6)

TRUST

[For 98 Halsbury's Laws of England (5th Edn) (2013) paras 1, 5, 24 see now 98 Halsbury's Laws of England (5th Edn) (2019) paras 1, 5, 24.]

Constructive trust

[For 98 Halsbury's Laws of England (5th Edn) (2013) para 124 see now 98 Halsbury's Laws of England (5th Edn) (2019) para 114.]

Discretionary trust

[For 98 Halsbury's Laws of England (5th Edn) (2013) para 94 see now 98 Halsbury's Laws of England (5th Edn) (2019) para 94.]

Executed or executory trust

[For 98 Halsbury's Laws of England (5th Edn) (2013) para 33 see now 98 Halsbury's Laws of England (5th Edn) (2019) para 33.]

Precatory trust

[For 98 Halsbury's Laws of England (5th Edn) (2013) para 34 see now 98 Halsbury's Laws of England (5th Edn) (2019) para 34.]

Private trust

[For 98 Halsbury's Laws of England (5th Edn) (2013) para 38 see now 98 Halsbury's Laws of England (5th Edn) (2019) para 38.]

Public trust

[For 98 Halsbury's Laws of England (5th Edn) (2013) para 37 see now 98 Halsbury's Laws of England (5th Edn) (2019) para 37.]

Resulting trust

[For 98 Halsbury's Laws of England (5th Edn) (2013) para 132 see now 98 Halsbury's Laws of England (5th Edn) (2019) para 131.]

Secret trust

[For 98 Halsbury's Laws of England (5th Edn) (2013) paras 35, 87 see now 98 Halsbury's Laws of England (5th Edn) (2019) paras 35, 87.]

Voluntary trust

[For 98 Halsbury's Laws of England (5th Edn) (2013) para 36 see now 98 Halsbury's Laws of England (5th Edn) (2019) para 36.]

TRUSTEE

Bare trustee

[For 98 Halsbury's Laws of England (5th Edn) (2013) para 195 see now 98 Halsbury's Laws of England (5th Edn) (2019) para 194.]

U

UNABLE

Unable to admit or deny

[CPR 16.5(1): in his defence, the defendant must state—(b) which allegations he is unable to admit or deny, but which he requires the claimant to prove.] '[49] In my judgment, a number of factors point towards the conclusion that a defendant is "unable to admit or deny" an allegation within the meaning of r 16.5(1)(b) where the truth or falsity of the allegation is neither within his actual knowledge (including attributed knowledge in the case of a corporate defendant) nor capable of rapid ascertainment from documents or other sources of information at his ready disposal. In particular, there is no general obligation to make reasonable enquiries of third parties at this very early stage of the litigation. Instead, the purpose of the defence is to define and narrow the issues between the parties in general terms, on the basis of knowledge and information which the defendant has readily available to him during the short period afforded by the rules for filing his defence.' *SPI North Ltd v Swiss Post International (UK) Ltd* [2019] EWCA Civ 7, [2019] 2 All ER 512 at [49], per Henderson LJ

UNABLE–UNWILLING

Canada [Refugee status was available to certain persons who inter alia were unable or unwilling to seek the protection of their home state.] 'I would agree with the court below that "unable" and "unwilling" have different meanings, which are fairly apparent on their face. One can say that "unable" means physically or literally unable, and that "unwilling" simply means that protection from the state is not wanted for some reason, though not impossible. This would, at first sight, seem to be a clear distinction, but as we shall see it has become somewhat blurred... .

'With respect to "unable", it would appear that physical or literal impossibility is *one* means of triggering the definition, but it is not the *only* way. Thus ineffective state protection is encompassed within the concept of "unable" and "unwilling", and I am left with the conclusion that the appellant here could have pursued his claim under either category.' *Canada (A-G) v Ward* [1993] 2 SCR 689 at 717, 718, 719, per La Forest J

UNCONSCIONABLE BARGAIN

[For 22 Halsbury's Laws of England (5th Edn) (2012) para 298 see now 22 Halsbury's Laws of England (5th Edn) (2019) para 98.]

[For 76 Halsbury's Laws of England (5th Edn) (2013) para 850 see now 22 Halsbury's Laws of England (5th Edn) (2012) para 298; 88 Halsbury's Laws of England (5th Edn) (2019) para 457.]

UNDERTAKING

[Patents Act 1977, s 40(1): employee entitled to compensation where he has made an invention belonging to the employer for which a patent has been granted and the patent is (having regard among other things to the size and nature of the employer's undertaking) of outstanding benefit to the employer.] '[41] In this context I understand the word "undertaking" to mean simply a unit or entity which carries on a business activity, and here the undertaking of interest is that of the company or other entity which employs the inventor. In many cases the identification of that undertaking will be comparatively straightforward. It will be the whole or, if it is divided into economic units, the relevant unit of the employer's business. So, as Aldous J observed in *Memco-Med Ltd's Patent* [1992] RPC 403 at 414 and I agree, the undertaking may be the whole or a division of the employer's business.' *Shanks v Unilever plc* [2019] UKSC 45, [2020] 2 All ER 733 at [41], per Lord Kitchin

UNDUE INFLUENCE

A court of equity will set aside a transaction entered into as a result of conduct which, though not amounting to actual fraud or deceit, is contrary to good conscience. Such conduct includes the procurement of a gift or other benefit by the exertion of undue influence and the making of an unconscionable bargain. Many of the cases in which undue influence arises relate to gifts, but the same principles apply to contracts where one party (A) may be said to have exercised undue influence over another party (B) in order to induce B to enter into the contract. (22 Halsbury's Laws of England (5th Edn) (2019) para 94)

A party to a transaction, though consenting to it, may not give a free consent because he is exposed to such influence from the other party as to deprive him of the free use of his judgment. In such a case equity will set the transaction aside, and, if property has passed, will order restitution, and, if necessary, follow the property into the hands of innocent third parties. In appropriate cases there may also be an account of profits or an award of fair compensation where the taking of an account would not do practical justice between the parties. The doctrine of undue influence is capable of extending to a situation where the wrongdoer, for his own reasons, wanted the complainant to deal with a third party.

Although the wisdom of the practice of making a classification of cases of undue influence has been questioned, a distinction should still be drawn between actual undue influence and presumed undue influence. (47 Halsbury's Laws of England (5th Edn) (2014) para 18)

A will or part of a will may be set aside as having been obtained by undue influence. If the execution of the will is not in dispute the party alleging undue influence has the right to begin, and must discharge the burden of proof by clear evidence that the influence was in fact exercised. ... To constitute undue influence there must be coercion; pressure of whatever character, whether acting on the fears or the hopes, if so exerted as to overpower the volition without convincing the judgment, is a species of restraint under which no valid will can be made.
...

A person may exercise an unbounded influence over another, which may be a very bad influence, without its being undue influence in the legal sense of the word. Undue influence may be found against a person who had died before the execution of the will, on the ground that the testatrix was under that person's complete control until his death, and was therefore rendered incapable of making a fresh will free from such undue influence. (102 Halsbury's Laws of England (5th Edn) (2016) para 56)

(1) A person shall be guilty of a corrupt practice if he is guilty of undue influence.

(2) A person shall be guilty of undue influence—

(a) if he, directly or indirectly, by himself or by any other person on his behalf, makes use of or threatens to make use of any force, violence or restraint, or inflicts or threatens to inflict, by himself or by any other person, any temporal or spiritual injury, damage, harm or loss upon or against any person in order to induce or compel that person to vote or refrain from voting, or on account of that person having voted or refrained from voting; or

(b) if, by abduction, duress or any fraudulent device or contrivance, he impedes or prevents, or intends to impede or prevent, the free exercise of the franchise by an elector or proxy for an elector, or thereby compels, induces or prevails upon, or intends so to compel, induce or prevail upon, an elector or proxy for an elector either to vote or to refrain from voting.

(Representation of the People Act 1983, s 115(2) (as amended by the Electoral Administration Act 2006, s 39 and the Local Electoral Administration and Registration Services (Scotland) Act 2006, s 14))

'It is said that ... jurymen, not being men with legal minds, are extremely likely to fall into great error, and might think undue influence was established where a man who was not of strong mind, united to a woman of very strong mind, should be led to devise away large family estates from his own relations to hers, whereas in truth that would not of itself be undue influence according to the construction which the law would put upon that term. Undue influence, in order to render a will void, must be an influence which can justly be described, by a person looking at the matter judicially, to have caused the execution of a paper pretending to express a testator's mind, but which really did not express his mind, but expressed something

else, something which he did not really mean....
I am prepared to say that influence, in order to
be undue within the meaning of any rule of law
which would make it sufficient to vitiate a will,
must be an influence exercised either by coercion or fraud.... In order to come to the conclusion that a will has been obtained by coercion, it
is not necessary to establish that actual violence
has been used or even threatened.... Imaginary
terrors may have been created sufficient to
deprive him [the testator] of free agency.... So
as to fraud. If a wife, by falsehood, raises
prejudices in the mind of her husband against
those who would be the natural objects of his
bounty, and by contrivance keeps him from
intercourse with his relatives ... such contrivance may, perhaps, be equivalent to positive
fraud.... It is, however, extremely difficult to
state in the abstract what acts will constitute
undue influence.... it is sufficient to say, that
allowing a fair latitude of construction, they
must range themselves under one or other of
these heads—coercion or fraud.' *Boyse v Ross-
borough, Boyse v Colclough* (1857) 6 HL Cas 2
at 33–34, 48–49, per Lord Cranworth LC

'It is obvious that when a mob has possession of a town, and beats those who come to the
polling booth, or otherwise intimidates them,
that is plainly exercising intimidation, and is
undue influence, and in my opinion it is the very
worst kind of undue influence. It is very bad for
a master to threaten and dismiss his men: it is
very bad in a landlord to eject his tenant. All
these are very bad, improper acts, but they are
justifiable acts if it were not for the effect they
would produce upon the freedom of election,
because they have a right to do so if it were not
done to interfere with the freedom of election.'
Stafford (Borough) Case, Chawner v Meller
(1869) 21 LT 210 at 211, per Blackburn J

'We are all familiar with the use of the word
"influence"; we say that one person has an
unbounded influence over another, and we
speak of evil influences and good influences,
but it is not because one person has unbounded
influence over another that therefore when exercised, even though it may be very bad indeed,
it is undue influence in the legal sense of the
word. To give you some illustrations of what I
mean, a young man may be caught in the toils of
a harlot, who makes use of her influence to
induce him to make a will in her favour, to the
exclusion of his relatives. It is unfortunately
quite natural that a man so entangled should
yield to that influence and confer large bounties
on the person with whom he has been brought

into such relation; yet the law does not attempt
to guard against those contingencies. A man
may be the companion of another, and may
encourage him in evil courses, and so obtain
what is called an undue influence over him, and
the consequence may be a will made in his
favour. But that again, shocking as it is, perhaps
even worse than the other, will not amount to
undue influence. To be undue influence in the
eye of the law there must be—to sum it up in a
word—coercion.' *Wingrove v Wingrove* (1885)
11 PD 81 at 82, per Hannen P

'The expression "undue influence" is, to my
mind, one of ambiguous purport. It is not
confined to those cases in which the influence is
exerted to secure a benefit for the person exert-
ing it, but extends also to cases in which a
person of imperfect judgment is placed or
places himself under the direction of one pos-
sessing not only greater experience but also
such force as that which is inherent in such a
relation as that between a father and his own
child.' *Bullock v Lloyds Bank Ltd* [1954]
3 All ER 726 at 729, per Vaisey J; see also
[1955] Ch 317

'The doctrine of undue influence ... merely
arises out of the fact that, while equity approves
of gifts by a father to a child, and therefore
invented the doctrine of presumption of ad-
vancement, so on the other hand it dislikes and
distrusts gifts by a child to a parent, and
therefore invented the presumption of undue
influence. Both these presumptions merely
mean, in our opinion, that in the absence of
evidence, or if the evidence on each side be
evenly balanced, in the first case equity will
presume that the parent who puts property in a
child's name intends to make a gift or give a
benefit to the child, while on the other hand
money or property passing from the child to the
parent cannot be retained by the latter, because
it is assumed that so unnatural a transaction
would have been brought about by undue use of
the natural influence that a parent has over a
child, and of the filial obedience which a child
owes to his parent. Both presumptions may be
rebutted; each is in truth a convenient device in
aid of decisions on facts often lost in obscurity,
whether owing to the lapse of time or the death
of the parties.' *Re Pauling's Settlement Trusts,
Younghusband v Coutts & Co* [1963] 3 All ER
1 at 9, CA, per cur

'What has to be proved to raise the presumption of undue influence is first a gift so substantial (or doubtless otherwise of such a nature)
that it cannot prima facie be reasonably ac-

counted for on the ground of the ordinary motives on which ordinary men act; and secondly, a relationship between donor and donee in which the donor has such confidence and trust in the donee as to place the donee in a position to exercise undue influence over the donor in making such a gift. This is just plain common sense to which the ordinary man in the street would readily arrive. In order to provide remedies for abuses of relations of trust and confidence where from the nature of the relationship proof of abuse might be difficult, if not impossible, lawyers established a strong foundation for the presumption of undue influence on public policy. But the courts have refused, rightly in my respectful opinion, to define either undue influence or such relationships of trust and confidence. To do otherwise would be to assume a power of divination more than human, and might exclude from relief for undue influence cases where such relief should readily be available to serve the purpose of the law. Thus both undue influence and those relationships of trust and confidence which raise the presumption are left, unlimited by definition, wide open for identification on the facts and in all the circumstances of each particular case as it arises. As the law has been developed and become established, the presumption seems to me in general at any rate to amount substantially in practice now to no more than the passing of the onus of proof where the amount (or nature) of the gift and the relationship of trust and confidence would, in the ordinary course of a trial, pass, independently of any special formulation of the raising of the presumption.' *Re Craig (decd), Meneces v Middleton* [1970] 2 All ER 390 at 395–396, per Ungoed-Thomas J

'There is no precisely defined law setting limits to the equitable jurisdiction of a court to relieve against undue influence. This is the world of doctrine, not of neat and tidy rules. The courts of equity have developed a body of learning enabling relief to be granted where the law has to treat the transaction as unimpeachable unless it can be held to have been procured by undue influence. It is the unimpeachability at law of a disadvantageous transaction which is the starting point from which the court advances to consider whether the transaction is the product merely of one's own folly or of the undue influence exercised by another. A court in the exercise of this equitable jurisdiction is a court of conscience. Definition is a poor instrument when used to determine whether a transaction is

or is not unconscionable: this is a question which depends on the particular facts of the case.' *National Westminster Bank plc v Morgan* [1985] 1 All ER 821 at 831, HL, per Lord Scarman

'Undue influence is of two kinds: (1) express or, as it is nowadays more usually known, actual undue influence; and (2) that which in certain circumstances is presumed from a confidential relationship, by which in this context is meant a relationship wherein one party has ceded such a degree of trust and confidence as to require the other, on grounds of public policy, to show that it has not been betrayed or abused. In cases where there is no confidential relationship actual undue influence must be proved. In cases where there is such a relationship it is sometimes alleged, but need not be proved and may never have occurred… . At least since the time of Lord Eldon LC, equity has steadfastly and wisely refused to put limits on the relationships to which the presumption can apply. Nor do I believe that it has ever been distinctly held that there is any relationship from which it cannot in any circumstances be dissociated. But there are several well-defined relationships, such as parent and child, superior and member of a sisterhood, doctor and patient and solicitor and client, to which the presumption is, as it were, presumed to apply unless the contrary is proved. In such relationships it would seem that you only have to look at the relative status of the parties in order to presume that the requisite degree of trust and confidence is there. But there are many and various other relationships lacking a recognisable status to which the presumption has been held to apply. In all of these relationships, whether of the first kind or the second, the principle is the same. It is that the degree of trust and confidence is such that the party in whom it is reposed, either because he is or has become an adviser of the other or because he has been entrusted with the management of his affairs or everyday needs or for some other reason, is in a position to influence him into effecting the transaction of which complaint is later made.' *Goldsworthy v Brickell* [1987] 1 All ER 853 at 865, CA, per Nourse LJ

'To make a good will a man must be a free agent. But all influences are not unlawful. Persuasion, appeals to the affections or ties of kindred, to a sentiment of gratitude for past services, or pity for future destitution, or the like, these are all legitimate, and may be fairly pressed on a testator. On the other hand, pressure of whatever character, whether acting on the fears or the hopes, if so exerted as to overpower the volition without convincing the judgment, is a species of restraint under which no valid will can be made. Importunity or threats, such as the testator has not the courage to resist, moral command asserted and yielded to for the sake of peace and quiet, or of escaping from distress of mind or social discomfort, these, if carried to a degree in which the free play of the testator's judgment, discretion or wishes, is overborne, will constitute undue influence, though no force is either used or threatened. In a word, a testator may be led but not driven; and his will must be the offspring of his own volition, and not the record of someone else's.' *Hall v Hall* (1868) LR 1 P & D 481 at 482, per cur

[See also *Re T* [1992] 4 All ER 649, CA.]

'Leaving aside proof of manifest disadvantage, we think that a person relying on a plea of actual undue influence must show: (a) that the other party to the transaction (or someone who induced the transaction for his own benefit) had the capacity to influence the complainant; (b) that the influence was exercised; (c) that its exercise was undue; (d) that its exercise brought about the transaction.' *Bank of Credit and Commerce International SA v Aboody* [1992] 4 All ER 955 at 976 CA, per cur

'A person who has been induced to enter into a transaction by the undue influence of another (the wrongdoer) is entitled to set that transaction aside as against the wrongdoer. Such undue influence is either actual or presumed. In *Bank of Credit and Commerce International SA v Aboody* [1988] 4 All ER 955 at 964, [1990] 1 QB 923 at 953 the Court of Appeal helpfully adopted the following classification.

Class 1: actual undue influence. In these cases it is necessary for the claimant to prove affirmatively that the wrongdoer exerted undue influence on the complainant to enter into the particular transaction which is impugned.

Class 2: presumed undue influence. In these cases the complainant only has to show, in the first instance, that there was a relationship of trust and confidence between the complainant and the wrongdoer of such a nature that it is fair to presume that the wrongdoer abused that relationship in procuring the complainant to enter into the impugned transaction. In class 2 cases therefore there is no need to produce evidence that actual undue influence was exerted in relation to the particular transaction impugned: once a confidential relationship has been proved, the burden then shifts to the wrongdoer to prove that the complainant entered into the impugned transaction freely, for example by showing that the complainant had independent advice. Such a confidential relationship can be established in two ways, viz:

Class 2A. Certain relationships (for example solicitor and client, medical advisor and patient) as a matter of law raise the presumption that undue influence has been exercised.

Class 2B. Even if there is no relationship falling within class 2A, if the complainant proves the de facto existence of a relationship under which the complainant generally reposed trust and confidence in the wrongdoer, the existence of such relationship raises the presumption of undue influence. In a class 2B case therefore, in the absence of evidence disproving undue influence, the complainant will succeed in setting aside the impugned transaction merely by proof that the complainant reposed trust and confidence in the wrongdoer without having to prove that the wrongdoer exerted actual undue influence or otherwise abused such trust and confidence in relation to the particular transaction impugned.' *Barclays Bank plc v O'Brien* [1993] 4 All ER 417 at 423, HL, per Lord Browne-Wilkinson

UNDULY HARSH

[Nationality, Immigration and Asylum Act 2002, s 117C(5); Immigration Rules, para 399. Deportation of foreign criminals; exception where effect of deportation of a parent on a child would be 'unduly harsh'.] '[23] On the other hand the expression "unduly harsh" seems clearly intended to introduce a higher hurdle than that of "reasonableness" under s 117B(6), taking account of the public interest in the deportation of foreign criminals. Further the word "unduly" implies an element of comparison. It assumes that there is a "due" level of "harshness", that is a level which may be acceptable or justifiable in the relevant context. "Unduly" implies something going beyond that level. The relevant context is that set by s 117C(1), that is the public interest in the deportation of foreign criminals. One is looking for a degree of harshness going beyond what would necessarily be involved for any child faced with the deportation of a parent. What it does not require in my view (and subject to the discussion of the cases in the next section) is a balancing of relative levels of severity of the parent's offence, other than is inherent in the distinction drawn by the section itself by reference to length of sentence. Nor (contrary to the view of the Court of Appeal in *IT (Jamaica) v Secretary of State for the Home Dept* [2016] EWCA Civ 932, [2017] 1 WLR 240 (paras [55], [64])) can it be equated with a requirement to show "very compelling reasons". That would be in effect to replicate the additional test applied by s 117C(6) with respect to sentences of four years or more.

...

'[27] Authoritative guidance as to the meaning of "unduly harsh" in this context was given by the Upper Tribunal (McCloskey J President and Upper Tribunal Judge Perkins) in *MK (Sierra Leone) v Secretary of State for the Home Dept, MK (section 55 – tribunal options) Sierra Leone* [2015] UKUT 223 (IAC), [2015] INLR 563 (para [46]), a decision given on 15 April 2015. They referred to the "evaluative assessment" required of the tribunal:

"By way of self-direction, we are mindful that 'unduly harsh' does not equate with uncomfortable, inconvenient, undesirable or merely difficult. Rather, it poses a considerably more elevated threshold. 'Harsh' in this context, denotes something severe, or bleak. It is the antithesis of pleasant or comfortable. Furthermore, the addition of the adverb 'unduly' raises an already elevated standard still higher."

...

'[33] However, when one comes to the actual decision of Judge Southern in *KO*, it is not clear that his approach was materially different from that of the President in *MK* or indeed the tribunal in *MAB* [*MAB (para 399; 'unduly harsh')* [2015] UKUT 435 (IAC)]. He adopted with one qualification the guidance in *MAB* as to the meaning of [the] "unduly harsh" test:

"The consequences for an individual will be 'harsh' if they are 'severe' or 'bleak' and they will be 'unduly' so if they are 'inordinately' or 'excessively' harsh taking into account all of the circumstances of the individual. Although I would add, of course, that 'all of the circumstances' includes the criminal history of the person facing deportation." (para [26])'

KO (Nigeria) v Secretary of State for the Home Department (Equality and Human Rights Commission intervening) [2018] UKSC 53, [2019] 1 All ER 675 at [23], [27], [33], per Lord Carnwath

UNLAWFUL ACT MANSLAUGHTER

Canada [Criminal Code, RSC 1985, c C-46, s 222.] '**25** The *actus reus* of unlawful act manslaughter under s 222(5)(a) requires the Crown to prove that the accused committed an unlawful act and that the unlawful act caused death (*R v Creighton* [1993] 3 SCR 3, at pp 42–43; *R v DeSousa* [1992] 2 SCR 944, at pp 959 and 961–962). The underlying unlawful act is described as the "predicate" offence (*DeSousa*, at p 956; *Creighton*, at p 42). The predicate offence in Ms Javanmardi's case is administering the intravenous injection contrary to s 31 of Quebec's Medical Act, a strict liability offence.

'**26** There has been some uncertainty around whether the Crown must prove that the predicate offence was "objectively dangerous" (see Larry C. Wilson, "Too Many Manslaughters" (2007), 52 Crim LQ 433, at p 459 citing Isabel Grant, Dorothy Chunn and Christine Boyle, *The Law of Homicide* (1994), at pp 4-15, 4-16 and 4-20; Stanley Yeo, "The Fault Elements for Involuntary Manslaughter: Some Lessons From Downunder" (2000), 43 Crim LQ 291, at p 293). In my view, the "objective dangerousness" requirement adds nothing to the analysis that is not captured within the fault element of unlawful act manslaughter — objective foreseeability of the risk of bodily harm that is neither trivial nor transitory (*Creighton*, at pp 44–45). An unlawful act, accompanied by objective foreseeability of the risk of bodily harm that is neither trivial nor transitory, is an objectively dangerous act.

...

'**30** As a result, the *actus reus* of unlawful act manslaughter is satisfied by proof beyond a reasonable doubt that the accused committed an unlawful act that caused death. There is no independent requirement of objective dangerousness.' *R v Javanmardi* [2019] SCJ No 54, 2019 SCC 54 at paras 25–26, 30, per Abella J

UNSEAWORTHY

[For 7 Halsbury's Laws of England (5th Edn) (2015) para 420 et seq see now 7 Halsbury's Laws of England (5th Edn) (2020) para 224 et seq.]

UNTRUE STATEMENT

New Zealand [Securities Act 1978, s 56(1): Compensation for loss or damage sustained by reason of an untrue statement. Section 55(a): a statement included in an advertisement or registered prospectus is deemed to be untrue if (i) it is misleading in the form and context in which it is included; or (ii) it is misleading by reason of the omission of a particular which is material to the statement in the form and context in which it is included.]

'[77] The definition of "untrue" in s 55(a) is very broad. It is clear that at least s 55(a)(ii) extends the meaning of the term "untrue statement". The term "misleading" is used in both (i) and (ii) of s 55(a). The breadth of the term "misleading" is illustrated by reference to s 37A(1)(b), which refers to a prospectus being false or misleading "by reason of failing to refer, or give proper emphasis, to adverse circumstances". Although those words do not appear in s 55(a), we consider a broad interpretation of the term "misleading" is appropriate. Because of the breadth of the definition in s 55(a), we do not consider that it makes any difference (at least for the purposes of the present appeal) whether it is seen as an exhaustive definition or not. We will therefore treat the definition as exhaustive for the purposes of this judgment.

'[78] We do note, however, that the term "untrue statement" and the definition in s 55(a) must be interpreted in the context of the Act and its investor protection purpose. This means that, to be an untrue statement in terms of s 56(1), any statement must be on a topic that may be relevant (either on its own or in combination with other considerations) to a decision to invest. Statements (even if incorrect) that are incapable of being relevant to an investment decision will not be untrue statements for the purpose of s 56(1). For example, trivial errors, such as an error in the middle name or address of a director or a clear typographical error, are unlikely to be capable of being relevant to an investment decision.

...

'[80] ... A claim that a prospectus is, in its entirety, an untrue statement will be able to be substantiated only if it can be shown that statements in (or omissions from) the prospectus have a cumulative effect, making the overall document misleading. While such an argument may be broadly described as an argument that the prospectus itself is an untrue statement, the reality is that it is unlikely to be successful unless it is supported by identified misleading statements or omissions.

'[81] The High Court found that the failure to achieve the FY04 revenue forecast was not material and, at least implicitly, that it was not therefore an untrue statement. The Court of Appeal accepted that a statement could be an untrue statement under s 55(a)(i) whether or not it was material. The respondents submit that the High Court was correct and that a statement is not an untrue statement if it is not materially untrue.

'[82] There is nothing in the wording of s 55(a) that requires that a statement be misleading to a material extent. Section 55(a)(i) uses the term "misleading" without any reference to materiality. It is true that s 55(a)(ii) refers to a statement that is misleading by reason of the omission of a particular which is material to the statement. That does introduce the word "material", but not as a qualifier of the word "misleading". Rather, it is a qualifier of "a particular". The effect of para (ii) is that a statement that is otherwise true can become an untrue statement for the purposes of s 56(1) if a particular is omitted and the particular that is omitted is such that its omission makes the otherwise true statement misleading. There is nothing in s 55(a)(ii) that supports the proposition that a misleading statement will not breach s 55(a)(i) unless it is misleading to a material extent.

'[83] In the present case, Mr Houghton argues that the FY04 revenue forecast was an untrue statement. To the extent that Mr Houghton relies on s 55(a)(i), we, like the Court of Appeal, do not think there is any requirement that an untrue statement be misleading to a material extent. All that is required is that the statement is misleading in the form and context in which it is included in the prospectus.'
Houghton v Saunders [2018] NZSC 74, [2019] 1 NZLR 1 at [77]–[78], [80]–[83], per Elias CJ, Glazebrook, O'Regan, Arnold and Kós JJ

USAGE

[For 32 Halsbury's Laws of England (5th Edn) (2012) para 50 see now 32 Halsbury's Laws of England (5th Edn) (2019) para 50.]

USER PRINCIPLE

New Zealand '[12] It was common ground that damages for infringement were to be assessed by the application of the user principle which is a technique for assessing damages in circumstances where the right holder neither sells nor licenses production of its work. As the Judge explained:

[379] It is plain from the authorities and the parties' positions that the user principle is the approach to be adopted in determining relief when it is not possible to establish a normal synchronisation licence fee. The threshold has been met for the user principle to apply, because Eight Mile Style would not have licensed *Lose Yourself* for use in the National Party's election advertising and the National Party was unlikely to have negotiated a licence with Eight Mile Style.

(Footnote omitted).

...

[26] The object of damages is to compensate for loss or injury. The general rule in relation to economic torts is that the measure of damages is to be, so far as possible, that sum of money which will put the injured party in the same position as that party would have been if it had not sustained the wrong. Where intellectual property rights relating to a product are infringed, the measure of damages will vary depending upon the manner in which the holder of the right chooses to exploit the right.

[27] Hence, where the benefit of the right is realised through the sale of a product and infringement results in a diversion of sales, the measure of damages will normally be the profit which would have been realised by the owner of the intellectual property right (IPR) if the sales had been made by him. By contrast where IPRs are exploited through the granting of licences for royalty payments, and an infringer uses the right without a licence, the measure of the damages for infringement will be the sums which the IPR holder would have received by way of royalty. Those alternative modes of exploitation comprise the first and second scenarios identified in Lord Wilberforce's well-known analysis in *General Tire & Rubber Co v Firestone Tyre & Rubber Co Ltd* [[1975] 1 WLR 819, HL, at 824–825].

'[28] If neither of those scenarios applies, recourse is generally had to the approach known as the "user principle." This involves the assessment of a notional licence fee or royalty, being the price that the IPR holder would reasonably have charged for permission or authorisation to carry out the infringing act. ...

...

'[38] Mr Arthur argued that the user principle is not restitutionary. User damages are compensation for loss, albeit not loss of a conventional kind. He contended that by classifying the user principle as partly restitutionary the Court inappropriately invoked an unjust enrichment concept and a notion of forcing a defendant to disgorge wrongful gains.

'[39] Mr Williams for Eight Mile did not contest the substance of that criticism. He pointed out that user principle damages have sometimes been said to be restitutionary in the sense that they compensate the owner of a valuable right for the loss of the value of its exercise. However he accepted that the orthodox view is now that user damages are compensatory in nature, a view we share.' *New Zealand National Party v Eight Mile Style, LLC* [2018] NZCA 596, [2019] 2 NZLR 352 at [12], [26]–[28], [38]–[39], per Brown J

V

VEIN

[For 76 Halsbury's Laws of England (5th Edn) (2013) para 14 see now 76 Halsbury's Laws of England (5th Edn) (2019) para 14.]

VERDICT

[For 61 Halsbury's Laws of England (5th Edn) (2010) para 847 see now 61A Halsbury's Laws of England (5th Edn) (2018) para 256.]

VEST

[For 102 Halsbury's Laws of England (5th Edn) (2010) para 413 see now 102 Halsbury's Laws of England (5th Edn) (2016) para 412.]

VIOLENCE

See also DOMESTIC VIOLENCE

[For 60 Halsbury's Laws of England (5th Edn) (2011) para 553 see now 60 Halsbury's Laws of England (5th Edn) (2018) para 530.]

W

WAIFS

[For 29 Halsbury's Laws of England (5th Edn) (2014) para 285 see now 29 Halsbury's Laws of England (5th Edn) (2019) para 290.]

WAR

[For 3 Halsbury's Laws of England (5th Edn) (2011) para 6 see now 3 Halsbury's Laws of England (5th Edn) (2019) para 6.]

WARD OF COURT

[For 9 Halsbury's Laws of England (5th Edn) (2012) para 264 see now 9 Halsbury's Laws of England (5th Edn) (2017) para 301.]

WARRANTY

[For 22 Halsbury's Laws of England (5th Edn) (2012) para 557 see now 22 Halsbury's Laws of England (5th Edn) (2019) para 348.]

Insurance generally

[For 60 Halsbury's Laws of England (5th Edn) (2011) para 114 see now 60 Halsbury's Laws of England (5th Edn) (2018) para 91.]

Marine insurance

[For 60 Halsbury's Laws of England (5th Edn) (2011) para 114n see now 60 Halsbury's Laws of England (5th Edn) (2018) para 91 n 2.]

Sale of goods

[For 91 Halsbury's Laws of England (5th Edn) (2012) paras 64–65 see now 91 Halsbury's Laws of England (5th Edn) (2019) paras 63–64.]

WASTE

[For 91 Halsbury's Laws of England (5th Edn) (2012) para 887 see now 91 Halsbury's Laws of England (5th Edn) (2019) para 776.]

Equitable waste

[For 91 Halsbury's Laws of England (5th Edn) (2012) para 898 see now 91 Halsbury's Laws of England (5th Edn) (2019) para 785.]

Meliorating waste

[For 91 Halsbury's Laws of England (5th Edn) (2012) para 894 see now 91 Halsbury's Laws of England (5th Edn) (2019) para 781.]

Permissive waste

[For 91 Halsbury's Laws of England (5th Edn) (2012) para 896 see now 91 Halsbury's Laws of England (5th Edn) (2019) para 783.]

Voluntary waste

[For 91 Halsbury's Laws of England (5th Edn) (2012) para 888 see now 91 Halsbury's Laws of England (5th Edn) (2019) para 777.]

WAYLEAVE

[For 76 Halsbury's Laws of England (5th Edn) (2013) para 335 see now 76 Halsbury's Laws of England (5th Edn) (2019) para 332.]

WILL

[For 102 Halsbury's Laws of England (5th Edn) (2010) para 1 see now 102 Halsbury's Laws of England (5th Edn) (2016) para 1.]

Informal or nuncupative will

[For 102 Halsbury's Laws of England (5th Edn) (2010) para 81 see now 102 Halsbury's Laws of England (5th Edn) (2016) para 81.]

Mutual wills

New Zealand

'[17] Section 30 of the Wills Act 2007 has codified the equitable doctrine of mutual wills.

However, Lorraine's Will and the Second Will were executed before the Wills Act 2007 came into force. This case is therefore to be determined by applying the equitable doctrine of mutual wills as set out in *Lewis v Cotton* [[2001] 2 NZLR 21, CA]. In that case, the Court of Appeal observed that while a will can always be revoked, where non-revocation has been contractually promised, the executors and trustees of any replacement will may be required to hold affected assets upon a constructive trust in terms of the revoked will. The origin of this doctrine is in cases of joint wills, that is, a will signed by two testators. Such a document would ordinarily be read as two wills with the mutual intention that neither should be revoked.

'[18] The relevant promise for the purposes of the doctrine of mutual wills may be either to not revoke a will at any time whether secretly or openly, or to not revoke a will secretly during the other will maker's lifetime and to not revoke it at all after the other will maker's death. However, the crux of the matter is not the non-revocation promise but rather the obligation to not deal with property contrary to the agreement or understanding.

'[19] The Court of Appeal in *Lewis v Cotton* held that the courts are "very slow" to find mutual wills simply because two parties have made corresponding or mirror wills. More is needed to satisfy the doctrine. ...

...

'[27] Thus, the equitable doctrine of mutual wills recognises that the executors and trustees of a will may be required to hold affected assets upon a constructive trust in terms of a revoked will. The doctrine applies where:

(a) there is an underlying consultation and coordination between two testators which resulted in an agreement or an arrangement as to how they would make their respective wills;

(b) the two testators made wills consistent with their agreement or arrangement;

(c) there is a contract or mutual understanding (intended to bind each testator to a future course of action) that neither testator would deal with the property in a manner inconsistent with the agreement or arrangement (and therefore the provisions of the corresponding wills); and

(d) one of the testators has died without revoking their will.'

McNeish v McArthur [2019] NZHC 3281, [2020] 2 NZLR 287 at [17]–[19], [27], per Doogue J

WITHOUT ISSUE

[For 102 Halsbury's Laws of England (5th Edn) (2010) para 442 see now 102 Halsbury's Laws of England (5th Edn) (2016) para 450.]

WORD

[For 102 Halsbury's Laws of England (5th Edn) (2010) para 247 see now 102 Halsbury's Laws of England (5th Edn) (2016) para 245.]

WORKER

[Delete the entry for *Gilham v Ministry of Justice* [2017] EWCA Civ 2220, [2018] 3 All ER 521 and substitute the following.]

[Employment Rights Act 1996, ss 191, 230(3): whether district judge was a 'worker' and thus able to claim whistle-blower's protection.] '[1] This case is about the employment status of district judges, but it could apply to the holder of any judicial office. The issue is whether a district judge qualifies as a "worker" or a "person in Crown employment" for the purpose of the protection given to whistle-blowers under Pt IVA of the Employment Rights Act 1996 ("the 1996 Act"). If a district judge does not on the face of it qualify for whistle-blower protection, the further question is whether this is discrimination against her in the enjoyment of her right to freedom of expression under the European Convention on Human Rights ("ECHR"). And if it is, what is the remedy?

...

'[11] On appeal to this court, the appellant continues to argue that she is a "worker" within the meaning of s 230(3)(b) of the 1996 Act. She also raises for the first time a new argument, that she is in "Crown employment" within the meaning of s 191 of the 1996 Act. If she fails in each of those, she continues to argue that her exclusion from whistle-blowing protection is a breach, either of her rights under art 10 or under art 14 read with art 10 of the ECHR and that either s 230(3)(b) or s 191 of the 1996 Act should be read and given effect so as to bring her within that protection.

'[12] It is not in dispute that a judge undertakes personally to perform work or services and that the recipient of that work or services is not a client or customer of the judge. The issue is whether that work or services is performed pursuant to a contract with the recipient of that work or services or pursuant to some different legal arrangement. Nor is it in dispute that judges hold a statutory office.

...

...

'[21] Taken together, all of these factors point against the existence of a contractual relationship between a judge and the executive or any member of it. Still less do they suggest a contractual relationship between the judge and the Lord Chief Justice.

...

'[23] Section 191(3) provides that "In this Act 'Crown employment' means employment under or for the purposes of a government department or any officer or body exercising on behalf of the Crown functions conferred by a statutory provision". Clearly, "employment" in this section cannot mean "employment under a contract" because it would then add nothing to the definition in s 230(3). The predecessor to s 191 was inserted into the Industrial Relations Act 1971 because historically Crown servants had not been seen to be employed under contracts of service and had not been able to complain of wrongful dismissal. The object was to enable them to complain of unfair dismissal and enjoy the other employment rights listed in s 191(2). Thus, argues the appellant, s 191 is apt to give her the protection of Pt IVA even if she is not employed under a contract.

'[24] The definition in s 191(3) has two limbs: employment under or for the purposes of a government department; and employment under or for the purposes of an officer or body exercising on behalf of the Crown functions conferred by a statutory provision. For the reasons given earlier, it is impossible to regard the judiciary as employed under or for the purposes of the Ministry of Justice. They are not civil servants or the equivalent of civil servants. They do not work for the ministry. It is slightly more plausible to regard them as working under or for the purposes of the Lord Chief Justice, who since the 2005 Act [Constitutional Reform Act 2005], has had statutory responsibilities in relation to the judiciary: under s 7 of that Act, he is responsible for the maintenance of appropriate arrangements for the welfare, training and guidance of the judiciary of England and Wales (within the resources provided by the Lord Chancellor) and for their deployment and the allocation of work within the courts. As already

noted, he also shares some responsibility for appointments, discipline and removal with the Lord Chancellor. But it is difficult to think that, by conferring these functions upon the Lord Chief Justice, the 2005 Act brought about such a fundamental change in the application of s 191. Judges do not work "under and for the purposes of" those functions of the Lord Chief Justice but for the administration of justice in the courts of England and Wales in accordance with their oaths of office. Mutatis mutandis, the same reasoning would apply to the identical definition of crown employment in art 236(3) of the Employment Rights (Northern Ireland) Order 1996, SI 1996/1919.

'[25] It is perhaps worth noting that s 83(2) and (9) of the Equality Act 2010, passed since the 2005 Act, defines "employment" as covering "Crown employment" as defined in s 191 of the 1996 Act. But it also makes express provision, in ss 50 and 51, prohibiting discrimination in relation to, among other things, appointment to public offices. These are defined to include officers appointed by or on the recommendation of a member of the executive (such as the Lord Chancellor) or by the Lord Chief Justice or Senior President of Tribunals. Thus judicial office-holders are clearly protected by these provisions, which would have been quite unnecessary had they already been protected as persons in Crown employment. Sections 50 and 51 do not apply in Northern Ireland, but this does not affect the force of this point.

...

'[37] As no legitimate aim has been put forward, it is not possible to judge whether the exclusion is a proportionate means of achieving that aim, whatever the test by which proportionality has to be judged. I conclude, therefore, that the exclusion of judges from the whistleblowing protection in Part IVA of the 1996 Act is in breach of their rights under art 14 read with art 10 of the ECHR.

...

'[46] I would therefore allow this appeal and remit the case to the Employment Tribunal on the basis that the appellant is entitled to claim the protection of Pt IVA of the 1996 Act.'
Gilham v Ministry of Justice [2019] UKSC 44, [2020] 1 All ER 1 at [1], [11]–[12], [21], [23]–[25], [37], [46], per Lady Hale P

Y

YEARLY INTEREST

[Income Tax Act 2007, s 874; Insolvency (England and Wales) Rules 2016, SI 2016/1024, r 14.23(7).] '[1] ... The short question, which has generated different answers in the courts below, is whether interest payable under r 14.23(7) is "yearly interest" within the meaning of s 874, so that the administrators must first deduct income tax before paying interest to proving creditors.

...

'[8] ... There is no definition of the phrase "yearly interest" anywhere in the 2007 Act. Nonetheless there is this deeming provision in s 874, added by Sch 11 to the Finance Act 2013:

"(5A) For the purposes of subsection (1) a payment of interest which is payable to an individual in respect of compensation is to be treated as a payment of yearly interest (irrespective of the period in respect of which the interest is paid)."

'[9] This is unfortunately another case in which the full meaning of an apparently innocent-looking simple statutory phrase can only be addressed by reference to the historical deployment of that phrase, or equivalent phrases seeking to express the same concept, in early legislation.

...

'[19] At first instance, Hildyard J was persuaded that the absence of any accrual over time (prior to the identification of a surplus and its quantification after payment of all proved debts in full) was fatal to the categorisation of statutory interest as yearly interest. By contrast, the Court of Appeal could discern no requirement from the authorities that yearly interest should accrue due over time. Since it was compensation for the proving creditors being kept out of their money for a substantial time, the interest had the requisite long-term quality sufficient for it to be categorised as yearly.

...

'[51] It is true, as the administrators submitted, that some of the second group of cases were primarily concerned with the question whether payments described as interest were truly interest at all for income tax purposes, rather than whether they were yearly interest. ... By contrast in the present case it has been common ground throughout that statutory interest under r 14.23 is interest for the purposes of income tax.

'[52] But those cases nonetheless provide the answer to the conundrum: what period of durability is to be identified for interest payable in a single lump sum as compensation for the payee being out of the money in the past, for the purpose of deciding whether it is to be treated as yearly interest, under the *Hay* principles [*IRC v Hay* 1924 SC 521, (1924) 8 TC 636]? The simple answer, supplied by all the second group of cases, is that it is the period in respect of which the interest is calculated, because that is the period during which the loss of the use of money or property has been incurred, for which the interest is to be compensation.

'[53] This appears also to have been the assumption made by the drafter of what is now s 874(5A), quoted above. It deems payment of interest to an individual in respect of compensation to be yearly interest "irrespective of the period in respect of which the interest is paid". This suggests that, but for the deeming provision (introduced, so the court was told, to deal with compensation for mis-selling of Payment Protection Insurance), the question whether the interest would or would not have been yearly interest would have depended upon the duration of the period in respect of which the compensatory interest was calculated.' *Revenue and Customs Commissioners v Joint Administrators of Lehman Brothers International* [2019] UKSC 12, [2019] 2 All ER 559 at [1], [8]–[9], [19], [51]–[53], per Lord Briggs JSC